Best Practices for Co-Teaching & Collaboration:

The HOW of Co-Teaching—Implementing the Models
Third Edition

Best Practices for Co-Teaching & Collaboration:

The HOW of Co-Teaching—Implementing the Models
Third Edition

Susan Gingras Fitzell, M.Ed.

Cogent Catalyst Publications

Printed in the United States of America.

Library of Congress Cataloging-in-Publication Data

Fitzell, Susan Gingras

Includes bibliographic references

ISBN 978-1-932995-39-8 (pbk.)

Teaching Teams 2. Classroom Management

Best Practices for Co-Teaching and Collaboration: The HOW of Co-Teaching—Implementing the Models, Third Edition

If you have questions or would like customized school in-service or ongoing consultation, contact:

Susan Gingras Fitzell

PO Box 6182

Manchester, NH 03108-6182

603-625-6087 or 210-473-2863

sfitzell@susanfitzell.com

www.susanfitzell.com

Dedication

I dedicate this book to Ed Burgess, my favorite co-teaching partner, ever, as well as all the amazing, motivated, inspiring co-teachers I have worked with over the years. Many of you deeply impacted my life, my ideas about co-teaching, and my understanding of how it needed to work.

Thank you to Pat Tunstall, Brent Williams, Elaine Smith, Tracy Cartas, Stacey Leonard, Karen Wasilenko, Rosanna Moran, Pamela Tognoli, Helene Anzalone and so many other instructional leaders for trusting me to work with your co-teachers as a coach. I hope they learned as much from me as I learned from them.

Thank you to the pioneers and researchers who have embraced the idea of inclusion and fostered understanding and belief in co-teaching and collaboration. Thank you to Marilyn Friend, Wendy Murawski, Lisa Dieker, Anne Beninghof, Sonya Kunkel, Paula Kluth, and Rebecca Hines for being willing to share your insights, ideas, and research. Without the body of research, experiences, and reflection of my colleagues in inclusion and co-teaching, the strategies and approaches in this book would be without a strong foundation.

And, lastly, I thank my family for their support as I work to make a difference in the world and for my children's willingness to let me experiment on them as they faced their educational challenges.

GET YOUR BONUS RESOURCES HERE:

http://Bonus398.susanfitzell.com

Table of Contents

Introduction .... **i**
Table of Abbreviations i
Educational Specialists as Experts, Collaborators, and Consultants iii
High Standards for All Students iii
College and Career Readiness Standards: Application to Students with Disabilities vi
CHAPTER 1 ~ Co-teaching 101 .... **1**
Co-Teaching: The Basics 3
What Is Co-Teaching? 3
What Is Not Co-Teaching? 3
Special Education Teacher as Consultant 4
Who Can Co-Teach? 5
Does Co-Teaching Work? 7
The Co-Teaching Label Is Often Wrong 7
Co-Teaching Will Not Work When... 7
Co-Teaching Done Well Works! 8
Co-Teaching With Teachers Who Are Willing 8
So, Does Co-Teaching Work? 9
But What About the Research? 9
One Teach, One Assist 13
Co-Teaching With Data-Driven Instruction 13
Benefits of One Teach, One Assist 15
Challenges of One Teach, One Assist 15
Parallel Teaching 16
Double the Participation 16
Consistent with UDL Framework 16
The Logistics of Parallel 17
Teachers Get Distracted, Not the Students 18
Benefits of Parallel Teaching 18
Challenges of Parallel Teaching 18
Alternative Teaching 19
Alternative Teaching 19
Benefits of Alternative Teaching 21
Challenges of Alternative Teaching 21
Station Teaching 22
Benefits of Station Teaching 23
Challenges of Station Teaching 24

Teaming 25
Benefits of Teaming 25
Challenges of Teaming 26
The Bottom Line on Co-Teaching Approaches & Differentiated Instruction 27
Chapter 1 Review and Discussion Questions 28
Reflection Questions 28
Reflecting on the Models 28
CHAPTER 2 ~ The HOW of Implementing the Models 31
Co-Teaching Models Have Evolved 33
Beyond the Models: Two Dozen Co-Teaching Implementations 33
#1 Two Teach and Debate 35
A High School English Classroom Example 35
A High School Social Studies Classroom Example 37
#2 One Teach—One Summarize 40
Listening Skills Are Critical to Effective Summarization 41
But My Co-Teacher Does Not Know the Content! 42
#3 Both Facilitate Participation and Collect Data 43
Both Facilitate Participation and Collect Data 43
An Effective Participation Activity: Know, Want to Know, Learned 45
The Solution: An "Oral K-W-L" 45
Share What Your Partner Said 46
Tying "Oral K-W-L" and "Both Facilitate Participation and Collect Data" into the Standards 46
Variation of the Oral K-W-L: Use a Picture as the Cue for Discussion 47
Oral K-W-L: What Did You Learn? 48
Take It Up a Level: Teach Questioning Skills 48
Take It Up a Level: Teach Listening Skills 49
#4 Two Support Student Participation and Engagement 50
#5 One Teach—One Collect Data 52
#6 One Lead and One Student Support 55
#7 One Teach and One Interpret 57
#8 One Guide Tech and One Facilitate Discussion 60
Backchanneling 60
#9 One Silent & One Oral: Reading, Tests, Worksheets 64
Reading the Tests Aloud 64
Reading Aloud Texts, Worksheets, and Short Stories 66
Read Alouds and Student Choice 66
#10 Two Teach with Different Teaching Styles 67
Both Teach the Same Standard Differently 67

#11 Two Facilitate Speed Partnering 71
#12 One Large Group and One Focus Group 74
An Opportunity for Enrichment 76
How Might One Large Group and One Focus Group Look? 76
#13 Both Teach Half—Same Objective, Same Way 78
#14 Teach Half Then Switch—Skills & Rigor 80
Follow These Steps to Implement Teach Half Then Switch—Skills and Rigor:....... 82
#15 Teach Half Then Switch—Pre-Teach or Enrich 84
#16 Teach Half Then Switch—Reading in the Content Area 86
#17 Teach Half Then Switch—One Review and One Run Lab 89
Implementation Suited to Vocational and Technical Schools 90
#18 Two Facilitate Group Process and Collect Data 92
#19 One to Manage Logistics—One for Safety and Questions 94
#20 Two Individualize with Station Teaching 97
#21 Three Mixed-Ability Rotations 99
#22 Three Same-Ability Stations—Re-Teach, Reinforce, Enrich 101
How to Implement Same-Ability Rotations with Flexible Grouping 101
#23 Two Run Acceleration Centers 103
Fitzell Acceleration Centers™ - A Better Alternative 103
You Make It Once and Use It All Year 104
Fitzell Acceleration Centers Respond to All Learners 104
Keep It Simple—Start Small and Enhance Over Time 105
#24 Team Teaching 107
Your Co-Teaching Approach 109
How to Choose the Best Implementation for Your Classroom 109
Co-Teachers Might Choose Approaches Based On 110
Which Co-Teaching Implementations Are Most Effective at the Elementary and Secondary Levels, and Why? 110
Dealing with Large Class Sizes When Co-Teaching 110
A Side Benefit: Staying on Schedule 111
Chapter 2 Review and Discussion Questions 112
Reflection Questions 112
Practical Application 112
CHAPTER 3 ~ The HOW of Co-teaching with Specialists 113
Co-Teaching and Collaboration with Specialists 115
RTI Specialists 116
Title One Specialists—Reading Specialist 117
Speech and Language Pathologists 118
An SLP's Thoughts on Co-Teaching 118

Teachers of English as a Second Language ... 122
Chapter 3 Review and Discussion Questions ... 125
Reflection Questions ... 125
Practical Application ... 125
CHAPTER 4 ~ The HOW of Fitting It All In: Chunking Lesson Plans® ... 127
A Lesson Planning Productivity Strategy ... 129
Chunking Lesson Plans® ... 129
Managing Lesson Chunks with Timer Apps ... 140
Using Timers in the Classroom ... 140
On-Screen Timer to Keep Students on Track! ... 141
Chapter 4 Review and Discussion Questions ... 142
Reflection Questions ... 142
Practical Application ... 142
CHAPTER 5 ~ The HOW of Logistics & Co-planning ... 145
Co-Planning Time ... 147
Co-Planning Time Is Sacred ... 147
Minimum Co-Planning Time ... 148
Effective Use of Co-Planning Time ... 148
I Do Not Have Built-in Co-Planning Time! ... 149
Co-Planning Meeting Agenda ... 151
Fundamental Questions for Your Co-Planning Session ... 151
Co-Planning in the Cloud ... 152
Chapter 5 Review and Discussion Questions ... 156
Reflection Questions ... 156
Practical Application ... 156
CHAPTER 6 ~ The HOW of Healthy Collaboration ... 157
Looking at Personality Types ... 159
Full Glass, Empty Glass Personality Types ... 160
How Can Understanding Personality Types Help Co-Teachers? ... 163
Collaboration Challenges and Solutions ... 164
First Five Minutes of Class ... 164
Potential Roadblocks: Challenges ... 165
Overcoming Roadblocks: Solutions ... 168
Ten Tips that Foster Positive Co-Teaching and Collaboration ... 170
The Essential Ingredients for Effective Collaboration ... 172
How to Woo Your Co-Teacher ... 172
When the Special Education Teacher Isn't Sold on Co-Teaching ... 174
Co-Teaching and Parity ... 174
Maintaining Trust in the Co-Taught Classroom ... 177

Collaboration Tips that Foster Trust and Respect 178
Questions to Consider When Preparing to Teach Together 179
Co-Planning Time 179
Instruction 179
Student Behavior 180
Communication 180
Co-Teaching Preparation Questionnaire 182
Scripts for Effective Communication 184
Choose Words Strategically 187
Denotations Versus Connotations 188
Prepare for Communication 188
Incorporate Active Listening Practices 189
What to Do When in Conflict 190
Stopping Conflict in Its Tracks! 191
We Convey More Than Our Words 192
"What Do I Say When My Colleague Says..." 194
Phrases That Shift the Dynamic Without Escalating Conflict 194
Comebacks That Don't Escalate the Conflict 194
Ask a Question 195
Offline Coping Techniques 195
What's Working? Card 195
How Is Co-Teaching Going? 197
Co-Teaching Observation Form 198
Chapter 6 Review and Discussion Questions 200
Reflection Questions 200
Practical Application 200
CHAPTER 7 ~ Effective Small Groups and Stations 201
What Constitutes Effective Small-Group Instruction? 203
Effective Small-Group Instruction 203
Ineffective Small-Group Instruction 203
Some Effective Flexible Grouping Options 203
Strategies for Effective Group Processes 204
Class Plan for Differentiating Within Groups 205
Train Student Experts 205
Practice the Station Teaching Process 206
Options for Determining Which Students Should Be in Which Groups 207
Implementing Ongoing Assessment Within a Classroom as a Means to Defining Groups 208
Use Student Talent and Interest to Define Groups 209

Use Grade Book to Determine High-Low Partners 212
High-Middle-Middle-Low 214
Arrange Your Classroom Environment for Success 215
Develop a Class Plan for Differentiating Within Groups 217
Standing Stations in Your Classroom! 219
Behavior Management for Small Groups & Acceleration Centers 221
Introducing the Group Activity 222
Establishing Group Ground Rules 222
Behavior Management Cue Card 224
Develop a Positive Reinforcement System for Small Group and Fitzell Acceleration Centers™ Work 225
Grading Small Group Work 227
Chapter 7 Review and Discussion Questions 231
Reflection Questions 231
Practical Application 231
Reflection Questions 232
CHAPTER 8 ~ SCHOOL LEADERS AND THEIR ROLE IN COLLABORATION SUCCESS 233
Considerations for School Administrators Implementing Co-Teaching Initiatives 235
Should Co-Teaching Be Voluntary? 235
How to Match Co-Teachers for Success 235
A School Principal's Role in a Successful Co-Teaching Initiative 236
Co-Teaching Initiatives: The Bottom Line 236
Speaking of High-Stakes Testing 238
Where Does Co-Teaching Take Place? 239
How Many Days a Week Should We Co-Teach? 239
Co-Teaching, Inclusion, and Student Numbers 240
Types of Inclusion 241
Effective Methods of Distributing Students in Co-Taught Classrooms 243
Scheduling Co-Teaching 245
Remember: Co-Teaching Time Is Sacred—Don't Break Trust 249
How Do We Measure the Success of a Co-Teaching Initiative? 250
What Should a Co-Taught Class Look Like? 251
Chapter 8 Review and Discussion Questions 252
Reflection Questions 252

BIBLIOGRAPHY **255**
APPENDIX **261**
How to Facilitate a Successful Book Study **263**
Individual Book Study 265
Group-Oriented Book Study 266
Tips for Being a Good Facilitator 267
Book Study Activities 269
Fishbowl Activity 269
Search-Pair-Share 270
What Worries You? 272
Is Homogenous Tracking Better Than Heterogeneous Grouping? 275
Introduction 275
Current Limitations in Evidence 276
Challenges in Tracking 277
Enrichment Activities: SDI & Challenge Activities in the Mixed-Ability Classroom 288
Ten-Minute Acceleration Center Activities Across the Content Area 289
Enrichment Using Technology in the Classroom—Nine Ways to Use Google Images to Teach Vocabulary 291
Technology in the Classroom Using Google Images 292
About the Author 293
Bring Susan to Your School for Consultation or In-Service 294
School Professional Development License Agreement 296

Table of Abbreviations

ACT	American College of Testing
ADHD	Attention Deficit Hyperactivity Disorder
CBM	Curriculum-Based Measurement
CCSS	Common Core State Standards
ELA	English Language Arts
ELD	English Language Development
ELL	English Language Learners
ESL	English as a Second Language
IEP	Individualized Education Program
KWL	Know, Want to Know, Learned Activity
MI	Multiple Intelligences
NAEP	National Assessment of Educational Progress
OTR	Opportunities to Respond
SAT	Scholastic Aptitude Test
SDI	Specially Designed Instruction
SLP	Speech and Language Pathologist
UDL	Universal Design for Learning

Introduction

Educational Specialists as Experts, Collaborators, and Consultants

Often, the educational specialist's expertise in understanding and teaching academic content in the standards or competency-based classroom is the key to whether a student with learning disabilities or special needs will make academic growth or not. When implementing state standards, content area teachers have expertise with content objectives, and how to teach those objectives to the general population. The special education teacher's or specialist's role in the co-instruction process is to ensure that lesson plans are differentiated to meet the needs of all students, as well as provide Specially Designed Instruction (SDI) when students with special needs are not making gains.

Without proper support or training, however, content area teachers can easily become overwhelmed with the task of trying to meet the needs of a heterogeneously grouped co-taught classroom. Whereas some content area teachers are skilled in working with students with disabilities, and some may even have certification in special education, we cannot assume a general education teacher has that knowledge and background.

Special education teachers can play a critical role in helping content area teachers analyze the standards or competency-based lesson plan and design lessons and support all learners in reaching challenging expectations. The implementation of state standards, or College and Career Ready Standards, places new demands on content area teachers as well as special education teachers.

It is important that both teachers take an active role in professional development that enables the special education teacher to become skilled in the content, as well as enabling the general education teacher to understand how to differentiate lesson plans and deliver SDI when necessary.

High Standards for All Students

Unlike previous structures to support students with special needs, teaching for standards-based grading or competency-based education requires that students with disabilities be challenged to excel within the general curriculum, and be prepared for success post-graduation as well as in college or their careers.

In the past, the emphasis for students with special needs was often a modified curriculum that demanded less of students as well as an abundance of accommodations to make work easier for students to support their success in school. In many states, students with disabilities took a modified state test that was less rigorous than that of their peers.

This reality is addressed in the Individuals with Disabilities Education Act update in 2017 which states (IDEA, 2017):

> *"Almost 30 years of research and experience has demonstrated that the education of children with disabilities can be made more effective by—*
>
> *(A) having high expectations for such children and ensuring their access to the general education curriculum in the regular classroom, to the maximum extent possible, in order to*
>
> *(i) meet developmental goals and, to the maximum extent possible, the challenging expectations that have been established for all children; and*
>
> *(ii) be prepared to lead productive and independent adult lives, to the maximum extent possible*

Standards-based and competency-based models require teachers to provide scaffolding, and differentiated instruction, so that students who struggle with traditional instruction can participate in rigorous curriculum and be successful.

Students with disabilities are a heterogeneous group with one common characteristic: the presence of disabling conditions that significantly hinder their abilities to benefit from general education.

Therefore, how these rigorous standards are taught and assessed is critical to co-teachers' ability to reach students with special needs and or learning disabilities. Consequently, for students to meet standards and demonstrate learning, co-teachers must implement:

- High quality, evidence-based instruction
- Instructional materials that are accessible for all students
- Embedded support such as
    - Universal Design for Learning (UDL)
    - Appropriate accommodations
    - Assistive technology
- Instructional strategies to include
    - Universally designed units and lessons
    - Individualized supports via accommodations and academic modifications
    - Positive Behavior Supports

Promising service delivery models that work well for students with disabilities, as well as the general student population, are co-teaching approaches and paraprofessional support. The key to the success of these approaches, however, is to implement co-teaching correctly and provide highly skilled paraprofessionals. Co-teaching fails when school districts implement the initiative without proper planning, scheduling, teacher buy-in, and training. Co-teaching will also fail if campus (and district) leadership is not sold on the approach.

College and Career Readiness Standards: Application to Students with Disabilities

The College and Career Readiness Standards **(US Department of Education, n.d.)** articulate rigorous grade level expectations in the areas of mathematics and English language arts (ELA). These standards identify the knowledge and skills students need to be successful in college and careers.

Students with disabilities, students eligible under IDEA, must be challenged to excel within the general curriculum and be prepared for success in their post-school lives, including college and/or careers. These common standards provide a historic opportunity to improve access to rigorous academic content standards for students with disabilities. The continued development of understanding about research-based instructional practices and a focus on their effective implementation will help improve access to mathematics and ELA standards for all students, including those with disabilities.

For students with disabilities to meet high academic standards and to demonstrate fully their conceptual and procedural knowledge and skills in mathematics, reading, writing, speaking, and listening, their instruction must incorporate supports and accommodations, including:

- Supports and related services designed to meet the unique needs of these students and to enable their access to the general education curriculum.
- An Individualized Education Program (IEP) that includes annual goals aligned with and chosen to facilitate their attainment of grade level academic standards.
- Teachers and specialized instructional support personnel who are prepared and qualified to deliver high quality, evidence-based, individualized instruction and support services.

Promoting a culture of high expectations for all students is a fundamental goal of state standards. To participate with success in the general curriculum, students with disabilities, as appropriate, may be provided additional supports and services, such as:

- Instructional supports for learning—based on the principles of UDL—which foster student engagement by presenting information in multiple ways and allowing for diverse avenues of action and expression.

- Instructional accommodations—changes in materials or procedures—which do not change the standards but allow students to learn within the framework of the standard.
- Assistive technology devices and services to ensure access to the general education curriculum and the standards.

Some students with the most significant cognitive disabilities will require substantial supports and accommodations to have meaningful access to certain standards in both instruction and assessment, based on their communication and academic needs. These supports and accommodations should ensure that students receive access to multiple means of learning and opportunities to demonstrate knowledge but retain the rigor and high expectations of the state standards.

CHAPTER 1

Co-teaching 101

Co-Teaching: The Basics

When I first started co-teaching, I firmly believed it was a setup for failure for students with learning disabilities to be in the general classroom. However, within the first year of co-teaching, I realized there were some significant benefits. The first benefit of including students with special needs and behavioral problems in the general classroom was that their behavior improved when surrounded by positive peer role models. The second benefit was that the bar had been raised and, when provided with proper support and learning strategies, students with special needs not only rose to the challenge, but they also gained the benefit of having more resources available to them in the general education classroom.

In a co-teaching situation, students not only have the benefit of a content expert providing instruction, but they have the benefits of a learning strategies expert to provide necessary scaffolding, adaptations, accommodations, interventions, and modifications.

What Is Co-Teaching?

Co-teaching is two or more teachers working together to provide instruction, typically, to students in a heterogeneous inclusive setting. Within a well-implemented co-teaching initiative, teachers plan together, instruct the class together, and collaborate with grading and differentiating instruction. In an ideal educational setting, teachers have common co-planning time to support their work in the inclusive classroom. Co-teaching allows educators to meet the needs of students at risk, gifted or with disabilities, who may be struggling in the classroom.

In a co-taught classroom that fully utilizes the talents of the two teachers and any other adult staff in the room, students are more likely to achieve high standards, to be successful, and to behave more appropriately than they would in segregated, pull-out, or self-contained classrooms.

What Is Not Co-Teaching?

- Co-teaching is ***not*** tag-team teaching. For example, sometimes teachers in a co-teaching situation consistently split the instruction so that while one person is teaching, the other is planning lessons, making copies, running errands, correcting papers, or doing any number of things that are not providing instruction or supporting the instruction of the teacher up front.

- Co-teaching is ***not*** one teacher teaching while the other teacher consistently waits in submission to the content teacher's bidding or allowances. Co-teaching requires that both certified teachers are involved in providing instruction or direct support to students in the classroom as needed.
- Co-teaching is ***not*** inclusion and inclusion is not co-teaching. In many areas of the country, there is a marriage of these terms where they are used interchangeably. However, inclusion refers to a philosophy and practice where all students—gifted, learning-disabled, and of mixed-ability—are in the same classroom as a learning community. Co-teaching is only one way to implement inclusion.
- Co-teaching is ***not*** general education teachers working with a special education teacher who is in and out of the classroom inconsistently and, consequently, does not have a realistic way to deliver instruction, plan with the classroom teacher, share responsibilities in the classroom on a regular basis, or in any other way be a person in the room but not someone the general education teacher can count on.
- When students with special needs are included in the general education classroom and classroom teachers are assigned a special educator who is not scheduled in that specific classroom a minimum of two days a week, the special education teacher is acting as a consultant within a collaboration model.

Special Education Teacher as Consultant

In this inclusion model, the special education teacher acts as "consultant" to the general classroom teacher. The special education consultant works primarily outside the classroom with the general education teacher and may work directly in classrooms as needed. The general classroom teacher in this situation makes most, if not all, of the classroom adaptations, accommodations, and modifications using the IEP, and the special educator is available as a guide and resource. If a paraprofessional is assigned to the general classroom, the special education teacher works closely with both the paraprofessional and the general classroom teacher. While this model is a good way to implement inclusion, it is not co-teaching.

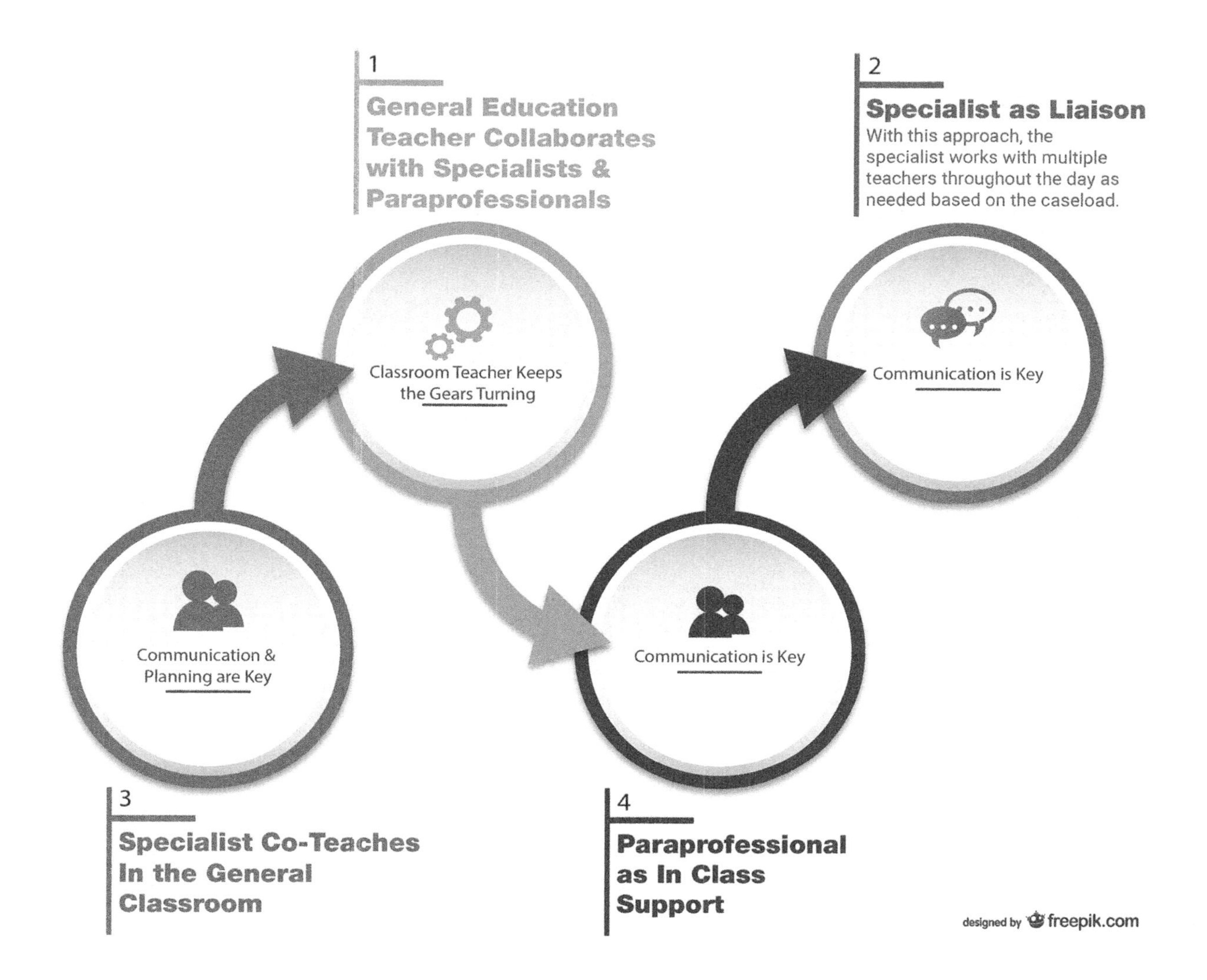

Who Can Co-Teach?

During a recent seminar on the topic of inclusion strategies, two women came up to me with huge concerns about the co-teaching initiative their district was starting. I was astounded when I was told they were paraprofessionals rather than certified teachers. They were very uncomfortable with what was being asked of them by their building principal; however, they did not feel they had the power to challenge the district decision to have paraprofessionals in a co-teaching role.

Paraprofessionals can re-teach or implement a lesson plan written by a certified teacher, under the supervision of a certified teacher. However, a paraprofessional is not qualified to co-teach, nor does the paraprofessional receive a salary commensurate with the responsibility of teaching.

Paraprofessionals are employed as non-certified personnel. This directly affects the responsibilities they should have in the classroom. Co-teaching is a service delivery system that requires two or more certified teachers or licensed staff to collaborate and provide instruction to the diverse classroom. The essential point is that certified teachers and the licensed staff co-teach and paraprofessionals support in the classroom.

Does Co-Teaching Work?

Do you have research to prove that co-teaching works? I was asked this question during a public seminar on inclusion strategies that I was delivering in the Chicago area. The teachers asking the question had experienced great success for their students and themselves through co-teaching. Their administrator, however, didn't believe that co-teaching worked. A national guru, who will remain nameless, on teaching strategies (not co-teaching) announced in one of her in-services that co-teaching does not work. That guru did not give an explanation, rather just made the statement, the teachers explained. (I wondered whether that guru had any experience with co-teaching since it was not her area of expertise.) Regardless, these two teachers were devastated. They asked me, "Do you have research that it works?" They emphatically exclaimed, "We know it works." They saw the growth in their students while co-teaching. They were passionate about continuing the co-teaching model in their school. However, that model was threatened because of misinformation.

The Co-Teaching Label Is Often Wrong

Well, here's the nitty-gritty: No matter what the research says, the label is often wrong. What I mean by that is: School districts that put two teachers in an "inclusive" classroom can call it co-teaching, yet it may not be co-teaching at all. And, if it is called co-teaching on paper simply because two bodies are in the room and it doesn't work, it's decided that co-teaching does not work.

Co-Teaching Will Not Work When...

Co-teaching (in name only) will not work

- when a general education teacher and a special education teacher are put together in a room and the special education teacher is constantly pulled for "other" responsibilities.
- when administration is not supportive and/or does not provide training and follow-through.
- when administration does not hold teachers accountable for best practice teaching methods.

- when administrators hold an in-service for the teachers but do not attend—how can they possibly know how to follow through with the training if they were not there?
- if schools use it as a budget-cutting endeavor.
- when teachers don't want to cooperate and one or both deliberately sabotage the process.

You see, the bottom line is: None of the above is co-teaching. It's a weak attempt at something that might, at a glance or on paper, look like co-teaching, but it's not co-teaching. Co-teaching means exactly that: co-, together, two, both—teaching. Not one teacher teaching and one teacher standing in the background waiting for permission to work with students.

Co-Teaching Done *Well* Works!

I've been co-teaching and working with co-teachers since 1993. Co-teaching done well, scheduled well, received well, and combined with best practice teaching strategies to differentiate instruction ***does*** work. It works a whole lot better than

- one teacher, all alone, trying to deal with a classroom of thirty-plus students at different ability levels.
- self-contained classrooms where the bar is often too low for students to make significant gains.
- co-taught classrooms are heterogeneous and schools are not putting the lowest achievers with the students with special needs and filtering out all the academically successful students into more challenging classes. (That's not inclusion; rather, that's one big, tracked, low-level class).

Co-Teaching With Teachers Who Are Willing

If a district has two teachers who are willing to practice co-teaching with fidelity and are co-teaching together on a consistent basis, their co-teaching marriage is respected by the "powers that be" so that the general education teacher isn't alone half the time (pulling the special education teacher out for coverage, meetings, trainings, crises, etc. is commonplace), ***and*** those teachers are using best practice strategies and differentiating instruction, the co-teaching model works better than almost any other model available to accelerate quickly all—yes, I said all—students' achievement. When you tier lesson plans in a co-taught class, high achievers also have the opportunity to accelerate!

So, Does Co-Teaching Work?

Does co-teaching work? Yes—when the district commits to implementing it correctly and supports teachers in the process. Yes—when the teachers' personalities mesh and they are willing to use best practice strategies to reach all learners. (I heard an "expert" say once that personality styles don't matter in co-teaching. I strongly disagree!) Yes—co-teaching works when schools don't segregate learners into classes of high, medium, and low and place the students with special needs in a tracked low-level class. Yes—it works when one of the two teachers doesn't fight the process every step of the way, but instead keeps an open mind and is willing to teach with best practice strategies. Yes—it can work when done well. It can even work when done half well.

Yes. Co-teaching, implemented correctly, works.

But What About the Research?

Valid research in dynamic, changing environments with varying controls, subjects, demographics, etc., is difficult to attain. A researcher I worked with to compile data from studies done on the efficacy of heterogeneous versus homogenous groupings[1] told me that trying to compare studies in education is like comparing apples to oranges. In "Co-Teaching: An Illustration of the Complexity of Collaboration in Special Education," the authors acknowledge:

> Most inquiry on co-teaching has emphasized co-teachers' roles and relationships or program logistics rather than demonstrating its impact on student achievement and other key outcomes, and far more literature exists describing co-teaching and offering advice about it than carefully studying it. (Friend, Cook, Hurley-Chamberlain, & Shamberger, 2010)

Through a literature review on the topic of co-teaching, Hannover Research summed up the problem:

> [T]he general lack of empirical data appears largely due to the fact that co-teaching is not conducive to large-scale, standardized research. Not only do definitions of co-teaching vary across the literature, but classes are also typically not similar enough to provide meaningful comparative data. For instance, the implementation of co-teaching—including the

1 See "Is Homogenous Tracking Better than Heterogeneous Grouping?" in the appendix.

> roles and responsibilities of co-teachers and the mode and quality of instruction—may differ not only among districts, but even among individual classrooms in a single school. (Hannover Research, 2012)

"A Meta-Analysis of Co-Teaching Research" (W. W. Murawski & Lee Swanson, 2001) stated, "Of the 89 articles reviewed on co-teaching, only 6 met the criteria set for selection" in the meta-analysis. Also, "none of the studies reported explicit measures of treatment integrity. Without a measure of treatment integrity, it is difficult to determine whether the studies genuinely adhered to their reported interventions as described."

To complicate matters further, there is no clear, consistent working definition for inclusion. "[M]any definitions of inclusive education have been advanced and many efforts to effect fundamental change to the structures and practices of special education have been undertaken. Divergent definitions reflecting distinct but complementary ideas developed simultaneously in different parts of the world." (Florian, 2014)

Despite the lack of large-scale research, there are some research highlights from studies that have been conducted on the topic of co-teaching:

- A great area of controversy is co-teaching in the mathematics classroom. One study included two fourth-grade classes in an elementary school, one with a regular education (solo teaching) and the other with the same regular education teacher and a special education teacher for the co-taught class. The researchers determined: "It is concluded that both solo teaching and co-teaching were beneficial to the two different groups of students within their various learning environments." (Almon & Feng, 2012)
- Although the following study did not focus on co-teaching, "the study was to assess the general effectiveness of placing special education students in inclusive classroom settings. This quantitative study used archived statewide data to measure changes in placement and make comparisons. Results from this study indicated an increased number of special education students meeting the expectations of the state accountability system." (Roden, Borgemenke, & Holt, 2013)
- A meta-analysis (Oh-Young & Filler, 2015) "was conducted using the findings from 24 studies published in peer-reviewed journals from 1980 through 2013. Results from the analyses suggest that there were significant differences (. p<. 0.0001) between placement settings with the majority of students with disabilities in more integrated settings outperforming those in less integrated settings on both academic and social outcome measures."

- Co-teaching is more likely to be successful when school culture supports inclusive practice. A qualitative study that researched the sustainability of responsible inclusive practices in a public elementary school identified five themes that support the sustainability of inclusion." (Richmond-Cullen, Bauman, Ferrance, & Kunkel, 2017) "The data revealed the following five consistent themes as integral to responsible inclusive practices: (1) Public Service with a Moral Purpose, (2) Culture and Commitment, (3) Data-Driven Decision-Making, (4) Leadership Qualities, and (5) Co-Teaching and Community Involvement." Essentially, the best practices identified in the research study were co-teaching and strong and effective parent-school relationships.
- Rivera, McMahon, & Keys (2014) "confirmed that schools are implementing some of the best practices of inclusion and students benefit from co-teaching, yet significant barriers impede co-teaching of students with disabilities. Longitudinal research on the processes and development of school-, teacher-, and student-level factors that contribute to successful co-teaching will lead to school settings that maximize inclusion to promote learning and well-being among all students."
- Walsh & Jones (1995) observed that "Of 16 instructional indicators from classroom observation forms, two instructional areas show particular differences between co-taught and self-contained classrooms. Teachers in co-taught classrooms (n = 39; 95%) were much more likely to provide "instruction reflecting the general education curriculum" than were teachers in self-contained classrooms (n = 64; 78%). Likewise, teachers (81%) in co-taught classrooms were more likely to provide instruction that involved students in the higher dimensions of learning needed for success on the critical thinking tasks of the Maryland Student Performance Assessment Program (MSPAP/DOL incorporated) than were teachers (58%) in self-contained classrooms. In light of the critical need to find effective ways to enable students with disabilities to truly and consistently access the general education curriculum, the results of these classroom observations provide additional support for efforts to expand opportunities for students with disabilities to receive instruction in co-taught settings."

Dr. Marilyn Friends' Co-Teaching Approaches

One Teach, One Observe. One of the advantages in co-teaching is that more detailed observation of students engaged in the learning process can occur. With this approach, for example, co-teachers can decide in advance what types of specific observational information to gather during instruction and can agree on a system for gathering the data. Afterward, the teachers should analyze the information together. The teachers should take turns teaching and gathering data, rather than assuming that the special educator is the only person who should observe.

Station Teaching. In this co-teaching approach, teachers divide content and students. Each teacher then teaches the content to one group and subsequently repeats the instruction for the other group. If appropriate, a third "station" could give students an opportunity to work independently. As co-teachers become comfortable with their partnership, they may add groups or otherwise create variations of this model.

Parallel Teaching. On occasion, students' learning would be greatly facilitated if they just had more supervision by the teacher or more opportunity to respond. In parallel teaching, the teachers are both teaching the same information, but they do so to a divided class group. Parallel also may be used to vary learning experiences, for example, by providing manipulatives to one group but not the other or by having the groups read about the same topic but at different levels of difficulty.

Alternative Teaching: In most class groups, occasions arise in which several students need specialized attention. In alternative teaching, one teacher takes responsibility for the large group while the other works with a smaller group. These smaller groups could be used for remediation, pre-teaching, to help students who have been absent catch up on key instruction, assessment, and so on.

Teaming: In teaming, both teachers share delivery of the same instruction to a whole student group. Some teachers refer to this as having "one brain in two bodies." Others call it "tag team teaching." Most co-teachers consider this approach the most complex but satisfying way to co-teach, but it is the approach that is most dependent on teachers' styles.

One Teach, One Assist. In a final approach to co-teaching, one person would keep primary responsibility for teaching while the other professional circulated through the room providing unobtrusive assistance to students as needed. This should be the least often employed co-teaching approach.

One Teach, One Assist

In the One Teach, One Assist instructional approach, one teacher has the primary responsibility for planning and teaching while the other teacher supports students, the learning process, and the classroom teacher.

- The special education teacher or highly skilled paraprofessional may:
- Deliver SDI.
- Provide instructional interventions to support tier two response to intervention.
- Implement behavior plans.
- Assist students with assessments.
- Document learner performance.
- Assist related service personnel.

Co-Teaching With Data-Driven Instruction

After high school, I worked in a factory to put myself through college. The assembly line I worked on had production quotas that dictated how many "pieces" we were required to produce per hour. One of the first things I learned on that assembly line was to look busy. Being a young college student, my energy level was high, and I would often finish the piecework quickly. After I was done, I would socialize with my friends who were also working with me to pay their way through college. The seasoned workers on the line quickly informed us that finishing the job and then chatting together afterward looked bad. They explained that when the foreman came by it was important to look busy. If we did not look busy, we would be assigned a higher production quota. And while we young people could meet our quota quickly, those who had been working the line for decades were not able to keep up the same pace. Not only that, if we looked like we were goofing around and had time to waste, that was a concern to management.

That lesson holds true in every job I have ever held. A couple of years ago, I was sitting next to a principal who had just received an edict from his superintendent that he had to let go of three teachers. He was upset with this news and struggling with decisions regarding his staff. He asked me whether I had been in the classroom to observe a certain co-teaching pair. I had been in that class and validated that with him. He then asked whether I saw the special education teacher sitting in the back of the room on the aisle focusing on one or two students. He asked whether I had seen a teacher do anything other than sit there while the general education teacher delivered the lesson. I could not deny that I had observed exactly what he had described. He then asked me a question that, from my teacher viewpoint, I had never considered. "How can I justify keeping that teacher when I can replace her with a paraprofessional who could do the same job?" He explained that every single time he walked by that classroom, the special education teacher was sitting in the same spot, working with those same few students. This teacher had resisted all coaching to change her practice and be more involved in using her professional skills to co-teach. If he had to choose a teacher to let go, why not choose that one?

Unfortunately, this reality exists in more than one district. I have heard this story repeated multiple times since the first occasion. In a time of budget crunches, school principals are asked to make difficult decisions regarding their staff. With this in mind, it becomes even more imperative that special education teachers in co-taught classrooms truly co-teach.

This is why I deliberately exclude One Teach, One Observe from the co-teaching approaches. Although it's supposed to be observation for data collection, some co-teachers, without proper training, only observe. I feel the term is misleading.

In Chapter 2, you'll find two dozen options for maximizing the talents of both co-teachers.

One of these options, that I'll expand upon in Chapter 2, is One Teach, One Collect Data. It's a method that can be quickly implemented in the situation above with almost no change on the special education teacher's part.

While the general education teacher delivers the lesson as usual, the special education teacher can be in the usual spot, but this time holding a clipboard with a chart, noting student behavior. How are students responding to the lesson? Which are attentive? Which students seem confused?

After the lesson, the data collector—in this case, the special education teacher—can share this objective data with his or her co-teacher to help enhance lesson planning.

Even better, when an administrator or a parent walks through the room where "One Teach, One Collect Data" is implemented, the question, "What are you doing?" now has a solid response: "We are collecting data. In this classroom, we plan data-driven instruction."

Benefits of One Teach, One Assist

- Students receive individual help in a timely manner.
- It is easier to keep students on track.
- The model allows for student observation and data collection.
- Each teacher brings his or her own perspective into the lesson.
- Although co-planning is required and strongly recommended, this model requires minimal co-planning.

Challenges of One Teach, One Assist

- Students may consider one teacher as the "real" teacher and the other teacher as the teacher's aide.
- The second teacher's activity in the classroom might be distracting, or considered distracting to the students or the other teacher.
- Students may begin to expect immediate personal assistance, especially if the class is structured so that all students with special needs are seated together with the special education teacher in close proximity and easily available for immediate help.

Parallel Teaching

Parallel Teaching allows teachers to split the class in half. Group size is smaller, allowing greater supervision by the teacher. While teachers are teaching the same information with this approach, working with a smaller group allows them to identify students who may be having difficulty understanding. In a larger class setting, identifying these students is much more difficult.

Double the Participation

Typically, when using a direct teaching approach, if you ask a question, two or three students will answer it (unless you teach kindergarten!). When direct teaching using a Parallel Teaching approach, if you ask students a question, three students might answer. The other teacher asks the same question and three students answer. You now have six students participating as opposed to three!

Also, your attention is more closely focused on your half of the class because those students are nearer to you. (Sometimes you might pull that class out into another space if there's an empty classroom down the hall.) In this approach, twice as many students are participating.

Consistent with UDL Framework

Two teachers in the room, both of whom are comfortable with the topic and can teach it equally as well, may teach the same topic; however, though they are teaching the same topic at the same time and covering the same goals, they might teach it a little differently. Consequently, they reach a wider range of learning styles in the classroom, which is consistent with UDL framework. Co-teachers may also minimize behavior problems by separating students who feed off each other.

Some co-teachers—I hope you are not in this situation—are dealing with class sizes of forty-five students. I have sat in these classrooms as an empathetic coach wracking my brain for solutions to the co-teacher's daily challenge. Parallel Teaching can make the group smaller, with each co-teacher taking twenty-two and twenty-three students, respectively.

Two teachers in the room, both of whom are comfortable with the topic and can teach it equally as well, may teach the same topic and cover the same goals; however, they may each teach it a little differently. Consequently, they reach a wider range of learning styles in the classroom. Co-teachers can also minimize behavior problems by separating students who feed off each other.

One challenge to Parallel Teaching is that it requires co-planning. If you do not have planning time, you really cannot do the Parallel Teaching model unless—there is one exception—the co-teachers really work well together.

Two math teachers with whom I once worked had taught together for years. They would often finish each other's sentences. They had been teaching Algebra I and II together for four years, so they did not always have to plan together because they both knew the topic well. Planning for these teachers often consisted of short, frequent check-ins and periodic planning.

Both teachers may need to be competent in the topic being taught for Parallel Teaching to be a viable option. This model will not work if the special educator part of the math co-teaching team does not really know math as well as the general education teacher does (at least enough to teach the specific topic they are teaching together).

The Logistics of Parallel Teaching

Logistically, depending on the physical classroom set-up, one group of students may be facing a board at the front of the room and the other group may be facing the side. When they are not writing on the board, the teachers can move into the group a little bit. Proximity to the students allows the teacher to be heard.

You will need space in the classroom to divide the class in half, or an empty classroom down the hall. Note: This does not mean that every day you Parallel Teach you should take your group and leave the room. That is not co-teaching; that is divide and conquer. However, at times, co-teachers may feel using two rooms is the best method for a particular lesson. For example, if half the class is participating in a science lab, the noise and activity may disturb the other half of the class if both groups are in the same classroom.

Teachers Get Distracted, Not the Students

Noise level must be controlled when Parallel Teaching. Teachers who find this model successful make a deliberate effort to talk quietly. Interestingly, when teachers model that "quiet," students follow suit. If you have two loud teachers, you are going to disturb each other, not to mention distract the students.

Educators often ask, "Does the Parallel Teaching environment disturb the students with Attention Deficit Hyperactivity Disorder (ADHD)?" Amazingly, I have not seen that to be the case when the co-teachers keep their voices down. What happens is that, instead of being in front of the whole room as in traditional teaching, when Parallel Teaching, co-teachers are a lot closer to their students and they speak more softly. That proximity, that closeness, really helps students with ADHD. They will function better than when they are way at the back of the room. When in a larger group, students with ADHD and Attention Deficit without Hyperactivity (ADD) may struggle to focus on the lesson because the teacher is at the front of the room and other things are going on in the room around them and behind the teacher's back.

Benefits of Parallel Teaching

- Co-planning—Two heads are better than one.
- Allows teachers to work with smaller groups.
- Each teacher has the comfort level of working separately to teach the same lesson.
- Can separate students who feed off each other.

Challenges of Parallel Teaching

- Requires co-planning time.
- Both teachers need to be competent in the content.
- The pace of the lesson must be the same.
- There must be enough flexible space in the classroom.
- The noise level must be controlled.

Alternative Teaching

Alternative Teaching provides the option to divide the class into two groups, a large group and a small group. This approach is useful for groupings such as one advanced and one at grade level, or one at grade level and one needing intervention.

Alternative Teaching

- Meets individual needs—both teachers' needs and student needs.
- When you are co-planning, two heads are better than one.
- Allows you to work with smaller groups, just like Parallel Teaching.
- Teachers can be at their comfort level—their own private bubble, whether it is with a certain level of student need, a teaching methodology, or a process.
- You can separate students who feed off one another and disrupt the learning environment.

When using frequent progress monitoring to form groups, the groups will vary, thus reducing stigma for students who are typically "pulled out" of the larger group because they are struggling.

When Alternative Teaching is combined with immediate ongoing assessment as a foundation for forming groups, sometimes students with special needs might be in a higher-level group because they understand the topic taught that day.

Alternatively, if co-teachers always have the special education teacher with the lowest-level students in the smallest group, the students may start viewing the special education teacher with the small group as the teacher who is not in control. The teacher with the big group is the "real" teacher and, therefore, the one in control.

The groups need to vary. If you always have the students with special needs in the same small group, everybody will know, "Oh, those are the sped students." That stigma kills their spirit.

I have seen that slow death of morale and spirit through my years teaching high school. Students would come to me in ninth grade with such low self-esteem, feeling like they were stupid because they had always been in special education classes. When including students in general education classes that are set up for success, teachers have the opportunity to turn that negative message around. Wilson and Michaels surveyed 346 secondary students (127 special education and 219 general education) about their perceptions of co-teaching. While significant differences were discovered between groups, all students responded favorably to co-teaching: They indicated they were getting better grades and developing better literacy skills, and they said they would choose to participate in co-taught classes again. The special education students thought that co-taught English classes gave them a unique opportunity to gain access to the general education curriculum and develop literacy skills. The general education students thought that co-teaching afforded them exposure to higher levels of abstraction, concept development, and literacy skill development (Wilson & Michaels, 2006).

Consider this example: As teachers, we know that sometimes students with Autism Spectrum Disorder will perseverate on a topic. When they are into something, they are all the way into it!

A student was very interested in NASA and space travel. He watched every Discovery Channel program on the solar system and NASA. He read all the books; he had all the action figures; he had accumulated years of knowledge on the topic. In the science class, when we started teaching the solar system, ***he*** was the expert. He was in the higher level of every activity involving the solar system unit.

The other half of the story is that he usually struggled and was on an IEP. He did not even have the basic reading skills for his grade level!

This exact situation is addressed in an alternative co-teaching scenario. Students are placed in groups based on their level for any given activity. They might not always be in the lowest-level group. Everyone gets a chance to shine.

Another challenge is that if you always have the special education teacher with the lowest-level students in the smallest group, the students may start viewing the teacher with the small group as the teacher who is not in control. The teacher with the big group is "The Teacher"—the real teacher and the one in control. Consider the two previous examples: the learning strategies specialist (special education teacher) taught the main lesson with the larger group, and the content area specialist (general education teacher) taught the group that was struggling to grasp the concepts.

Again, when using the Alternative Teaching approach with one large group and one small group, it is important that the small group varies. The small group should not be the lowest achievers on a regular basis. That would be the same as segregating and tracking within the class.

Benefits of Alternative Teaching

- It meets individual needs—both teacher needs and student needs.
- When you are co-planning, two heads are better than one.
- It allows you to work with smaller groups, just like Parallel Teaching.
- Teachers can be at their comfort level—their own private bubble, whether it is with a certain level of student need, a teaching methodology, or a process.
- You can separate students who feed off one another.

Challenges of Alternative Teaching

- Groups must vary or the students in the group will quickly become labeled (e.g., the "smart" group).
- The students might view the teacher working with the larger group as the teacher in control.
- Noise level must be controlled.
- There must be adequate space.

Station Teaching

I had the opportunity to work with a talented pair of co-teachers who maximized the benefits of Station Teaching: Aaron and Jaimie, Lebanon Middle School.

They typically had students working in stations for a twenty-minute chunk of time. During that time, some students were reading, some students were writing, and some students were on laptops. They were all working on the same objective, the same standard, and the same assignment; however, they were working at their own pace. Students had the choice of strategies and tools they could use to complete the assignment. Some students hand-wrote their drafts, some used laptops to draft their essays, some used both. They were all reading the same book.

Station Teaching is an advanced co-teaching structure that can be combined with any other approach.

Generically, Station Teaching may take two forms:[2]

1. There is a "station" in a corner of the room, a piece of the room, a setup in the room, or a crate in the room. Its purpose is to have your students focus on one topic. That topic might be the area in your subject where your students did not do well on the state test last year. Or it might be an aspect of your curriculum that you need to repeat for students who struggle. It may be advanced material for students who need to be challenged beyond the standard curriculum. The goal is to give all your students an opportunity to succeed.
2. There are stations in four or more areas of the room with specific activities geared toward individualized instruction, cooperative learning, investigating, or reinforcing instruction for learning targets in multiple topic areas or standards. Students rotate through the stations at timed intervals.

2 Station teaching may be described in other resources differently. In this volume, it is presented as an advanced co-teaching strategy clearly differentiated from alternative and Parallel Teaching models.

Benefits of Station Teaching[3]

- Each teacher has a clear teaching responsibility; both can actively teach.
- Students benefit from individual or small group work.
- Teachers can cover more material more quickly if stations are well-planned and coordinated.
- There are fewer discipline problems when students are engaged in active, hands-on learning appropriate to their ability level. Worksheets and solely verbal-linguistic approaches should be kept to a minimum.
- Talkative students can be separated to minimize off-task behavior and classroom disruptions.
- Station teaching maximizes the use of volunteers and extra adults in the classroom because there are always students who need one-on-one or extra support.

---

3 Adapted from ***Partners for Student Achievement: A Co-Teaching Resource Handbook for Cooperating Teachers in VA by the MidValley Consortium for Teacher Education***.

Challenges of Station Teaching

- Flexible grouping requires ongoing co-planning, assessment, and, ideally, tiered lesson plans and activities.
- There may be increased noise in the room, unless teachers consistently teach and enforce the rules of engagement and provide incentives.
- All stations must be paced so teaching ends at the same time or students have options when finished.

Teaming

Teaming is an advanced method of co-teaching. This approach usually requires that both teachers feel competent in the subject area.

Co-teachers can equally present the content being taught, ask critical thinking questions, play "devil's advocate" in order to make a point, debate with each other and the students, and take advantage of both teachers' knowledge of the subject. Students clearly see no difference in hierarchy between the co-teachers using this approach. Teachers often find this approach satisfying, stimulating, and fun. Students are usually stimulated and motivated by having this double dynamic in the classroom. Some co-teachers become so effective in planning and working together that they feel their work is cut in half using a Teaming approach.

Normally, Teaming does not occur unless both teachers are comfortable with each other. Usually they have been together for a while and know the topic equally well.

Exceptions exist, such as when two people click. They are comfortable with each other. In English or social studies co-teaching, for example, both read the story, banter off each other, talk about each other, talk about different points, and share the classroom equally. Sometimes they do not even have time to plan together, but they can still pull it off. It depends on the personalities, but usually this situation occurs when teachers are very comfortable with each other and both know the content equally well.

It can be fun when you have reached the level where you can truly team teach. You play off one another, team with one another, and support each other. It can be amazing to watch an expert team managing the behavior, the instruction, and the activities all at once. When the two teachers really jell, and they both know the subject well, Teaming is something to behold.

Benefits of Teaming

- Creates effective, fun learning
- Teachers can use their knowledge effectively together
- Keeps co-teacher involved in class

- Allows for shared ideas including enrichment and differentiation
- Breaks up the monotony of one person doing all instruction
- Creates many spontaneous teachable moments

Studies have shown that when students in general education have co-teachers, they do not always make significant gains with Teaming. However, they enjoy the class more. They are more motivated. They may meet the other teacher in the halls and say, "How come you're not in my other class?" The dynamics going on in the classroom keep students interested and motivated.

Challenges of Teaming

- Co-teachers must click, not conflict
- Requires supporting and carrying 100 percent of the load by both teachers
- Both teachers may have to be equally involved in the planning, grading, correcting, and supporting in the classroom
- Unless they are at the stage where they are finishing each other's sentences, planning may take a long time

The Bottom Line on Co-Teaching Approaches & Differentiated Instruction

If we want all students to meet state standards and/or College and Career Ready Standards and show growth, we need to examine honestly the implementation method used in the co-taught classroom. General education teachers cannot expect to teach the whole class all the time and at the same time reach a variety of learners. If teachers attempt to do so, they will not see the gains they are looking for ***no matter how many*** support staff and specialists are in the room. This situation is especially true if the class is teacher-directed with most of the time spent by students copying notes provided by the teacher.

This is because of who your struggling learners are:

- Those on an IEP
- Students whose first language is not English (the language of instruction)
- Those on a 504 plan
- Students who are not responding

They are struggling because they are unable to learn in the traditional, auditory-based, lecture-based, whole class, everybody-does-the-same-thing-at-the-same-time teaching approach. Sure, students who can learn auditorily and through verbal-linguistic strategies will do fine. We are not doing this for them; they are already learning. We are trying to reach the subgroups that are not making necessary gains.

Chapter 1 Review and Discussion Questions

Reflection Questions

After reading the chapter, consider the following questions:

- Is the grouping of your classroom heterogeneous or homogenous?
- Are you and your co-teacher(s) communicating well?
- Is one teacher primarily in the background with little time in the front of the room?
- Do both teachers have access to the lesson plan before the lesson is taught?
- How do you group your students when implementing Station Teaching? Do both teachers work together to ensure that stations are differentiated to meet all students' needs?
- If students are struggling with a lesson, who re-teaches that lesson: the general education teacher or the special education teacher?
- How often are both teachers in the room teaching together at the same time?

Reflecting on the Models

- Based on the benefits and challenges of co-teaching with the One Teach, One Assist approach, develop a logical argument for relying primarily on the One Teach, One Assist approach.
- Based on the benefits and challenges of co-teaching with the One Teach, One Assist approach, develop a logical argument for ***not*** relying primarily on the One Teach, One Assist approach.
- After reading suggestions for what co-teachers can do in a co-taught classroom, analyze which of the bulleted items could be implemented successfully in your co-taught classroom.
- If both teachers need to be competent in the topic to Parallel Teach, could a teacher without strong content knowledge Parallel Teach? Consider the following four scenarios:
    1. The objective is to review a lesson previously taught, and the delivery would be more effective with two smaller groups as opposed to one large class.

2. Time is needed to reinforce content area vocabulary. Dividing the class in half would enable the teachers to use more creative methods of instruction while closely supervising and facilitating student activity.
3. Students are working in groups and the teachers determine that if they visually divide the class in half, they can better support and facilitate student success by each working one side of the room.
4. Core instruction to deliver new concepts is on the schedule for the class period. One teacher has strong content knowledge and the other does not.

- Do both teachers need to have strong content knowledge in all the above scenarios?
- The general education teacher has a booming voice and is used to delivering instruction with a loud commanding presence. What adjustments will the co-teachers need to make to Parallel Teach successfully?
- Analyze your class makeup as well as you and your co-teacher's teaching style. Assess your, and your co-teacher's, knowledge base and determine at least four ways you might use Alternative Teaching to provide targeted and intense instruction in your classroom.
- Consider the pros and cons of Alternative Teaching and determine how you might implement the methods that support success and consider solutions for the challenges.
- Discuss with your co-teacher how you might use Station Teaching and Teaming for effectively meeting the wide range of ability levels in your classroom.
- Which model do you feel would be the hardest to do? Why?
- What benefit can you see for co-teaching in each of these models?
- Which of the approaches would you be more willing to try first? Why?

CHAPTER 2

The HOW of Implementing the Models

Co-Teaching Models Have Evolved

In Chapter 1, I reviewed five of the six basic co-teaching approaches coined by Dr. Marilyn Friend:

- One Teach, One Assist
- Parallel Teaching
- Alternative Teaching
- Station Teaching
- Teaming

But, depending on what source you read or workshop you attended, you may have adopted variations of those approaches, even if using the work of Dr. Marilyn Friend. Co-teaching models or approaches have evolved over the years as we have learned more about what works and what does not, and in relation to how education has changed since the late 1980s. Consequently, confusion often exists as to what co-teaching looks like.

I previously taught co-teaching methodology using broad strokes of information and a variety of names for each of the models in an attempt to use language that connected with my audiences' experience with the co-teaching vernacular. However, after presenting the models using the current broad categories, many teachers admitted to me that they were still unsure how to best utilize the information I had given them. It was not until I was in a coaching session with two co-teachers that my "Aha" moment came:

Why not present co-teaching using the same specific examples that I use when I coach teachers? What if I talked about the five basic models briefly, but focused more on the pragmatic aspects, as well as more specific examples and scenarios?

Beyond the Models: Two Dozen Co-Teaching Implementations

While I will touch on the models, as they are familiar co-teaching approaches for many educators, my focus is on specific examples for implementation of the models. That said, some options for implementing co-teaching do not fit neatly under one model. Some might be difficult to categorize in a specific model.

Also, it's been my experience that without clearly defined examples of what the models can look like, co-teachers often struggle to use more than one or two approaches. Consequently, students don't receive the benefit of having two licensed teachers in the classroom. Often, the special educator or specialist takes more of a subordinate role as an assistant (Mastropieri et al., 2005; Wendy W Murawski & Dieker, 2004). This situation is especially true when the special education teacher does not feel comfortable with the content common at the secondary level. When special educators feel comfortable with the content and both have a clear understanding of the lesson, co-teachers are more likely to share teaching responsibilities more equitably (Mastropieri et al., 2005).

To support specialists in the co-taught classroom who may not be comfortable leading the content area instruction, many of the following co-teaching implementations do not require strong content knowledge. The two dozen implementations list "specialist content expertise required" at the end of each description.

My belief is that it is more important to focus on The HOW of Co-Teaching: What each teacher specifically does in a collaborative classroom to maximize his or her talents and ensure student growth and learning.

The point of this chapter is to:

- Provide specific methods to implement co-teaching and collaboration with two (or more) adults in the room so there is absolutely no doubt as to what each person's role is during a lesson or class period. Many of these implementations take approaches found in co-teaching resources and drill down to be so specific that there's no doubt what each adult in the room can do. They have explicit titles to minimize any confusion.
- Utilize fully the talents of all adults, specialists, and paraprofessionals to support student learning.
- Provide teaching approaches and activities that foster professional respect and parity between all adults in the room.
- Create a dynamic, engaging, highly effective learning environment that fosters rigorous learning in an inclusive classroom environment.

#1 Two Teach and Debate

A High School English Classroom Example

In January 2003, I was coaching co-teachers in a high school located in a suburb of Pittsburgh. I met the assistant principal at the front door and was given a list of the classrooms I was to visit that day. She pointed to one co-teaching pair and warned me that the class had been having difficulties all year and that the students were extremely apathetic.

I walked into the classroom later in the day. Two teachers were in the front of the room, both were talking, and the discussion between them and the students was very lively.

All the students were engaged in a discussion about *The Odyssey*. They were responding to provocative questions such as: What was the author's intent? Why does the story take this turn? Can this character survive?

Students came up with a variety of well-thought-out viewpoints. I was thoroughly enjoying the discussion because the energy in the room was invigorating and *The Odyssey* intrigued me, too! I was enthralled; I was fascinated. This did not look like apathy! Then I realized that the teachers were disagreeing with each other!

Later during the debriefing session, I complimented the co-teachers, Amy and Emily, on how well they worked together and asked how they got the students to be so engaged.

Amy said, "We work at it. If you came into our classroom in September, you wouldn't have seen this." They explained that they couldn't even put students in pairs at the beginning of the school year. They had four gangs represented in that classroom!

Amy said, "The first mistake we made was putting two members from opposing gangs together. A fistfight broke out!" They quickly realized they couldn't sit certain kids together. Forget peer partners! The teachers couldn't even begin to worry about critical thinking skills because discussion led to fighting.

Amy and Emily concluded that they had to model respectful debate for their students. People have a right to an opinion. Disagreement does not mean disrespect. It took most of the semester for them to achieve their goal, but by January, it was all clicking.

The co-teachers told me that modeling student collaboration, playing devil's advocate with each other, and presenting opposite points of view was the best thing they could have done for the class. By taking the co-teaching approach, they could have class discussions that enriched everyone's experience, fostered critical thinking, and took learning up a level.

By the time I was there, they had it down. It was amazing. Amy and Emily felt that was one of the best things they were able to do for their class because now they could teach. That was the first time I was exposed to the idea that co-teaching is a wonderful model for the students to learn collaboration and debate.

A High School Social Studies Classroom Example

Colleagues of mine, Kathy and Peter, taught social studies together and loved to enliven the classroom with theatrics. They decided to role-play different sides of a political issue to accentuate the different points on two sides of an election debate.

They set the stage: Kathy stood on one side of the door and Peter stood on the other. As students entered through the doorway to class, they had to walk between two teachers who were debating a political issue—taking opposite stands. They feigned intensity and passion in their disagreement. The bell rang, and the students sat in their seats waiting for class to begin—and for the teachers to calm down. Instead, Kathy and Peter followed the students into the room and took it up a level. They got a little bit louder, and then they started pulling the students into the debate. "Trish, what do you think? What do you think about this issue? Do you agree with...?"

They made it personal but refrained from becoming disrespectful or antagonistic. They were successful in engaging their class in thoughtful discussion. The brain loves and learns through emotion. They had the emotion and the energy to draw in their students and create a powerful learning experience. What a wonderful way to convey two stances on an issue! It is difficult to do that all by yourself, so modeling disagreement and debate is a powerful benefit to co-teaching done well!

The co-teachers in the previous examples implemented the co-teaching model in ways that were surprisingly simple and highly effective. I call this implementation Two Teach and Debate.

Classic Teaming involves both teachers delivering instruction on core information. The idea is that the teachers are so in sync with each other that someone walking into the classroom would not be able to determine which teacher is the specialist and which is the general education teacher.

With Two Teach and Debate, instruction is shifted from presenting core information with one perspective to presenting alternative viewpoints on the same information with each teacher playing devil's advocate to the other. The team dynamic becomes electrically charged, thus making the lesson more engaging, yet also fostering critical thinking, analysis, and respectful debate.

Much of what is taught in our standards inherently has multiple perspectives—whether it is a historical event that could have turned out differently, a math problem being solved with another process, or a different interpretation of a metaphor in a book. Also, any subject or topic that requires evidence to build a case (which is 99 percent of them) can be used as a basis for Two Teach and Debate.

After delivering three to five minutes of core content, the co-teacher delivering that content gives a signal to his or her co-teacher. The signal could be as simple as making eye contact or pointing to the co-teacher, but once the signal is given, the other half of this teaching duo knows to interject and present another viewpoint or even disagree with what was said. The co-teacher presenting the alternate viewpoint or facts then has a set time to present his or her case before the lead teacher takes another two minutes for rebuttal.

Repeat as necessary, trading the floor every two minutes for as long as the lesson plan allows. Set a timer. This exercise can become so passionate that it is easy to lose track of time.

Discuss ahead of time whether you want one co-teacher to present a specific point, play devil's advocate, or whether you just want to have the debate on the fly. Part of the beauty of Two Teach and Debate is that it can be as simple or as complicated as the topic requires.

This approach requires minimal planning time and does not require both teachers to be content area experts! All your co-teacher really needs to do is to be able to think and hold an opinion. Take the learning up a level and make the debate livelier with more in-depth background on the same topic. The variability of debate intensity will depend on the levels of comfort with debate that each co-teacher may have. Two Teach and Debate also establishes parity between the teachers. Both are equally instructive in their roles during the debate.

Engaging the students in the debate and discussion takes that learning up another level. Rather than passively sitting and watching the debate, students can provide additional evidence for either argument. Having them actively participate in the debate by searching through textbooks, notes, or even their own personal experience to provide evidence encourages them to utilize all the information at their disposal and helps them learn to defend complex information in a timely manner—a skill easily applied to essay writing and exams.

Two Teach and Debate is a powerful way to co-teach, and a surprisingly simple and flexible one. It could take two minutes, or ten, or even half of a class period if you choose. Most notably, it teaches respectful debate. It is a live demonstration for the students on how to have a thoughtful discussion and defend a viewpoint, while listening to what another person has to say.

» **Specialist content expertise required:** Minimal to moderate depending on the content.

» **Planning time required:** Minimal. Can be implemented quickly and informally without preparation.

#2 One Teach—One Summarize

There may be a time when a special education teacher is assigned to a class or content area even though he or she does not have the content area expertise. This scenario poses a challenge to the collaborative team because the specialist is learning the content along with the students. It may seem at first glance that there is no value in that pairing. However, if we look beyond the traditional co-teaching approaches, there are approaches we can take that maximize the talents of both teachers in the room.

A co-teacher may be a certified, licensed teacher, yet not know the curriculum. Maybe the area being co-taught is not the co-teacher's subject area strength. Or possibly, the co-teacher is highly skilled at teaching a certain subject, like math, but there's a new math curriculum in place so he or she was not able to participate in the curriculum training.

We know from research (Duke & Pearson, 2002) that when students summarize information, their overall comprehension of the text improves. Also, the more they practice the skill of summarizing, the better they become at the skill. Students must comprehend the text, or in this case, the spoken word, to summarize it.

Summarization is a powerful learning strategy. And we can use this same strategy with co-teachers and with students by implementing One Teach—One Summarize.

Say I am the general education teacher delivering core information. I am teaching in ten-minute chunks to keep students engaged. Then I signal my co-teacher and say, "Could you summarize that, please?"

Now, my co-teacher summarizes the information. The students are hearing the content in a different way. My co-teacher might use different language, may explain it more concretely, or more abstractly. Because of the change in content delivery, there will be students who now understand the information better because it is being explained in a different way.

Provide students with practice summarizing. Say, "Okay, could someone in the room summarize it differently?" Or "Miss Smith summarized the information using different words. Is there something we could add to her summary?" By involving the students in the summarization task, you are also teaching them to listen because you must listen to be able to summarize well.

Listening Skills Are Critical to Effective Summarization

Recently, my new business coach, Michael, spent time with me on the phone, asking me targeted questions to understand fully my perspective on some key issues. After I answered his questions and we were at a transition point, he said, "Okay, let me see if I understood you correctly." He astounded me by repeating, in summary form, every answer I gave him. He did not miss a beat.

I asked, "Are you taking notes?" Michael did not admit to taking notes, but I suspect he was. He replied, "Well, this is just good listening skills and I am working on being a better listener."

There's something intrinsic that comes from being heard. Knowing that someone heard you because he or she repeated back what you said is powerful. With One Teach—One Summarize, we not only summarize, we teach in layers. You are teaching and modeling a strategy that supports learning, listening, and relationship skills as well as aiding comprehension and summarization skills.

But My Co-Teacher Does Not Know the Content!

To summarize what the teacher leading the lesson taught, a co-teacher does not need content or curriculum knowledge. The co-teacher just needs the ability to think and to be a good listener. Therefore, with One Teach—One Summarize, we are maximizing the talent of two adults in the room, and it is okay if one does not know the curriculum verbatim.

This is in contrast with One Teach, One Assist. With that strategy, what often happens is the teacher in the assist role is often distracted from the lesson by helping a student who is off track, or responding to a student asking permission to sharpen a pencil, or a helping student who is confused. It is difficult to be the assistant in the background and learn the content the lead teacher is presenting. With One Teach—One Summarize, both co-teachers are up front. By keeping the transitions between instruction and summary quick, students remain engaged.

» **Specialist content expertise required:** None to minimal.

» **Planning time required:** Minimal. Can be implemented quickly and informally without preparation.

#3 Both Facilitate Participation and Collect Data

Both Facilitate Participation and Collect Data

While students are sharing during an interactive activity, both co-teachers facilitate student participation by visually splitting the room in half. Each co-teacher observes a different side of the room. Or, one takes the front of the classroom, and the other takes the back of the classroom. You do not need to move desks. Do not make it harder than it needs to be.

While students are conversing, co-teachers are listening to the student pairs, and encouraging dialogue. They also walk around their section of the room with a clipboard collecting data. For example, you might take note of:

- Student behavior
- Which students may need supplemental instruction for background knowledge
- Students who have expertise or unique perspectives on the topic
- Misconceptions that need to be addressed

- Examples from students' lives—attaching the content to their "real world"
- Students who share something insightful, interesting, or from a different perspective, etc.

For example, let's say I was walking by Andy and I heard him say something that was insightful. I might say, "Andy, I love what you just said. Would you mind sharing that with the group?" Andy replies, "Not at all." Now I know we can call on him, and I jot that down on my clipboard.

But Andy might be shy, or he might know that if he lets his intelligence show, his classmates might tease him in the hallway. If I ask, "Andy would you be willing to share that with everyone?" Andy may reply, "I'd rather not."

You might then say, "You would rather not, okay. It was a wonderful idea and I would love to share it with the class, so everyone benefits. Do you mind if I share it for you?"

And Andy might say, "No, that's okay."

Sensitive to Andy's concerns, you then ask, "Would you like me to tell the group that you said it, or would you like me to keep that a secret between us?"

"You can tell them."

"Great, I can tell them. Thank you."

If Andy says, "No, I want it to be a secret," that is okay. Even if I am sharing and I am not giving him credit in front of class, that works for him. He knows I shared his idea. Now, imagine he is a student on an IEP. Imagine he is a student who does not always succeed. Imagine he is a struggling learner. And I, his co-teacher, have decided that something he said has enough value to repeat it to the whole class. Can you imagine what that does for that student?

It is a self-esteem booster. Some students who struggle in school are amazingly insightful and knowledgeable, but they do not do well on tests. This sharing provides an opportunity to recognize their talents in a way that often does not happen on a written assessment.

An Effective Participation Activity: Know, Want to Know, Learned

A Know, Want to Know, Learned Activity (K-W-L) is a graphic organizer used to engage students in reading text by finding out what they already know about the topic as well as what they want to know. The goal is to activate and connect to a student's prior knowledge. We ask students to write down what they ***know***, and what they ***want to*** know before instruction. Then after instruction, return their K-W-L form and ask them to fill in what they ***learned***. By completing the graphic organizer with what a student has learned, we utilize a formative assessment that can be used to adjust instruction and support student success.

The theory behind using the K-W-L method is sound. That said, what I found when I was teaching high school was when we gave students a K-W-L, student responses were inconsistent and often did not achieve the goal of the exercise.

Here is what often happened: I would say, "Students, here is a three-columned paper with one column labeled K, one W, and one L. Please fill out the first two columns."

After collecting the K-W-L forms, my co-teacher and I would review them. Too often, the typical response was this:

What do you know?
"Nothing."

What do you want to know?
"Nothing. This is boring," or "Nothing. When am I going to use this in life?"

Some did not write anything more on the handout. Some students tried but did not have the written language skills to give us accurate information regarding their interest or background knowledge. A few students wrote volumes. Consequently, we stopped doing them. Our conclusion was that K-W-Ls do not work if students do not fill them out or they do not write anything of value on them.

The Solution: An "Oral K-W-L"

Rather than have students write down what they know, ask students to invite their partners to share verbally what they know about the upcoming topic. It is an invitation to speak, which is excellent for students who are more reluctant to participate. Allow them two to three minutes to share with their partners.

The "Oral K-W-L" is an academic strategy that differentiates instruction because it reaches the students who do not write well. Also, an Oral K-W-L is easier to utilize than a written K-W-L if you are co-teaching kindergarten or first grade. At the lower elementary level, it is harder to use written K-W-L unless you have scribes because lower elementary students typically cannot write what they already know. They can only tell you or a scribe what they already know, and you or the scribe must write it down. Most kindergarten teachers I have worked with have twenty-four or more students. That is a lot of time scribing. But now, they can do it orally.

After two to three minutes of student participation in the Oral K-W-L, take a few minutes for students to share what they know as a whole-class activity. But let's do the share with a twist.

Share What Your Partner Said

It takes courage to share your own idea, so ask students to share ***what their partners said.*** It is a whole lot less intimidating to share what the other guy said! Sharing one's own idea is not an issue with kindergarten students; however, it is a significant game changer for students in the fourth grade and up.

Tying "Oral K-W-L" and "Both Facilitate Participation and Collect Data" into the Standards

- How might you tie Oral K-W-L into the standards?

Example standard: "Develop a model to describe the cycling of matter and flow of energy among living and nonliving parts of an ecosystem."

- Instruct students, "Ask your partner what he or she knows already about the flow of energy through the food web." By implementing Both Facilitate Participation and Collect Data, before you start to teach the food web, you will have a handle on what your students know and their misconceptions.

Example Standard: "Identify and explain the strategies for the safe and efficient use of computers (e.g., passwords, virus protection software, spam filters, pop-up blockers)."

- Instruct students, "Ask your partner how computers are used to store personal information." By implementing Both Facilitate Participation and Collect Data, you and your co-teacher will gain an understanding of student misconceptions about computer and internet security. Use when delivering instruction on the standard.

Variation of the Oral K-W-L: Use a Picture as the Cue for Discussion

For a different take on the Oral K-W-L, show students a picture that is relevant to the standard about to be taught. Instead of asking students to turn to their partners and ask what they already know about X, Y, or Z, say instead, "Take a look at this picture. Pretend you are a detective. What information can you draw from this image about...?"

If the Oral K-W-L is a precursor to a reading assignment, ask, "How does this picture create the mood for the story? What does it tell you about the characters? What does it tell you, if it is one of the characters in the story?" Now, students are looking at a picture and learning how to use pictures to make predictions and gain background knowledge before reading the story.

Photograph Ad Meskens

Using a picture to spur discussion, real-world connections, and engagement in the upcoming topic differentiates delivery for students who learn best when incorporating nonlinguistic representation into our instructional methods.

For example, a kindergarten-to-lower elementary co-teacher delivers instruction on geometric shapes. The teacher instructs students, "Ask your partner, are there any rectangles and circles in this picture?" With that prompt, students are discussing the shapes they see in the picture.

In the upper grade levels, after grade level instruction on geometric shapes, co-teachers might show a photograph of architecture or interior design and ask, "What do you think the diameter of the circular window is? Take a guess. Ask your partner what he or she thinks the diameter is." For a more advanced application, teachers might ask students, "What formulas do you think were needed to create this architectural design?" Same picture, different levels of complexity with your questions, different levels at which students can apply their knowledge.

Oral K-W-L: What Did You Learn?

Math K-W-L as formative assessment: Say you just taught a ten-minute core power teach for the objective on the wall, and you want to know, "Okay, did the students get it?" Rather than going on a little longer to make sure they got it, stop after ten minutes of delivering that instruction on grade level. Put a math problem on the board and have students talk to each other about how to solve the problem.

Both Facilitate Participation and Collect Data: Co-teachers facilitate discussion and problem solving, each taking one side of the room, while ascertaining whether students understand the concepts. This application of Oral K-W-L provides a timely opportunity for co-teachers to know exactly which students need more help. Below is a more detailed description of this assessment method.

Take It Up a Level: Teach Questioning Skills

Teach students questioning skills first before the Oral K-W-L. Do a mini-lesson on how to ask someone effective questions. Provide sample questions and instruct them to use the question examples as a script or template for questioning their partner. Questions will vary depending on grade and ability level. However, some generic starters could be:

- What do you think this picture represents?
- What could have happened next?
- What can you tell about the photographer or artist's point of view?
- What is wrong in this picture? Is there a problem?
- Can you see a possible solution to the problem represented in the picture?

Students can ask their partners questions from the scripted examples to discover what their partners know about the topic about to be taught.

Take It Up a Level: Teach Listening Skills

Consider adding a listening skills component. Teach students how to listen and repeat back what they heard their partners share. Many students have poor listening skills. By adding listening skills to your lesson plan, you take the Oral K-W-L up a level.

» **Specialist content expertise required:** Minimal to moderate depending on the content.

» **Planning time required:** Minimal. Can be implemented quickly and informally without preparation.

#4 Two Support Student Participation and Engagement

While this implementation of the co-teaching models is very similar to Both Facilitate Participation and Collect Data, there is one key difference: The focus is not on collecting data during student pair shares; rather, the focus is on engaging with students by asking essential questions that cause them to think more critically and more divergently. This implementation also ensures that students stay on task.

In addition to maximizing instructional time, research has shown that it's important to use effective strategies to promote learning, engagement, and participation in the instructional process. The co-teaching implementation, Two Support Student Participation and Engagement, provides teachers with a valuable opportunity to respond to students by increasing their use of Opportunities to Respond (OTR) and positive feedback (Mckenna, Muething, Flower, Bryant, & Bryant, 2015).

The most effective ways to facilitate this implementation include:

- Visually separate the room into two halves. There is no need to move desks.
- Each teacher should own one half of the room to support and engage students.
- Resist the urge to move to the other side of the room because two teachers on the same side spells trouble among students on the opposite side.
- Listen to students' conversations and interject questions, other perspectives, clarifications, etc. to provoke students into more meaningful interaction.
- Only collect data if the process of data collection does not take away from your ability to engage with the students and facilitate their participation in the activity.

» **Specialist content expertise required:** Minimal to moderate depending on the content.

» **Planning time required:** Minimal. Can be implemented quickly and informally without preparation.

#5 One Teach—One Collect Data

One Teach, One Assist can come in a lot of different forms, like One Teach—One Collect Data. One teacher will be in the front of the room direct teaching and the other teacher will be in the back of the room with a clipboard taking notes.

Let's consider the increasing demand on teachers to implement data-driven decision-making. When using the One Teach—One Collect Data approach, the supporting co-teacher is in a good position to observe students and collect data. Co-teachers can work together in advance to decide what types of information to collect, how to collect that information, and how they might use it to make adjustments in the lesson.

While one teacher is teaching, the other teacher can circulate through the room, provide assistance to individual students, use position control to manage behavior, consider ways to reinforce the current lesson later, put notes on the board, and ask questions for the students that they might not ask on their own.

The notes you take depend on the lesson and classroom but should be agreed upon with your co-teacher beforehand. You could take notes on student behaviors, on which students have their books open or who needs more support. For example, the data collector might look at how students are responding to the lesson:

- Are they engaged, sleeping, or off-task? Looking out the window or texting?
- Which students have come to class prepared?
- Which students are struggling to take down notes and may need additional support after class?
- Are specific students attentive, asking questions, looking confused, but not asking questions, or sleeping?
- Are there students off-task? Check that off next to their name.
- Is there a kid who is having a positive effect for the day? Check that off too and add comments.
- If there's time, like with a pair-share, check for comprehension and understanding.

Note these things on the chart.

Use the notes to adjust lesson plans. For example, a comment on your clipboard might read, "at 10:45, teaching biomes, six students not paying attention." When you debrief with your co-teacher after the lesson, you can discuss why the students checked out mentally at that point and what you can both do to change that in following lessons. Whatever data you need, these notes are to help you and your co-teacher objectively assess how the lessons are going.

Now, this is not only the role of the special education teacher. Data collection can, and should be, accomplished by both teachers, depending on who is teaching at the time. A wonderful extension of this data collection experience is for the general education teacher to collect data, while the special education teacher is leading the class.

Another variation to note-taking is more formal data collection. While one teacher is direct teaching, the other teacher can be in the background with a clipboard, a pen, and a chart that allows him or her to take note of specific targeted student behavior.

After the lesson, the data collector—who might be the general education or special education teacher—shares the results with the co-teacher. With this objective data (Please be sure it is objective. It is not wise to write on the data collection form that your colleague is boring the students to death, so they are fast asleep), co-teachers have the information necessary to enhance their next lesson plan to address the issues that might become known through data collection. This data may also be used in IEP meetings, a 504 meeting, an RTI (Response to Intervention) planning meeting, or for any other purposes where student data may be advantageous.

» **Specialist content expertise required:** Minimal to moderate depending on the content.

» **Planning time required:** Minimal. Can be implemented quickly and informally without preparation.

#6 One Lead and One Student Support

Many of us are familiar with the One Teach, One Assist approach. It may appear that an implementation that is named One Lead and One Student Support is just another way of saying the same thing. However, my goal in reframing this implementation is to shift our mindset from the paradigm that locks us into thinking that the teacher providing the One Teach is always a general education teacher and the teacher who is implementing One Assist is always the special education teacher or specialist in the classroom. I would like to see us expand our thinking and take co-teaching up a level.

In One Lead and One Student Support, the leader could be either adult in the room: the general education teacher, the paraprofessional or the specialist. In addition, I've worked with teachers who made a good case for the lead being another student! By switching the verbiage from "one teacher" to "one lead," we expand our thinking into other options for leading instruction in the classroom.

When we vary the person leading instruction, we can also vary which students need support. It is possible that support is being provided to students who are working on enrichment projects. Possibly, the students who need support are students who do not understand the instructional language and need an interpreter. Of course, it could also be the students who are struggling academically, yet that group may include students who are not on an IEP but simply having difficulty with that day's learning objective.

The goal for the One Lead and One Student Support co-teaching implementation is to break out of rigid mindsets that cause us to believe the lead is always the content area specialist or the general classroom teacher and the one providing student support is always the specialist. Expanding our language to be more inclusive of a variety of roles increases our ability to view co-teaching as an opportunity to reach all learners in a manner that is highly effective for a variety of goals and learning styles present in the classroom.

» **Specialist content expertise required:** Minimal to moderate depending on the content.

» **Planning time required:** Minimal. Can be implemented quickly and informally without preparation.

#7 One Teach and One Interpret

A powerful way to take co-teaching up a level is to use One Teach and One Interpret. Let's say one teacher is a content area expert who excels at delivering information through direct teaching. Meantime, the other teacher's strong suit is in converting verbal-linguistic information into a visual format.

How would the above example work in the classroom? Visualize this: The content specialist is delivering the information verbally, augmenting it with notes via PowerPoint. At the same time, the other teacher may be drawing a picture on the board—a "snapshot device" that incorporates the first teacher's concepts into a drawing that looks like a snapshot from a camera.

The Six Inventions that Settled the West

Both teachers can think up any number of implementations:

- While the subject matter expert is direct teaching the content, the other teacher is dramatizing the information. Imagine how using actions to act out the content, or even adding costumes and props to this dramatization, can engage students!
- If one teacher knows sign language, he or she could sign specific keywords and phrases and have the students repeat those phrases, and the correlating signs, at certain periods during the lesson.
- Teachers could convey the objectives being taught using analogies, real-world experiences, stories, or any other variation to reinforce the content by reframing it from a slightly different perspective.

- Interpreting, in a visual way, the material being taught provides a new dimension to co-teaching and fully engages both teachers. It can also appeal to the visual kinesthetic learner.
- In a classroom with students who are not proficient in the instructional language, the interpreter could literally be interpreting the content in their native language.

One Teach and One Interpret does not require extensive content area expertise, nor does it require substantial planning time. It is very possible that a specialist in the classroom knows little about the content yet can listen and interpret the content differently for the students, thereby providing instruction that reaches more learners and is increasingly memorable. It also supports the specialist in learning the curriculum. That is a win-win for everybody.

» **Specialist content expertise required:** Minimal to moderate depending on the content.

» **Planning time required:** Minimal. Can be implemented quickly and informally without preparation.

#8 One Guide Tech and One Facilitate Discussion

Backchanneling

If you have ever been to an educational conference, you might have been asked to use Twitter and a #hashtag during the event. Conference organizers asked you to tweet your notes from lectures, tweet updates about sessions, or to contact people through Twitter, all using their special hashtag. You can then use the hashtag during or after the event to look up notes from lectures you missed or get quotes from sessions you did not get to see. I have done that for conferences I was not able to attend. I found the conference hashtag, followed the event through posts with that hashtag, and got tons of great information without ever having to attend.

This activity is called backchanneling. Think of it as the online activity that goes on in the background of the conference. It is a way of using technology to increase audience participation and spread relevant information, even to people who were not at that event. It is also a great tool for teachers.

Jeff, a middle school social studies teacher, had a Twitter account specifically for his class. He and the students would tweet about history, homework, and assignments using the class-specific hashtag. He could even use it to send the students reminders, prompts, and answer student questions.

Now, most of us cannot use Twitter in school because most schools do not allow it. But what a lot of teachers are doing is using other technology platforms in the classroom to do backchanneling. Some teachers are using TodaysMeet.com, or Padlet; others are using Google Classroom. It can be a simple as creating a Google Docs file and sharing it with your class. Display the Google Docs file on the interactive whiteboard or a screen; then student responses, activity in the document, etc., are on display for the entire class to discuss.

Backchanneling can even be used in kindergarten. One co-teaching pair uses Today's Meet and asks questions that require a yes or no answer. As their writing skills progress, the children can participate with higher-level vocabulary. At the middle school and high school level, it is often left to the teacher's discretion whether students use their own devices instead of school-provided devices. It is easier to manage the technology with co-teachers because one teacher can teach the lesson and the other can facilitate participation using the technology. Typically, if the teachers are clear about expectations, the students will use their devices appropriately.

With platforms that facilitate backchanneling, co-teachers typically realize more student participation and engagement than the traditional oral Q&A. After analyzing private transcripts of backchanneled meetings with students, it was noted that students enjoyed the experience, were more engaged, and some of their feelings of isolation were alleviated (Toledo & Peters, 2010).

When backchanneling, students have processing time to think through their answers before they write. Or they see another student's answer and it triggers a connection for them that they would not have gained in traditional class discussion attempts.

I recommend that co-teachers do not ask questions that have a right or wrong answer because students will simply copy from "the smart students." Some students will wait for someone to put up the right answer before responding and copy that answer. Eventually, participation in the activity declines.

Use backchanneling for questions that require multiple examples or foster multiple ways of thinking about the topic. Consider having a rule that students cannot write the same thing as somebody else. Each student must post a different answer.

For example, say you and your co-teacher just taught the class a lesson on idiomatic expressions. Rather than have students write on paper or take more notes on the topic, instruct students to participate in a backchannel activity. You might say, "Okay, take out your device. Log into TodaysMeet. We want everyone to give us one example of an idiomatic expression, in your own words."

This is where One Guide Tech and One Facilitate Discussion comes in. While one teacher is presenting instructions and leading discussion based on student responses, the co-teacher is working the computer. Now, the co-teacher is not just monitoring student behavior, but is also interacting with the students, responding to student participation, using questioning techniques to foster critical thinking and provoke response. Because everything the students add is showing up on the screen, all of it is up there for interaction in real time. When a student brings up an interesting point, you can expand on it right away.

What I have found amazing with these platforms is, repeatedly, I see almost 100 percent student engagement. Students who struggle to type, or for whom English is a second language, finally have the time and "cues" to participate in discussion. Platforms like Google Classroom have a speech-to-text function that allows students to voice their ideas into the group document. And with all those varied answers on the same subject up on screen it allows processing time to English language learners (ELL) and students who might need a refresher on core information.

In a chemistry class I was working with at a high school in Texas, co-teachers showed a couple of BrainPOP videos as a review for the next day's test. Then the students participated in a BrainPOP quiz using their own phones. To maintain on-task behavior, the co-teachers established a rule whereas once a question was answered, students had to dock their devices in the upper left-hand corners of their desks. Consequently, the students knew that after they answered the question, they could not start texting. They had to put their phone down.

In a recent qualitative study, "Educators' perceptions of uses, constraints, and successful practices of backchanneling," the authors engaged educators from the United States and Canada in online interviews to determine their perceptions of the use of backchanneling in the classroom to enhance learning. On analysis of the data from the interviews, they deemed that educators saw backchanneling as a "non-disruptive, non-subversive, collaborative activity that expanded participation and interactions. When used with intentionality, educators determined that backchanneling enhanced learning" (Toledo, C.; Peters, S).

» **Specialist content expertise required:**

- Strong content knowledge is required in most cases when facilitating the discussion.
- Strong content knowledge is not required; however, the level of understanding of the content directly correlates with the academic level of engagement with students via the technology.
- Co-teacher guiding technology must be comfortable with the technology and have an understanding of the apps and programs used.

» **Planning time required:** Minimal to substantial depending on the topic, understanding of the technology and software, and lesson objective. If it is Kahootz or a game app, time is involved in creating the questions or finding ready-made games. If backchanneling, minimal prep time may be necessary. However, the time required depends on multiple factors.

#9 One Silent & One Oral: Reading, Tests, Worksheets

Reading the Tests Aloud

I was the special education teacher in a new co-teaching relationship. I wanted our different learners to be successful and get the support they needed without garnering the stigma of being "special ed." Co-teaching was a new initiative for our school, so all of us were figuring it out as we went along. This situation caused us often to feel anxious and uncertain about how to meet the rigor of the curriculum for all students in our heterogeneous classrooms.

Because of my special education training, I was fully aware that some students on an IEP could be more successful if they had tests read to them and needed that accommodation. It was very easy to support students by reading tests aloud when they were in a resource classroom; however, now we were faced with pulling them out of the classroom during a test and having it be obvious to everyone else that these students were getting something different. The possibility that it might cause students to be stigmatized made me feel very uncomfortable.

My solution was to extend an invitation to any of the students in the class who might want to have the test read to them. Assuming that only those who needed it, students on an IEP, would request the accommodation, I shared my idea with my co-teacher, Nicole. She gave me a look of disbelief and concern. "If you tell the class that anyone who wants the test to be read aloud can go with you down the hall to have it read orally, half of the class will go with you," she said. I denied that would happen, truly believing that general education students would never want to come out and have the test read aloud to them. I insisted that it would be okay.

On the day of our first test, I announced to the class that I would be taking a group down the hall to read the test orally and that anyone who felt they could benefit from that accommodation could come with me. To my horror and embarrassment, almost half the students raised their hands, indicating they wanted to come with me to take the test. My co-teacher gave me that look that spoke volumes: "I told you so!" Though the words never left her lips, they were written all over her face. Nicole was right.

As I guided everyone out of the room and down the hall, I wondered how I was going to recover from this fiasco with my co-teacher. After everyone settled down with his or her test, I began to read the test aloud. The process was slow, and everyone needed either to wait until I moved on to the next question or move ahead while I was talking. This quickly became uncomfortable for students who truly did not need that support. Not five minutes into the test, I had students asking to go back to the regular classroom to finish their tests. Fortunately, I was only a few doors down the hall. I was able to allow the students to return to the classroom while I observed them to ensure they didn't talk or cheat.

The interesting thing is nothing was lost in the process. Some students remained who were not on an IEP, which destigmatized the accommodation of reading the test aloud to students. Others returned to the classroom, yet felt they had a choice in the way they took the test. And the next time we gave a test and I offered the accommodation once again, only the students who needed the accommodation came with me. Some of those students were not on an IEP, yet they benefited from the support. In the end, it was a win-win. Both my co-teacher and I learned from the experience and all the students benefited without attaching stigma to students with special needs.

Reading Aloud Texts, Worksheets, and Short Stories

The One Silent and One Oral implementation of co-teaching can be used for more than just taking tests. It can support students who benefit from a read-aloud. Possibly, there are students who can decode text but lack fluency, comprehension, or sustained focus and who might prefer material read aloud. This co-teaching implementation affords students the choice. It also spares students who struggle to comprehend literature that is read aloud from having to sit through round-robin instruction.

Additionally, this implementation significantly supports students navigating complex instructions on worksheets. Often, instructions and worksheet questions are at a higher reading level than the grade level the worksheet is intended for.

Read Alouds and Student Choice

A key component of this co-teaching implementation is student choice. Even students who may have oral test specified on their IEPs may refuse this accommodation. If that happens, document that the choice was offered, and that the student refused the service. Understand, however, that especially with older students—middle-school aged and above—this choice is an important one for them to make for themselves. If they are forced to take a test that is read aloud to them, the negative impact on their emotional states and, therefore, their brain chemicals may hinder their ability to be successful on a test. This is a situation where it's important for teachers to understand fully their students' needs both emotionally and academically when in the co-taught environment.

» **Specialist content expertise required:** Minimal to moderate depending on the content.

» **Planning time required:** Minimal. Can be implemented quickly and informally without preparation.

#10 Two Teach with Different Teaching Styles

Both teach the same standard differently.

Every six to eight weeks, for over two years, I sat in on math lessons taught by co-teachers, Danna and Brandi, Permian High School. Individually, they were highly effective teachers with their own teaching styles. But together, they had managed to combine those styles into a lesson plan that built off each other's strengths and taught students the same concepts in different ways.

Danna rarely used technology. She was more old school and preferred a linear approach to math with a dry-erase board. It was very step-by-step, which was important, so students could:

- be prepared for standardized tests.
- understand initial concepts, such as simplification in math.
- extend that understanding to concepts that build on the basics.

While at the whiteboard working with the abstract number concepts, Danna began the lesson by asking, "What I prefer is good-old fashioned fractions. Now, what do you need to do to a fraction?" She pointed to the fraction 20/5 on the board.

"Divide it?" one students asked.

"What's another word for divide?" Danna asked.

The students responded, "Simplify."

Danna nodded. "Simplify or reduce." She wrote the synonyms on the board, then asked the students to divide/reduce the fraction and find the answer.

"Four," the students eventually responded.

"But all it says is four?" Danna pointed out. "We said a ratio is two numbers?"

Several students chimed in, "Four over one, four over one."

"Four over one, 4/1. Your final answer has to have the one under it."

In contrast, Brandi used technology to demonstrate the solution to the same number problem, and she solved the problem using a different method, thereby demonstrating to the students that there is more than one way to solve the math problem. She also brought the math to real-world application by using familiar, concrete examples from the students' neighborhood to explain the math concepts. She was up, out of her chair, using gestures and animated inflection to help students connect the abstract math presented on the whiteboard and text to real-world application.

Brandi asked, "If I said, I want to travel from Permian to Midland Lee, am I going to start halfway? I have to start here—" she pointed to the ground below her—"because it is asking for the distance. I cannot skip. I have to start from here and count all the way to there."

This connection to real-world application was more tangible for most students, making the math more relatable and easier to understand when they circled back to more traditional, abstract math problems.

In another example, she explained, "We are doing [problems] number one and number three, okay? It talks about means and extremes. In our notes, we talked about those and we labeled them for you...and we also gave you a phrase. We said, 'We go from one extreme to the other.'" The catchy mnemonic phrase clicked with several students who had not seemed to follow the earlier lesson and who were now nodding their heads slightly.

Brandi gestured to the overhead projector, where she had a color-coded worksheet outlining several math problems and the notes from earlier in the lesson.

Whereas Danna taught at the board, in one color marker, using traditional lecture style teaching, Brandi moved into the student audience, gestured, and provided examples that connected the abstract concepts to real-world application. She used color to categorize and clarify the math process and to reinforce mnemonics taught during initial instruction.

In addition, alternating teachers delivering instruction within lessons like this helped retain the students' focus and kept the teachers on task. The class was visually stimulating and engaging.

Danna and Brandi explained to me that early on in their work together they found one or the other of them would often keep talking and talking, and they would fall behind on their lesson plans. They now use timers to signal teaching switches, and they have found that they are more efficient than ever, bouncing ideas and concepts off each other easily.

On another note, the parity and respect for each other as co-teachers was evident in their dialogue with the students. For example, Danna pointed out, "She [Brandi] did the same conversion that we did, but she likes to put it in a different formula. We don't care how you do it as long as you get the right answer."

This approach let students know there is more than one way to solve a problem, which is critical to success in higher-level math.

The teaching styles these two teachers used were both very effective and only served to reinforce the other's lessons. They held the focus of students who might learn in different ways, re-teaching things for students who needed another go at the information.

This was one of the classes where I was given access to their benchmark scores. Every six to eight weeks, I reviewed their students' progress. It was astonishing to see the incredible gains they made in a co-taught class where both teachers taught the same standard differently.

» **Specialist expertise required:** A solid understanding of the skills they are teaching and their application to the curriculum.

» **Planning time required:** Each teacher prepares for the lesson he or she is teaching so their interaction with each other as well as their delivery is accurate and smooth. Communication is essential to ensure both are in agreement about what they are trying to achieve as it relates to the curriculum.

#11 Two Facilitate Speed Partnering

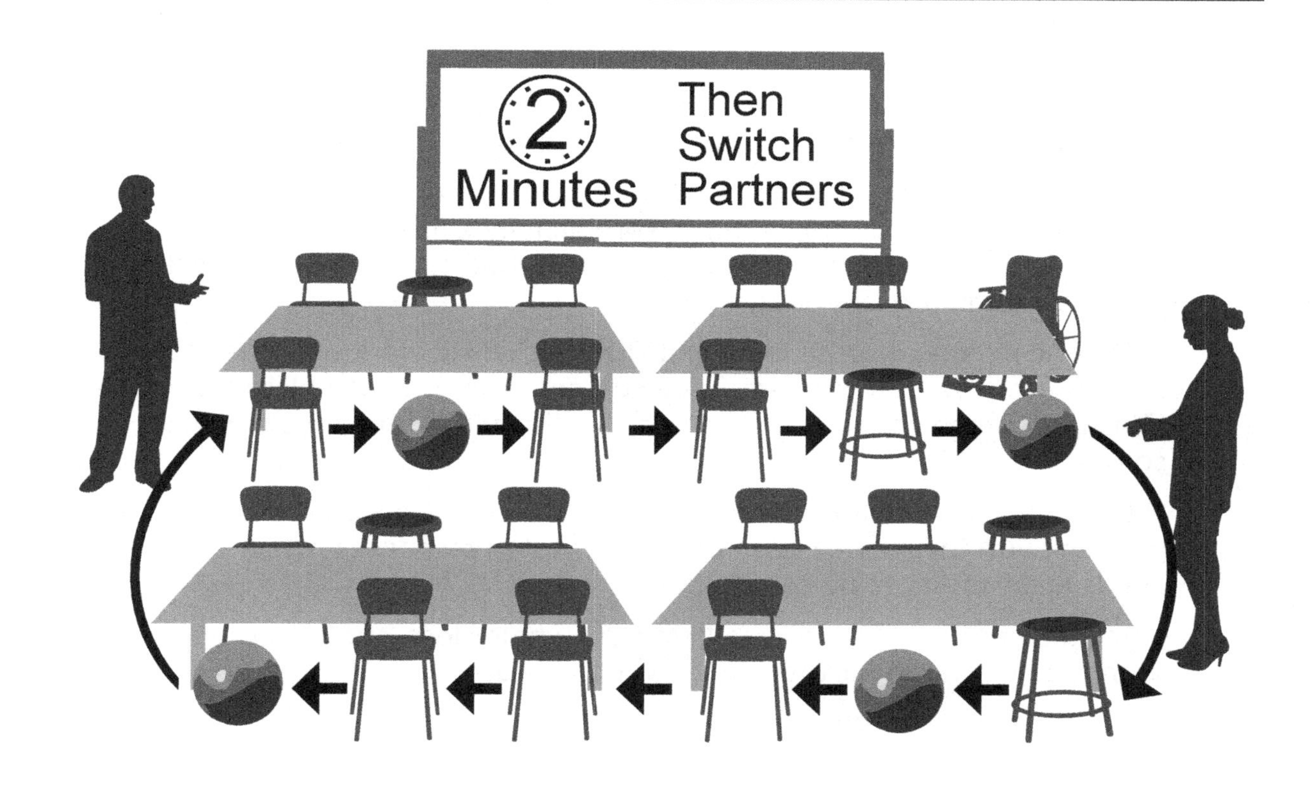

Another variation on Station Teaching, and one that works especially well with math lessons, is Two Facilitate Speed Partnering. Speed partnering is an adaptation of speed dating, as a method of pairing students for quick review and problem solving. In speed dating sessions, men and women spend three to eight minutes meeting a candidate for a date, and then they move on to the next candidate. After several speedy introductions and conversations, the men and women indicate whom they would like to date.

In Speed Partnering, students work with a partner for one to five minutes and then move on to the next partner in a predefined order (Wood & Perlman, 2017). Studies on the efficacy of Speed Partnering have demonstrated that the Speed Partnering protocol promotes the development of "soft" skills and improves the classroom environment. "Furthermore, research has demonstrated that a positive group environment has been linked with increased student learning" (Bacon, Stewart, & Silver, 1999).

I was introduced to Speed Partnering by co-teachers, Danna and Brandi. They called their speed partner variation "Speed Mathing." They chose a clearly defined process for Speed Mathing:

- One of the co-teachers reviewed the directions of a math problem, ensuring that students understood the directions and vocabulary used in problem.
- Students were given one minute to work out the math problem on their own. While students were working on the problem independently, the co-teachers walked around the room collecting data on whether individual students understood the process or struggled.
- After one minute, a timer rang, and students would work with their "speed partner" to solve the problem. They had one minute to complete the problem. (This time frame varied depending on the difficulty of the problem being solved.)
- When the designated time was up, one of the co-teachers reviewed the problem with the whole class. Students chanted responses rather than raising hands and waiting to be called upon.
- After the problem was reviewed with the whole class, students were prompted to switch partners by moving "one over."
- Repeat step number one.

This process keeps the students engaged in a continuous rotation of partners with new problems to work on each time they switch. It is a rapid-fire form of review, which is more dynamic and interesting than simply having the students work from a set of problems in the back of their textbooks. Speed Mathing was one chunk of a math lesson plan specifically targeted to ensuring that students understood the objective previously taught.

The general education teacher, Danna, taught a ten-minute core power teach of the day's objective. Rather than extend the direct instruction to twenty or thirty minutes and have students work independently on problems for review, she and Brandi engaged the students in Speed Partnering to work out the problems traditionally left to individual instruction or homework.

While the students worked, the co-teachers circulated around the room, assessing what the students could do on their own as well as with their partners. The Speed Mathing activity provided a valuable formative assessment that helped inform the rest of the lesson, letting the co-teachers know whether they needed to spend more time reviewing the problems or whether the students had a grasp on the content.

Something else noteworthy in the process was the added technique of rephrasing the directions and example questions. When explaining a problem, especially a word problem, Danna and Brandi often asked students to come up with different vocabulary for the same words or process than those found in the question. They pushed students to be more comfortable using language they were not as familiar with, particularly vocabulary from the standardized tests.

In combination with the limited time for solving math word problems, these aspects of Speed Partnering serve to give students practice at taking timed standardized tests without the added stress of an actual exam.

» **Specialist expertise required:** A moderate to solid understanding of the skills they are teaching or reinforcing and their application to the curriculum.

» **Planning time required:** Each teacher prepares for the lesson he or she is teaching so their interaction with each other as well as their delivery is accurate and smooth. Students may ask either teacher for help during step two and step three. Both teachers need to be prepared to respond to student questions. Communication is essential to ensure they are both in agreement about what they are trying to achieve as it relates to the curriculum.

#12 One Large Group and One Focus Group

Historically, when utilizing a big group with a small group pulled to the side, as in Alternative Teaching, the small group is usually the students on an IEP doing remedial work with the special education teacher. When I started co-teaching in 1993, I did not want to take the students with learning disabilities in a small group to a corner of the room because I did not want everybody in the class to look at the group and say, "That's the group with the special education teacher, so those are the dumb students." I am not a proponent of doing anything in the classroom that further stigmatizes students who have special needs or learning disabilities. Consequently, my co-teachers and I rarely used this co-teaching implementation. Since then, I have seen wonderful things happen with Alternative Teaching implementations when teachers do not rigidly hold on to the belief that the small group is the students on an IEP.

Renaming this grouping approach to One Large Group and One Focus Group reframes the co-teaching approach. I love the mind shift that takes place when we simply change the words "small group" and replace them with "focus group."

In the early 2000s, I observed co-teachers, Francine and Jenny, Woodington Middle School, implementing One Large Group and One Focus Group. I assumed the small group was the students on an IEP working with the special education teacher. I was wrong.

During the debrief later in the day, I learned the focus group was indeed composed of students with special needs; however, there were also students who were not on an IEP included that needed additional supports. For example, one of the students had missed school the day before, so for that student, it was initial instruction.

The biggest surprise was that the special education teacher had been instructing the large group while the general education teacher was re-teaching the math to the focus group.

At the beginning of the school year and through to the holidays, they facilitated the One Large Group and One Focus Group implementation with the general education teacher, Francine, teaching the large group and her special education co-teacher, Jenny, teaching the focus group. When Francine was home at the holiday break, she started reviewing her class data and assessing where the students were academically. She realized that the students in the focus group, the ones on an IEP, had not made gains in their math lessons. They had plateaued. It frustrated and concerned her because the state test was in three months, and there was tremendous pressure to make Adequate Yearly Progress because they had not yet achieved that goal as a school.

Francine explained, "I realized why the students were plateauing. Jenny was learning the math along with the students. When she was re-teaching, she didn't know any other instructional techniques beyond what she learned from my math lesson." Jenny had no other tools or methods to present the information. Francine explained, "I've spent my career teaching math. I love attending math conferences, so, I have gone to many workshops on differentiated instruction. I know how to teach math and figure out how to help students to understand the content."

When they returned in January, both teachers agreed that during math intervention, the special education teacher would take the large group and facilitate a review activity while the general education teacher, with her more specialized knowledge and tool bag of techniques, took the focus group. They also pulled other struggling students or students who had been absent into the group.

With this targeted teaching arrangement for One Large Group and One Focus Group, the students in the focus group made significant gains. Francine felt more confident in their ability to help students learn the curriculum, and Jenny was very happy in her role as facilitator. All students in the co-taught class benefited from having the two teachers.

One Large Group and One Focus Group is also a great tool for students who need to catch up. If there's an unplanned day off from school, One Large Group and One Focus Group can be used for students who missed assignments, need to make up quizzes, or need SDI.

An Opportunity for Enrichment

One Large Group and One Focus Group can also be implemented for students who need challenge work. Consider that you presented initial instruction on a core objective and most of the class needs additional time to go over basics. However, there's a handful of students who understand the content and are ready to move on.

The focus group could be used to enrich those students and ensure that their needs are met, also. I often hear co-teachers lament that they spend so much time supporting students with learning challenges that students who are academically advanced get left behind. This co-teaching implementation provides a viable solution for reaching all levels of learners in the classroom.

How Might One Large Group and One Focus Group Look?

The Large Group:

- Individual students working independently
- Student pairs or triads working collaboratively
- Students receiving direct instruction as a whole

The Focus Group:

- Students who need SDI
- Students who need to make up tests, or missed assignments
- Students who are ready for enrichment activities

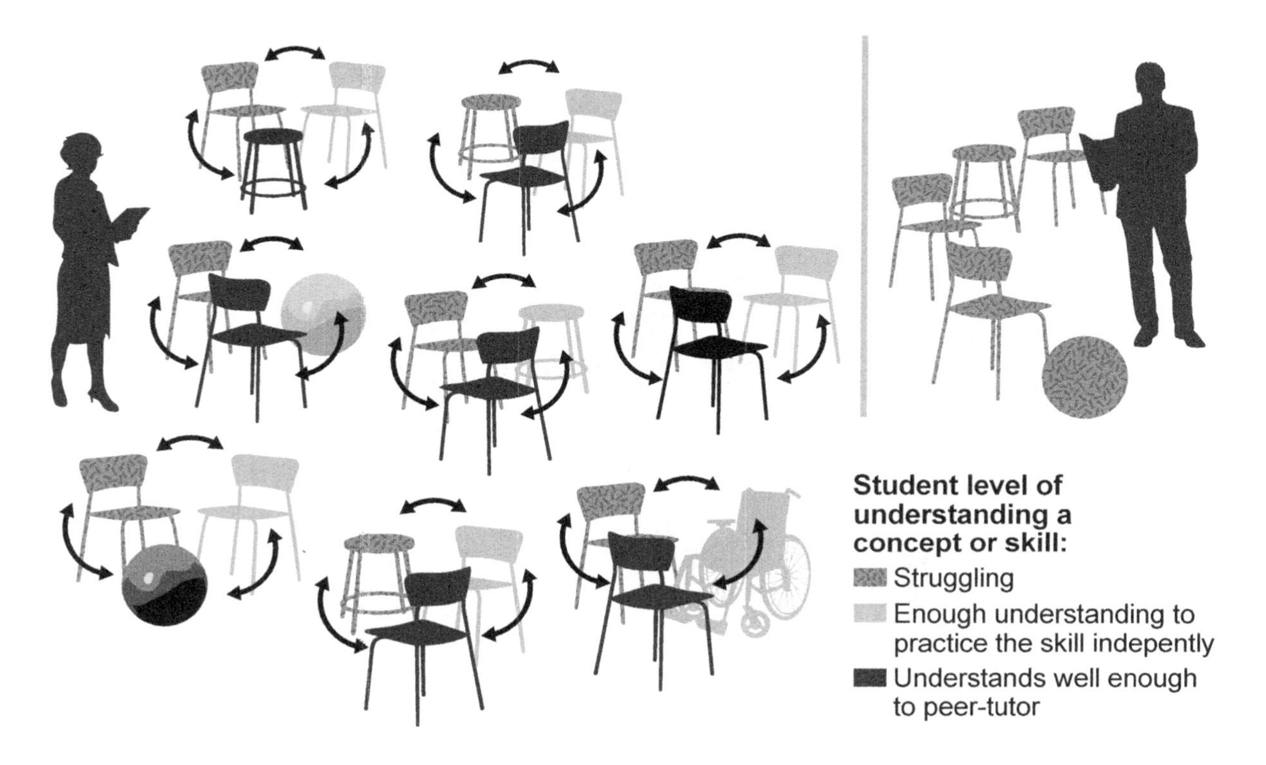

» **Specialist expertise required:** It depends on the goal of this implementation. If the specialist is facilitating the large group in review, moderate content understanding is necessary. If the specialist is supervising behavior, possibly minimal content expertise is required. However, if the specialist is teaching concepts critical to understanding the lesson's objective, then the specialist will need a solid understanding of the concepts he or she will be teaching. If the specialist is leading the focus group with an enrichment activity, the specialist will need to know how to facilitate the activity without giving students too much assistance. Also, if the specialist is delivering SDI to the focus group, strong content knowledge as well as an understanding of how to differentiate instruction is critical.

» **Planning time required:** Each teacher prepares the lesson(s) he or she is teaching to the group. Communication is essential to ensure both are in agreement about what they are trying to achieve as it relates to the curriculum.

#13 Both Teach Half—Same Objective, Same Way

This implementation is equivalent to the Parallel Teaching approach. Co-teachers divide the class into two equally sized mixed-ability groups. The implementation, Both Teach Half—Same Objective, Same Way, clearly describes the Parallel Teaching Approach. Each co-teacher takes half the class and instructs the students using the same methods to teach the same content. They are working together in parallel.

I observed co-teachers, David and Maggie, Bow High School, each work with one half of a social studies class to help students prep their side of a debate. The energy in the room was electric. Students were engaged, challenged, motivated, on task, and most importantly, learning. Interestingly, they were able to concentrate despite the increased noise level. This is not much different from a large dinner party that breaks up into two or three conversations that all go on at once. It worked! This would have been much more difficult for a single teacher to manage. With two teachers, however, the lesson went smoothly.

Essentially, the benefit to Both Teach Half—Same Objective, Same Way is having the ability to teach the content in two smaller groups instead of one larger group.

Using this format doubles the participation. It is also an opportunity to separate students who misbehave when together. With a smaller group, a co-teacher is better able to look in the students' eyes and read non-verbal signals that may convey understanding or confusion. It allows more opportunity to ask questions, and really dig into the content because of the smaller group and the proximity of the teacher to the students.

The key to making Both Teach Half—Same Objective, Same Way work is that both co-teachers need to a have solid knowledge of the content being taught. If you're delivering initial instruction, you both have to know that material 100 percent. But what about review? What about dig-deeper activities, facilitating discussion, or running a vocabulary review?

Review activities, facilitated discussion, vocabulary review, and similar activities that do not require content specific expertise are all ideal for implementing Both Teach Half—Same Objective, Same Way and do not require both co-teachers to be content experts.

» **Specialist expertise required:** It depends on the goal of this implementation. If the specialist is facilitating review or discussion, moderate content understanding is necessary. If the specialist is teaching concepts critical to understanding the lesson's objective, then the specialist will need a solid understanding of the concepts he or she will be teaching.

» **Planning time required:** This implementation requires planning time. Planning can be done face to face or in the cloud. Teachers need to plan together to ensure they are both teaching the same objective in the same way. Communication is essential to ensure they are both in agreement about what they are trying to achieve as it relates to the curriculum.

#14 Teach Half Then Switch—Skills & Rigor

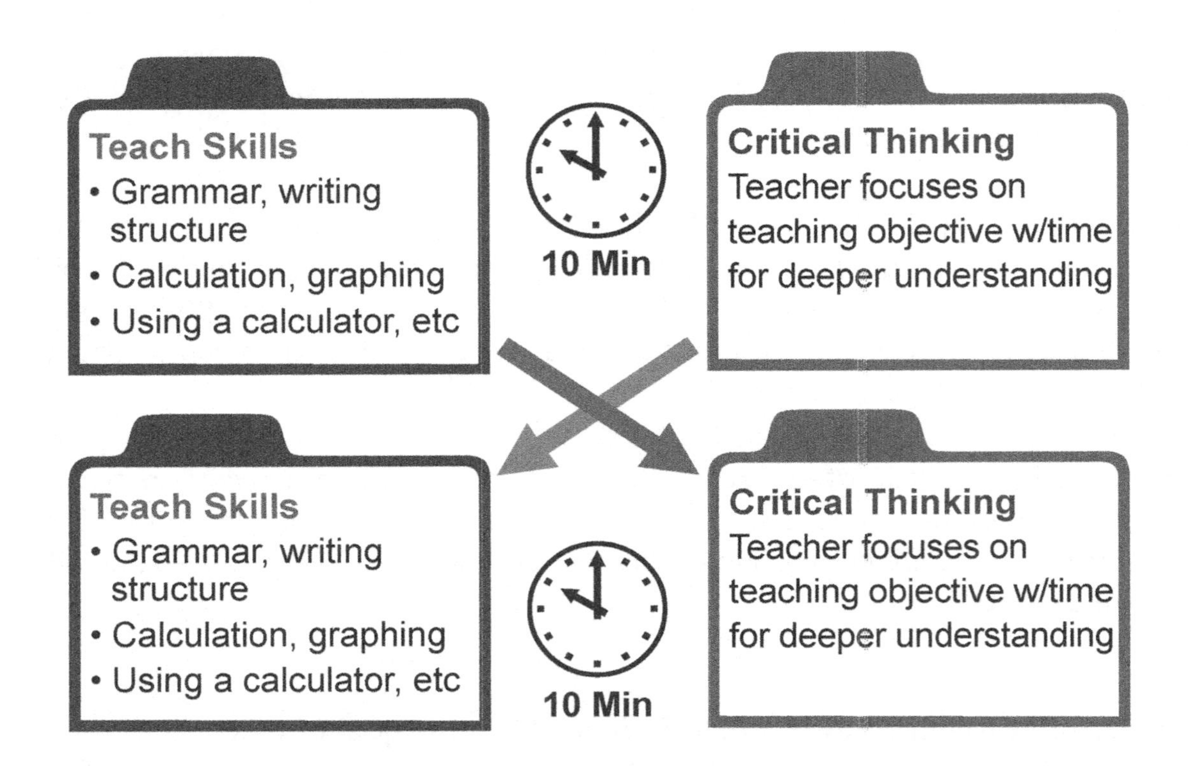

When I walked into an eighth grade language arts classroom at Rochelle Middle School, I was fascinated by the desk arrangement and co-teaching approach being implemented.

The co-teachers, Natasha and Dianne, had arranged the desks so there were two sections of desks and chairs. Seven desks and chairs faced seven more desks and chairs, creating a makeshift conference table. That same arrangement was repeated on the other side of the room. Each teacher was seated at one fourteen-student "conference table."

Natasha, the language arts teacher, was reviewing the skill of drawing inferences from text. She had several poems scattered about the desks. The students took turns reading the poems and discussing them. She expertly maintained their attention and asked questions to provoke their understanding. The students' focus and thoughtful responses impressed me. At one point, she responded to a student's look of confusion, engaging him in the lesson. It occurred to me that if this lesson was delivered to the whole class at once, this student would have been lost. Later, Natasha told me that with a smaller group in close proximity, she could quickly catch and support any student who was struggling.

The special education teacher, Dianne, was reviewing grammar and test-taking skills with the students. She had strips of paper with state test questions on the subject of grammar spread out over the multi-desk conference table. Students were reviewing grammar as well as analyzing the format of the test questions so they'd be prepared for the state test.

They each worked with their half of the class for ten minutes. Then, a timer went off and they switched groups. They taught half the class and then switched. Students who were reviewing grammar for the first ten minutes were now reviewing how to draw inferences from poetry during the next ten-minute chunk.

When I asked them about their experience, Natasha explained, "I love teaching poetry, but this is eighth grade and we have twenty-eight students in the class, mostly boys! Try to get eighth grade boys interested in poetry; it isn't easy!" she laughed. "But with this small group, I can do it."

I asked Dianne whether she enjoyed teaching grammar. She responded, "I'm not comfortable teaching poetry. I'm not comfortable drawing inferences. Natasha is so much better at it than I am; I'm still learning. However, I've spent my entire career as a special educator correcting grammar and teaching students how to take a test. I feel confident teaching those skills."

Let's put this in perspective. These co-teachers could've taken their twenty-eight students and implemented One Teach, One Assist. With that approach, Natasha would have reviewed drawing inferences from poetry by direct teaching the whole class. Dianne would have supported students in the background. She may have had some behavior problems because, as she explained, it's twenty-eight students, mostly boys, and keeping them engaged in a lecture format was challenging. They may have planned that chunk of the lesson for ten minutes.

After that ten minutes of review, they could have spent another ten minutes reviewing grammar and test-taking skills again, using the One Teach, One Assist model.

Which is a better use of instructional time? Teaching twenty-eight students at once and reviewing two topics for twenty minutes? Or teaching half the class, in two mixed ability groups, in focused, targeted instruction? Using Teach Half Then Switch—Skills and Rigor, they had smaller groups, divided the behavior problems, and then switched. They used the same amount of class time.

Using Teach Half Then Switch—Skills and Rigor is effective because a targeted objective can be covered in each station. This increases the students' and teachers' concentration and focus on that specific objective in a smaller group. It allows the teachers to analyze and respond to students' individual needs. This co-teaching approach was used in a study designed to investigate the efficacy of co-teaching in the instruction of reading comprehension. It was determined that students in the co-taught groups had a greater increase in comprehension skills than students in the control group (Haghighi & Abdollahi, 2014).

Follow These Steps to Implement Teach Half Then Switch—Skills and Rigor:

- Arrange student desks so there are two sections of desks and chairs. For example, seven desks and chairs facing seven desks and chairs to make what is akin to a long conference table. Repeat the same arrangement on the other side of the room.
- Strategically divide the class into two mixed-ability halves.
- Have each teacher sit at one student "conference table."
- Teachers should sit at the opposite ends of their "conference table" so they can signal each other and view the entire room.
- One teacher teaches half of the class that day's objective, with appropriate rigor for the class or grade level.
- The other teacher teaches half of the class focusing on a skill necessary for the subject. For example, students might be reviewing and relearning the skill of grammar, or reading, interpreting, and creating charts and graphs, or how to read a map (topographical, weather, or geographic), use MLA format, etc.
- After ten minutes, switch. Either the students can move, or the teachers can move.
- If teachers move instead of the students, engage students in a brain break to break up the sitting.

These co-teachers use a graffiti wall activity to review skills while the other half devise test questions for review.

» **Specialist expertise required:** A solid understanding of the skills they are teaching and their application to the curriculum.

» **Planning time required:** Each teacher prepares the lesson he or she is teaching to his or her half of the class. Communication is essential to ensure that both teachers are in agreement about what they are trying to achieve as it relates to the curriculum.

#15 Teach Half Then Switch—Pre-Teach or Enrich

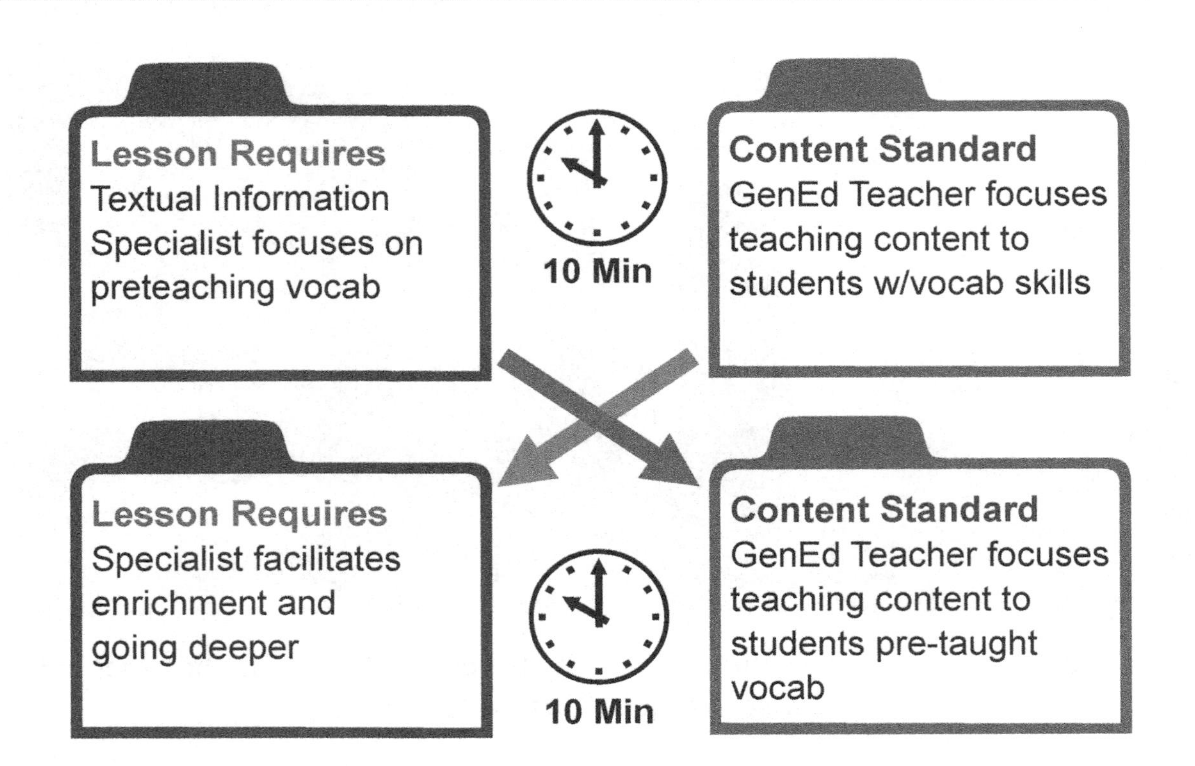

Another implementation of Teach Half Then Switch is Pre-Teach or Enrich: to pre-teach half the class while teaching the other half the day's objective, and then switching. After the switch, the half that was pre-taught learns the day's objective while the other half is challenged with an enrichment exercise.

For this implementation, we divide the class in half by ability level. One of the simplest ways to do this is to take your gradebook and sort it by grades as opposed to sorting by student names in alphabetical order.

- Sort by student grades so you have the highest grades at the top of the list and the lowest grades at the bottom.
- Then, divide the list in half as shown in the diagram.
- We are going to make an assumption, then adjust: Assume that the top half of the class does not need to spend instructional time being pre-taught background information or vocabulary for that lesson's objective. If you have students who are on the bottom half because of missed assignments or tests who truly belong in the top half of the class for that lesson, adjust your groups accordingly.

- The students in the top half of the grade roster (above and including the median) will spend the first ten minutes of instructional time with the content area teacher learning that lesson's objective.
- The students in the bottom half of the grade roster (below the median) will spend the first ten minutes of instructional time with the specialist pre-teaching concepts, vocabulary, or facts necessary for the lesson's objective.
- Set a timer for ten minutes.
- When the timer rings, switch groups.
- The students on the bottom half of the roster now gain instruction on the lesson's objective. They are prepped and ready for the lesson because they were pre-taught information critical for their understanding.
- The students on the top half of the roster are given a challenge activity to take their learning up a level. Find options for challenge activities in the appendix.

Because the grades will change over time, the halves will also change. This benefits students on all levels.

» **Specialist expertise required:** Minimal to moderate knowledge in the content area. If the specialist is pre-teaching vocabulary, content knowledge is not critical. If the specialist is teaching concepts critical to understanding the lesson's objective, then the specialist will need a solid understanding of the concepts. For the enrichment activity, the specialist will need to know how to facilitate the activity without giving students too much assistance.

» **Planning time required:** Each teacher prepares the lesson(s) he or she is teaching to his or her half of the class. Communication is essential to ensure both teachers are in agreement about what they are trying to achieve as it relates to the curriculum.

#16 Teach Half Then Switch—Reading in the Content Area

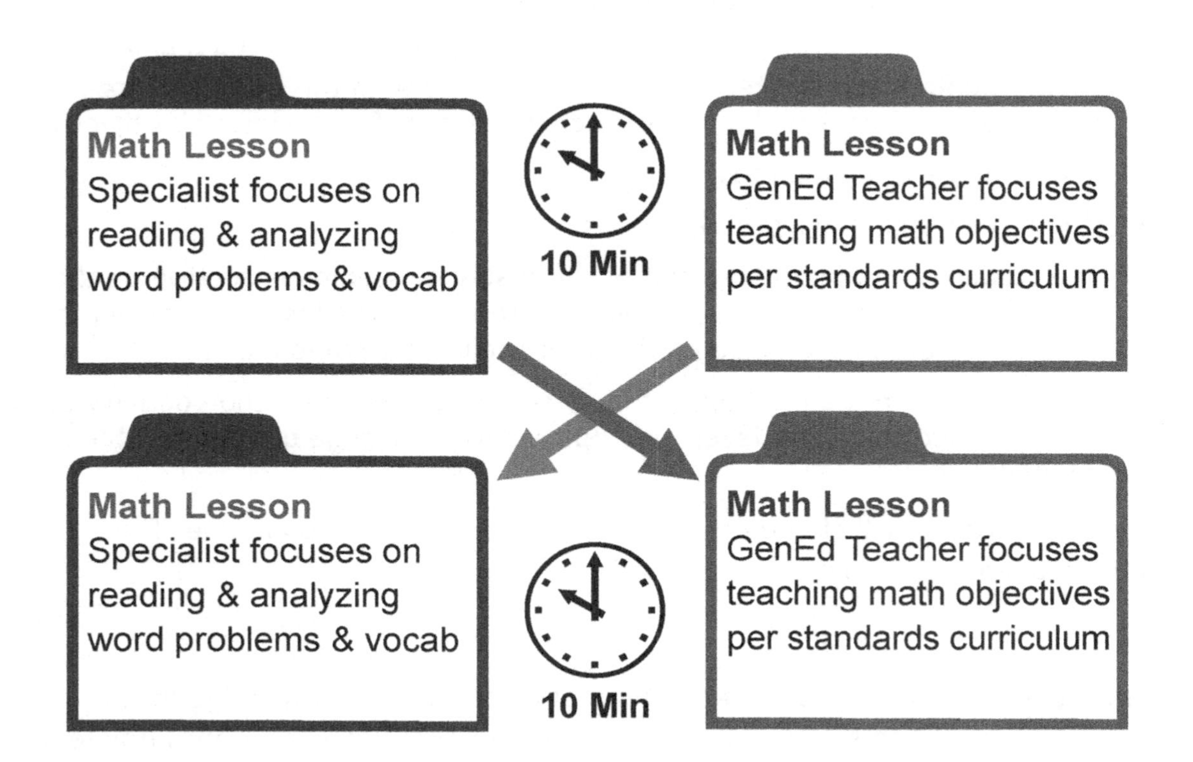

Jerry, a special education teacher newly assigned to a co-taught classroom at the middle school, approached me quite distressed. He felt he was doing a disservice to his co-teacher and his students. He explained that he had been an award-winning literacy specialist at the elementary level. His passion was teaching literature through literacy circles.

Because he continually wanted to better himself, he went back to school to get a second master's degree focusing on special education. After he turned in his credentials to say he was licensed in special education, the district moved him from the elementary school he loved into a middle school math classroom.

"I'm a literacy specialist! I do not know math!" he exclaimed. "I feel like I'm doing a disservice to my co-teacher."

Adam, Jerry's co-teacher, overheard the conversation and was astounded that Jerry did not realize the positive impact he had on the success of their students with the math curriculum. He explained, "In all my years of teaching, I never could teach students how to get through word problems like you have. By the way, their math vocabulary is amazing! They are doing so much better in word problems than I ever imagined possible!"

Adam realized he had not communicated to Jerry how much the students were benefiting from the co-teaching arrangement. He would split the class in half and have Jerry go over the word problems with the students. It was not just busywork like Jerry feared, but rather an intentional effort to support the students in their ability to read math vocabulary and word problems.

Now that Jerry understood the benefit he brought to this middle school math classroom, he was reenergized. Both he and Adam realized they could use Teach Half Then Switch to support students' ability to read in the math content area as well as teach them math calculation and problem solving.

What if instead of focusing on what our co-teacher can't do, we focus on what he or she can do that adds value to our instructional process? In one study, teachers resolved challenges in achieving a compatible relationship by learning from and relying on each other's differences and strengths. Contrary to the belief that co-teachers mismatched in content expertise is an obstacle to overcome, teachers achieved parity in their roles through using their expertise in content knowledge and differentiation to mentor each other (S. Pratt, 2014). Adam and Jerry used their individual skills and areas of expertise to benefit the students as well as learn from each other.

Follow these steps to implement Teach Half Then Switch—Reading in Content Area:

- Arrange student desks so there are two sections of desks and chairs. For example, seven desks and chairs facing seven desks and chairs to make what is akin to a long conference table. That same arrangement is repeated on the other side of the room.
- Strategically divide the class into two mixed-ability halves.
- Each teacher sits at one student-populated "conference table."
- Teachers sit so they are on opposite ends of their "conference table" to have the ability to signal each other and view the entire room.
- One teacher teaches half of the class that day's academic objective.
- The other teacher teaches half of the class reading in that content area.
- After ten minutes, switch. Either the students can move, or the teachers can move.

- If teachers move instead of the students, engage students in a brain break to break up the sitting.

» **Specialist expertise required:** Teaching reading in the content area.

» **Planning time required:** Each teacher prepares the lesson he or she is teaching to his or her half of the class. Communication is essential to ensure both teachers are in agreement about what they are trying to achieve as it relates to the curriculum.

#17 Teach Half Then Switch—One Review and One Run Lab

Manny and Ella co-taught middle school science in a poor district just outside of Albuquerque, New Mexico. The school budget was tight, and they often found themselves unable to replace material that had been broken during the science labs. Consequently, Ella often lacked the materials to run a proper lab with the entire class. She lamented that she had to do demos instead of engaging the students with labs because there was not enough lab equipment. We brainstormed solutions to the problem and realized that Teach Half Then Switch could be an excellent solution to the equipment shortage.

Manny could run a review lesson with half of the class on a topic essential for the curriculum, but not necessary for the lab's implementation. While he ran the review lesson, Ella could run the lab with the students in triads instead of lab partners. That easily set the stage for having enough equipment to engage students in science labs, despite their shortage of equipment.

In their effort to make science real, students studied forensics. The forensic techniques discussed and performed in class throughout the unit needed review. Manny took half the class to another room and played a PowerPoint version of *Jeopardy* with the students to review the forensic techniques. While he facilitated the review with the students, Ella ran the lab. The next day, they switched groups so that over the course of two days, all the students reviewed important concepts for forensic science as well as had the opportunity to participate in the science lab.

This same co-teaching implementation can be used with any lesson that would be more engaging if hands-on materials could be used during instruction. Sometimes teachers have a shortage of math manipulatives such as Unifix Cubes or Algebra Tiles. While one half of the class uses the math manipulatives, the other half of the class is engaged in a review game that reinforces concepts critical to that unit. In this situation, it is possible to shorten the chunks of instructional time to ten or fifteen minutes, thus making it possible to implement this co-teaching strategy during one class period.

Implementation Suited to Vocational and Technical Schools

This co-teaching strategy is a viable option for vocational classes such as culinary arts, electronics, programming, and web development. In the vocational setting, it provides teachers with the opportunity to reduce the teacher-student ratio when teaching critical concepts that require hands-on practice. Safety is increased as well as focus and the opportunity for deeper learning.

Follow these steps to implement Teach Half Then Switch—One Review and One Run Lab:

- Plan for classroom requirements. This implementation often requires that teachers use two classrooms. Some science classrooms have a lab station in the back of the room with lab tables supplied with electrical outlets, faucets, etc., and an instructional setting in the front of the room that utilizes traditional desks. Most schools, however, especially at the middle or junior high level, do not have the space or functionality to implement this co-teaching approach in one room. Consequently, it will be necessary for co-teachers to find another space to instruct the review. Find a space that's relatively close to the classroom to minimize instructional time wasted when walking to the next classroom and transitioning into that learning environment.
- Strategically divide the class into two mixed-ability halves.
- Decide which teacher is best skilled to instruct the lab and the review.
- One teacher facilitates the lab half of the lesson, incorporating the appropriate level of rigor for the class or grade level.
- The other teacher teaches his or her half of the class, reviewing a skill necessary for student understanding and recall of the curriculum.
- Decide whether the halves will switch the next class period or whether the lesson can be implemented in one class period. If implementing One Review and One Run Lab in one class period, limit the time of the lesson chunk to ten to fifteen minutes.

» **Specialist expertise required:** A solid understanding of the skills being reviewed and their application to the curriculum.

» **Planning time required:** Each teacher prepares the lesson he or she is teaching to his or her half of the class. Communication is essential to ensure both teachers are in agreement about what they are trying to achieve as it relates to the curriculum.

#18 Two Facilitate Group Process and Collect Data

During cooperative learning and group-work activities, co-teachers can be collecting data on which students are doing well with the material, which might need help, and how the individual students are interacting within their groups. Data collected can be used to calculate parts of the students' grades and to grade group progress. Data collection can also be done by both teachers at once, when implementing Two Facilitate Group Process and Collect Data.

Using specific observational data as part of a rubric for the final grade provides a viable solution to the fairness issue that frequently plagues group work. Parents and students often feel grading a group project on the end product is unfair. There is a belief that one student inevitably does the bulk of the work. Using a rubric that includes multiple checkpoints minimizes this issue.

Again, visually split the room in half. Each co-teacher focuses on one half of the room (one third if there's three of you, etc.). Resist the urge to move to another side because a student "over there" raises his hand. My experience has been that when both teachers are on one side of the room, some students on the other side will take advantage of the opportunity that being unsupervised presents. Sticking with one section of the room also affords teachers the opportunity to focus more completely on specific students or groups and their needs.

The Group Process Data Collection Form is a tool to target goals and behaviors you have determined are critical to success. List the behaviors you want to target to the form at the top of the page. Some may include:

Student(s) is (are)...

- Demonstrating respect toward peers
- Doing their share of the work
- Demonstrating good listening skills
- Contributing to discussion, solution, etc.
- Being Collaborative rather than competitive
- Understanding the objective of the activity

» **Specialist content expertise required:** Minimal to moderate depending on the content. Understanding of group process norms and best practices for facilitating effective groups recommended.

» **Planning time required:** Minimal. Can be implemented quickly and informally without preparation.

#19 One to Manage Logistics—One for Safety and Questions

Some classroom activities, such as experiments in physics or chemistry, or maintenance activities in a computer class, involve having students work with equipment or materials that could cause harm if not used correctly. For safety purposes, effective use of this model can even be applied at the elementary level during activities that employ certain manipulatives or equipment. The focus of this implementation is on moving about the room and engaging with students to answer questions and verify proper use of materials while ensuring safety during exercises and experiments. This implementation is well suited to Vocational and Tech Schools.

The most effective way to facilitate this implementation is:

- One teacher focuses on the logistics of making materials available, grouping students, data collection, etc. This adult is relatively stationary with a good view of the entire room.
- One teacher focuses on monitoring student safety and answering questions during the activity. This adult moves around the room and is actively engaged with students.
- Both adults listen to students' conversations and interject questions, offer perspectives, clarifications, etc. to provoke students into more meaningful interaction.

Metalworking Scenes

getting bar stock from the stockpile

cutting to length using the horizontal bandsaw

grinding a radius on both ends using the finishing machine

using a bending jig to "cold form" a scroll shape

the bench vise helps to make a scroll's edges "flush"

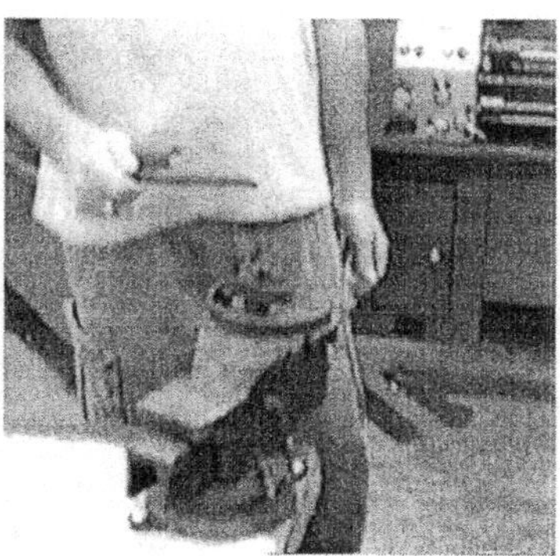
the bending jig

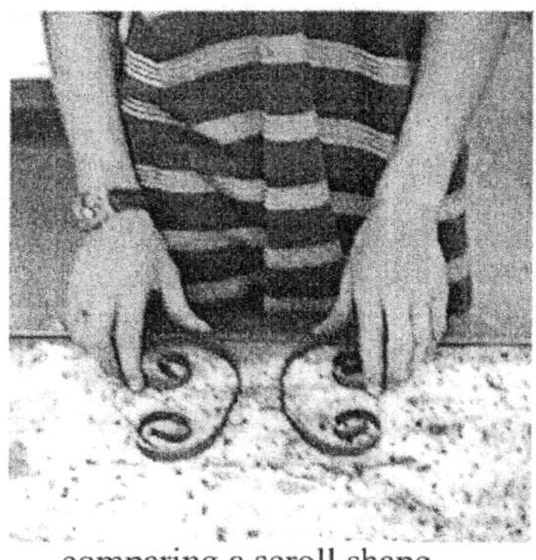
comparing a scroll shape to its matching "workpiece"

comparing a scroll shape for "symmetry"

comparing a scroll shape to check progress

George Jackman used his time while managing logistics to take photos of students performing the steps of the process and created reference manuals for students "with the students as the stars!"

» **Specialist content expertise required:** Should be able to model competently and monitor proper safety procedures. Subject matter expertise is minimal to moderate depending on the activity.

» **Planning time required:** Minimal. Can be implemented quickly and informally without preparation.

#20 Two Individualize with Station Teaching

There are as many ways to co-teach as there are types of students. The same is true of Station Teaching. Depending on the rapport between co-teachers and the atmosphere of the classroom, variations on Station Teaching can be used to maximize student success.

Remember Aaron and Jaimie, co-teachers at Lebanon Middle School, who used twenty-minute chunks of time for Station Teaching, almost exclusively? They took the first five minutes for warm-up, then the next ten to fifteen minutes for direct instruction with the whole class on the objective for that day. After the direct instruction, they instructed the students on the expectations and assignment for their stations.

Students could choose to work alone, with a partner, or in small groups. They also could choose their approach to completing the assignment. All students were required to complete the assignment, but they had choices on how they accomplished the tasks to achieve that goal. Some students used laptops to type while others wrote by hand. Some students read the book, while others listened to audio versions of the text. The result was that they were all working toward the same objective.

Both co-teachers rotated through the stations to make sure they supported every student, not just the ones who needed intervention. They checked in with students to see whether they were accelerating through the assignment or needed extra help. Using Station Teaching to provide time for instructional conferencing (Learned, Dowd, & Jenkins, 2009) allowed them to support students in a way that not only increased student skill level, but also provided students will a level of autonomy that fostered independence and motivation.

As their coach, I tried to get Aaron and Jaimie to try different co-teaching approaches and implementations. However, they felt that they had a system that worked, and honestly, they did.

Their students were making gains, and that is really the measure of good co-teaching. I am not as concerned about what approaches are being used as I am with whether students are making gains.

» **Specialist expertise required:** A solid understanding of the skills they are reviewing and their application to the curriculum.

» **Planning time required:** Minimal. Can be implemented quickly and informally without preparation.

#21 Three Mixed-Ability Rotations

High school math co-teachers, Elizabeth and Jason, effectively used Three Mixed-Ability Rotations for review before tests. Each co-teacher reviewed one segment of the test with a third of the class. One third reviewed independently. The groups rotated every ten minutes. After thirty minutes, each student participated in a small group review with each co-teacher and had the opportunity to practice test review questions independently.

To ensure the independent group stayed on track, each rotation was assigned a student leader. That student was available to answer questions or help any student in his or her rotation that might need some assistance solving the problems assigned. The student-led review was especially impressive to watch because the students having trouble would reach out to the student leader for help and the student leader would tutor them. They did not tell those students, "Hey, here is the answer," instead they tutored them effectively. Tutoring a peer reinforced the information in the student leader's mind. Summarizing and explaining information to other students helps the peer leader retain that information.

Station teaching, like co-teaching, involves finding your rhythm—finding the system or arrangement that works for you and your co-teacher as a unified pair. The rotations above worked well for Elizabeth and Jason because they took the time to smooth over kinks in their transitions and teaching systems in a conscious effort to work well together.

Crystal and Michelle, fourth grade co-teachers at Clara Love Elementary School, used Three Mixed-Ability Rotations successfully in their classroom for both language arts and math. They would deliver core content in a ten-minute chunk at the beginning of class. Then, the students would break into three groups. Desks were facing each other, conference-table style. Students at two of the stations worked with one of the co-teachers to reinforce the core content delivered at the start of the lesson. The third station worked individually on netbooks loaded with the MobyMax personalized learning system.

Contrary to the belief that students in an inclusive setting would be distracted by two teachers teaching at the same time, the students were highly focused on the teacher leading their group or the individualized curriculum they were working with on the netbook. Using this approach, by the fourth quarter of the school year, one child gained ten reading levels, students with behavioral difficulties exceeded expectations in social growth, and overall student achievement was significant.

» **Specialist expertise required:** A solid understanding of the skills being taught or reviewed and their application to the curriculum is necessary.

» **Planning time required:** Each teacher prepares the lesson he or she is teaching to his or her rotation. Communication is essential to ensure both teachers are in agreement about what they are trying to achieve as it relates to the curriculum.

#22 Three Same-Ability Stations—Re-Teach, Reinforce, Enrich

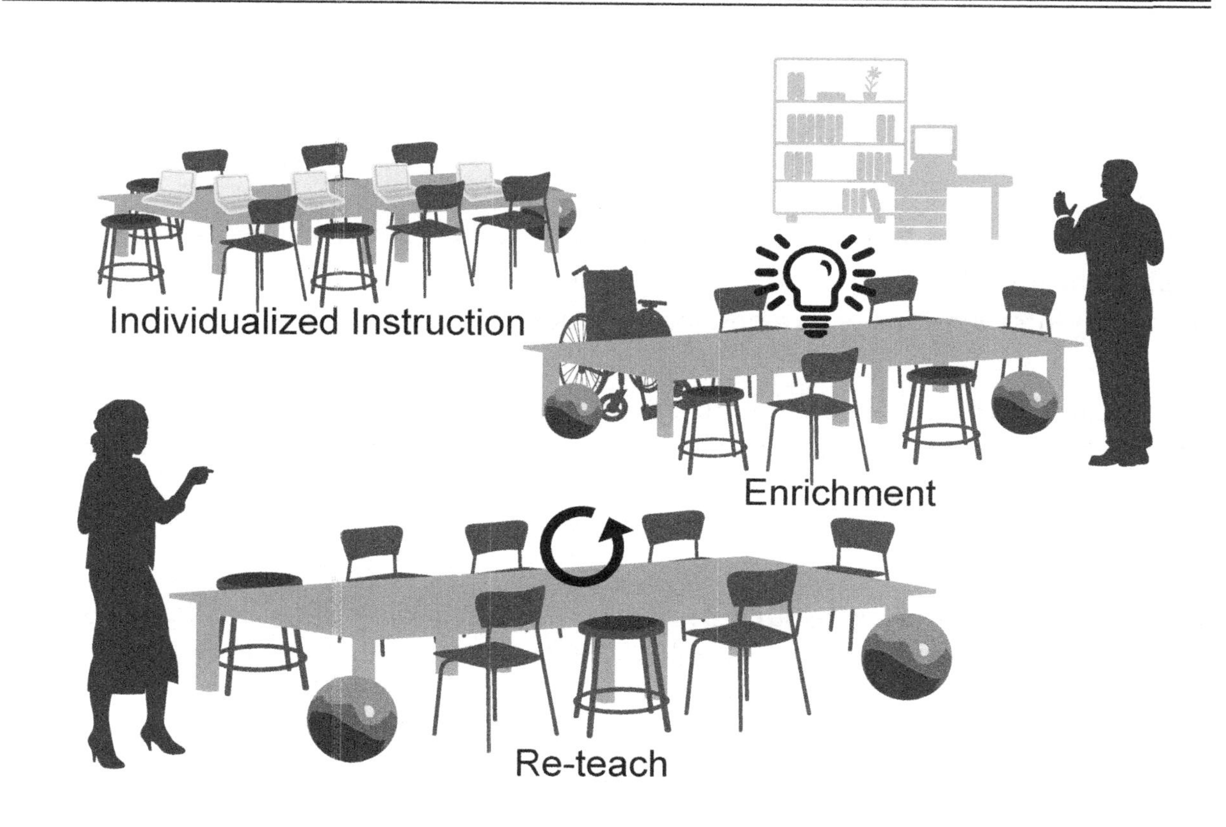

How to Implement Same-Ability Rotations with Flexible Grouping

Same ability groups have earned a negative reputation because too often they are used too much, thereby, sentencing students to a school career imprisoned in an academic caste system. Yet, there are times when same ability groups are beneficial. The key is ensuring that the groups are flexible and based on frequent formative assessment.

Flexible grouping can be a great strategy to incorporate into your lessons to meet the needs of all levels of learners. With flexible grouping, students' level of achievement is assessed before leaving class or ending a lesson. Typically, co-teachers use quick formative assessment tools such as exit cards.

After analysis of the formative assessment, students are grouped according to their level of understanding of that unit or lesson. The fluid nature of this strategy ensures that students are not put in a group and then forced to stay at that level throughout the school year; rather, they can advance or get additional instruction at their own pace.

Once we know where students are regarding their understanding of a lesson, we can group them based on their ability, for ten-minute chunks of time, two to three times per week to re-teach, reinforce learning, or enrich their understanding.

We so often lament that we must teach to the middle. However, this co-teaching implementation allows us to teach efficiently to students' level of understanding, providing interventions where needed, and advance instruction where warranted.

For instance, with this implementation, you might have one enrichment group, one on-track group, and one review group. Each teacher facilitates one of the two groups and one group works on its own.

» **Specialist expertise required:** A solid understanding of the skills being taught or reviewed and their application to the curriculum is necessary.

» **Planning time required:** Each teacher prepares the lesson he or she is teaching to his or her rotation. Communication is essential to ensure both teachers are in agreement about what they are trying to achieve as it relates to the curriculum.

#23 Two Run Acceleration Centers

Fitzell Acceleration Centers™ - A Better Alternative

A **Fitzell Acceleration Center**TM is a merging of several "station" methods. If you have ever created a learning center, implemented an Accelerated Reading program, or if you are familiar with Science Research Associates' individualized direct instruction for Reading Mastery (SRA), you have worked with stations. The Acceleration Center4 takes the best from each of these and combines them into a model appropriate for elementary and secondary levels.

Generally, teachers do not center-teach anymore. We do not have the time to prepare learning centers with the "one use" paradigm. For the most part, they are a foreign concept to secondary teachers and considered "elementary."

Acceleration Centers are similar to the concept of learning centers, except that teachers do not create a separate center for every unit. Instead, teachers focus

4 Note: For the purposes of readability and brevity, all references to "Acceleration Center(s)" in this text are understood to mean "Fitzell Acceleration Center(s)TM."

on a curriculum strand taken from the state standard. Activities in the center range from very basic skills to the highest skills, and possibly even college level material. One center or station is utilized for the entire year, and beyond.

You Make It Once and Use It All Year

You prep it once and possibly add to it during the school year. One or more small groups must work independently of the teachers.

The only maintenance required is student assessment and reassignment.

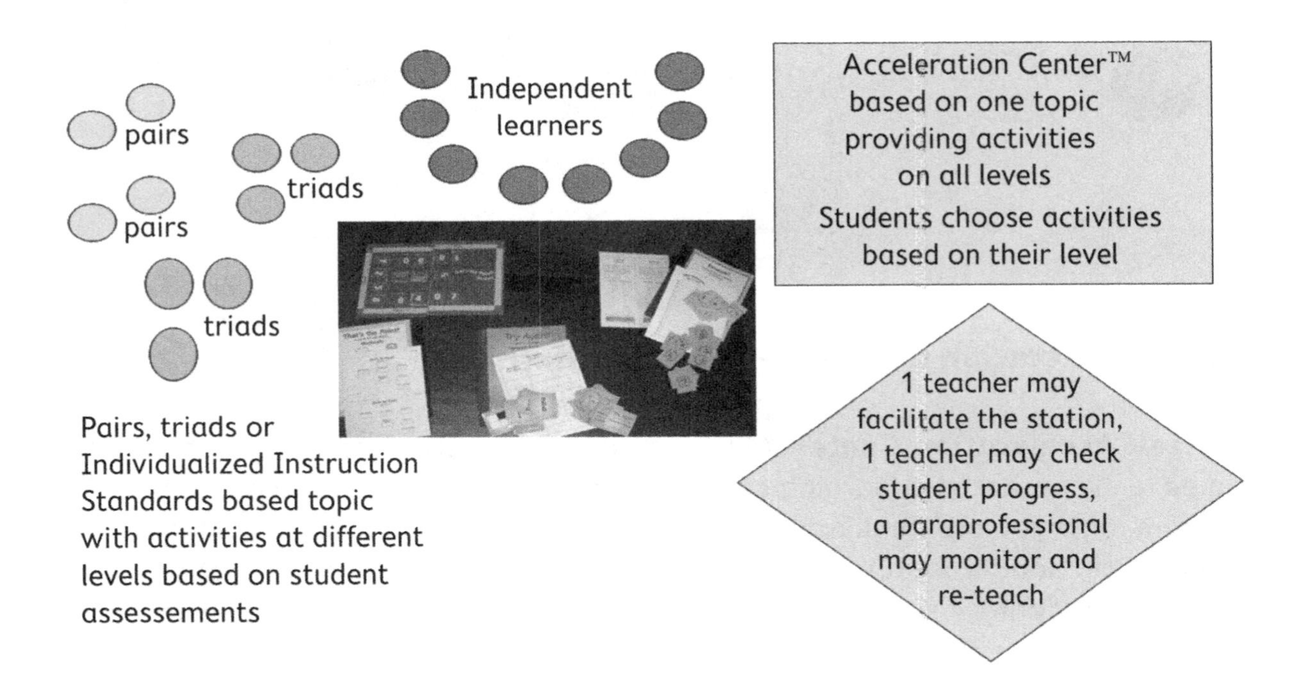

Fitzell Acceleration Centers Respond to All Learners

The Acceleration Center approach allows students to work at their ability levels. When co-teaching in diverse classrooms with a wide range of ability levels, few ways work better to bridge the gap than Station Teaching. With the Two Run Acceleration Center implementation, students can work at their ability level in either individualized or small group activities, geared toward accelerating their progress in meeting curriculum goals and state standards.

While students work with activities they have chosen from the Acceleration Center, teachers are free to become facilitators in student learning, as needed. Co-teachers might set up Acceleration Centers and each monitor one station. For example, one Acceleration Center might be for writing skills and another for grammar.

If you decide to implement Acceleration Centers, start small. Start with one standard and one Acceleration Center with multiple activities at varying levels. I have worked with teachers who get very excited about the concept and immediately start planning three different centers, or a center per teaching unit. Start with one. Co-teachers will be less likely to become overwhelmed with the planning and prep work involved, students have time to practice using centers, and the bugs can be worked out before a new Acceleration Center is planned.

Try an application of your chosen model. Start small. Take baby steps toward implementation. If it is overwhelming, you are probably trying to do too much all at once.

Additional Resources

For a more complete and detailed support, and instructions for implementing group work and Acceleration Stations™ refer to *RTI for Secondary Teachers* by Susan Fitzell. (Corwin Press)

For quick reads on the topic:

1. Navigate to SusanFitzell.com
2. Click on Articles in the header menu.
3. Type "Acceleration Center" in the search box.
4. Hit return.

You'll find several articles on the topic.

For program handouts:

Bonus398.susanfitzell.com

For professional development options:

SusanFitzell.com/Teachers/

Keep It Simple—Start Small and Enhance Over Time

Brett and Kate, a co-teaching pair from Penacook, New Hampshire, chose one standard strand: mastering multiples, multiplication and division for their Acceleration Center. They set up one center with four stations around the room to practice the strand at different levels. Each station presented a challenge activity using a different game format.

In a debrief session afterwards, Kate said, "Not only did all the students in the class increase their proficiency on the standard, but we had an unexpected surprise. One of our students has been numb to school all year. No matter what we did, we could not motivate him. After we introduced the Acceleration Center, he was so excited that he kept asking when we could do it again. We were amazed at his enthusiasm. Most encouraging, his assessment showed improvement! The Acceleration Center activity worked."

Brett and Kate started with one concept: multiplication. Now they can add to the foundation, incorporating more activities at different levels for skills in the math strand for multiplication.

The benefits of Two Run Acceleration Centers is:

- It makes differentiation easy to implement and timing is flexible.
- It provides an opportunity to respond to student learning (or non-learning).
- It supports multiple ability levels in the inclusive classroom.
- Often, because activities are varied and students have choices, apathy and lack of motivation are minimized or eliminated.
- It provides time for co-teachers to provide students with extra support.

» **Specialist expertise required:** A solid understanding of the skills they are teaching or reviewing and their application to the curriculum is necessary.

» **Planning time required:** The planning time is front loaded. Acceleration Centers are built prior to first use. They can be time consuming to build. This implementation is only worth the time and effort to build and implement if it can be utilized at least twice a week for a minimum of ten to twenty minutes. This implementation is to incorporate repetition and practice of skill deficits.

#24 Team Teaching

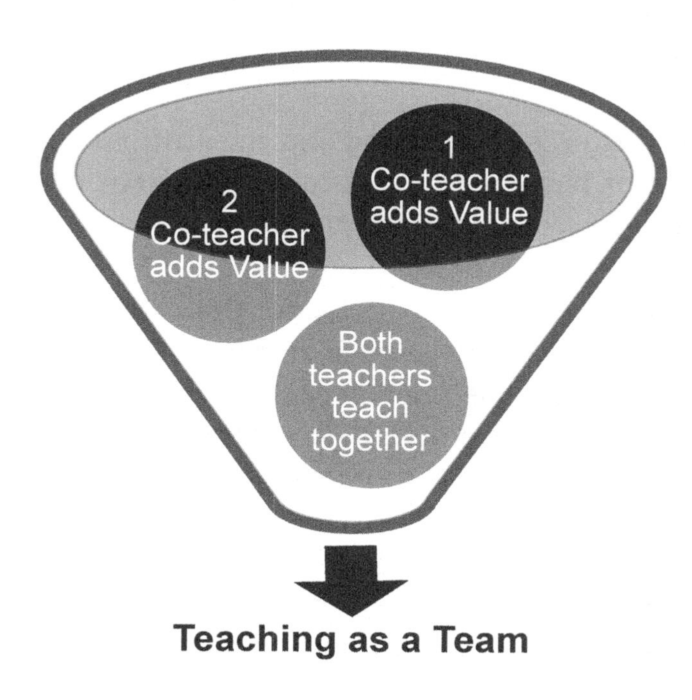

If there is one co-teaching term that instigates misinformation, conflict, and the demise of co-teaching efforts, it is Team Teaching. Although this term is no longer listed in the most recent iteration of Dr. Marilyn Friend's co-teaching models, it's still a widely used term.

Many teachers, administrators, and specialists equate Team Teaching with dividing everything in half. Everything must be done equally. Equal correcting, equal planning, equal work, equal interfacing with students, equal equal!

That expectation and misinformation about the Team Teaching model significantly impacts the success of many co-teaching initiatives. I am going to present a simpler definition of Team Teaching:

Two or more teachers working together as team players with the common goal of supporting student success and the success of the teaching team.

It is not equal workloads, nor specific roles. It is about collaboration, shared ideas, maximizing each individual's strengths—from the teachers' strengths to the students' strengths—and supporting each other with whatever it takes to create a successfully co-taught classroom.

Any one of the twenty-three co-teaching implementations shared in this chapter could be an example of Team Teaching because each implementation requires the adults in the room to be team players in the process.

Team teachers provide seamless instruction for their students through communication, persistence, perseverance, and mutual agreement on how to implement the co-teaching models and provide powerful, effective instruction. Team teachers are problem solvers, idea generators, and supportive co-players in the classroom field working toward a common goal.

Team teachers develop trust in each other and feel safe expressing their ideas and feelings. Team teachers each carry their own weight and respect the agreements made for how they would run the classroom and, consequently, achieve their goals as co-teachers.

Very simply stated: Team Teaching is implemented when teachers work as a healthy team together to support student learning and success.

» **Specialist expertise required:** Varied

» **Planning time required:** Varied.

Your Co-Teaching Approach

Co-teaching works best when educators make conscious choices about how to implement the co-teaching model. Each co-teaching implementation has benefits and challenges that should be considered for every lesson or class period. It is also important to consider the co-teachers' personalities and learning styles. Co-teaching doesn't work well when two teachers show up in a room together and "punt."

One Teach, One Assist is the most common co-teaching model; however, any one of the other approaches might be a better choice depending on the lesson plan, the class dynamics, available preparation time, availability of materials, etc. Some approaches are more appropriate for certain grade levels or subject areas, or at certain times of the year, than others.

Choose how you implement the co-teaching approaches based on the lesson's goals, class personality, behavioral dynamics, and teacher comfort levels. Consider each model's benefits and challenges, and then decide, with your co-teacher, what will work best. It is not uncommon to observe seasoned co-teachers using one implementation the first half of the class, another co-teaching implementation the second half, and totally different co-teaching approaches the following day.

How to Choose the Best Implementation for Your Classroom

No one approach works every time, all class period, in all classes. Co-teaching requires teachers to know their students and to know ***each other***. Knowing your co-teacher, understanding his or her personality, and maximizing individual teacher strengths will yield the greatest results. I speak from not only being a co-teacher myself starting in 1993, but from the experience of coaching co-teachers in a multitude of demographics and environments since 2002.

Do you co-teach? If so, what co-teaching approaches do you prefer? Why? Do you find that the approaches need to change based on what you are teaching? What positive advice can you give other co-teachers?

Co-Teachers Might Choose Approaches Based On

- The learning needs of the students, student behavior, and the level of student motivation.
- Teacher personality and learning style can significantly impact which approach is chosen.
- The lesson plan often dictates which approach might work best. If the lesson involves hands-on small-group work, teachers may choose Station Teaching. If the lesson is primarily direct teaching, teachers might choose One Teach, One Interpret.
- The physical space available in the classroom may significantly impact the approach implemented. Sometimes teachers must be very creative to figure out a way to differentiate presentation styles within the physical limitations of the classroom.

Which Co-Teaching Implementations Are Most Effective at the Elementary and Secondary Levels, and Why?

Which co-teaching implementation you should use depends on the lesson's goal, as well as a variety of other factors. There is no one most effective approach. For example, let's look at Parallel Teaching. This approach allows teachers to split the class in half. Group size is smaller, allowing greater supervision by the teacher. While teachers are teaching the same information with this approach, working with a smaller group allows them to identify students who may be having difficulty understanding. In a larger class setting, identifying these students is much more difficult.

Dealing with Large Class Sizes When Co-Teaching

There are teachers out there—I hope you are not in this situation—who are teaching classes of forty-five students. I have sat in these classrooms as an empathetic coach wracking my brain for solutions to the teacher's daily challenge. Both Teach Half—Same Objective, Same Way can make the group smaller. Even if you are teaching twenty students, using co-teaching implementations that forms smaller groups can be effective in reaching more students.

A Side Benefit: Staying on Schedule

Co-teaching implementations for set amounts of time keep teachers on schedule. Also, there's an unintentional advantage to this. Because you and your co-teacher are teaching the same thing, you know you must finish at the same time, so you can go on to the next activities. It keeps you both on track and you get more of the lesson done. You are less likely to let the students veer you off track with irrelevant questions.

Chapter 2 Review and Discussion Questions

Reflection Questions

- Consider the implementations outlined in the chapter and choose three you feel could be implemented in your classroom, with your co-teaching partner.
- What is it about these three implementations that you feel will work well in your classroom?
- What challenges might you face, either with your co-teacher or the students in your class, with each implementation?
- How will you apply each implementation to ensure the maximum benefit for your students? What roles will each co-teacher have?
- How will these implementations help to increase learning for all students in your classroom?

Practical Application

With your co-teacher, plan and implement a co-taught lesson using one of your three chosen implementations. Then reflect on the following questions:

- Did you feel successful/effective in what you wanted to accomplish? What worked? What did not work as planned? Why do you think that? What could you do differently next time?
- What is it that you have learned from your co-teacher and his or her style of teaching? About yourself? About your students?
- What is it that is wonderful in working with a variety of students in the classroom?
- What is it that is frustrating or challenging in working with a variety of students in the classroom? What could you tell colleagues about the needs of students who learn differently?
- What are your next steps?

CHAPTER 3

The HOW of Co-teaching with Specialists

Co-Teaching and Collaboration with Specialists

When a special education teacher is assigned to a general education classroom, it's often called co-teaching. With that arrangement, there's an expectation that the special education teacher may teach and have a role as an equal instructor in the classroom. Sometimes the expectation is clear that the special education teacher will implement a true co-teaching model taking a lead role in instructing all students, including students with special needs.

On the contrary, it's common for other specialists to work with ***only*** students on their caseload. Often, when specialists arrive in the classroom, the general education teacher does not even acknowledge their presence. Rather, specialists attempt to pull ***their*** students aside to deliver prescribed services. Consequently, the perception of being extraneous to the classroom, instead of an equal contributor to it, is a major hurdle that many specialists face.

That said, some specialists are effectively co-teaching with general education teachers at all grade levels. When it comes to co-teaching, some things are universal. For as many types of teaching specialists as there are, and despite the often highly specific nature of the services they provide, the expertise they contribute can positively impact the success of all students.

Following are contributions from specialists who have worked side-by-side with general education teachers to support students on their caseload as well as other students in the class. My hope is that more specialists will be invited to take a collaborative role in the classroom, maximizing the talent of both adults and supporting the success of all students.

RTI Specialists

While planning and coordination are critical for any effective co-teaching arrangement, they are doubly so for intervention specialists. Intervention specialists focus on physical, cognitive, communication, academic, or behavioral delays, and implement RTI plans for identified students.

The demands on an intervention specialist's time are extensive, so for Rae, a teacher in the Northmont City School District, the fact that her intervention specialist co-teacher was so willing to utilize her time to help the entire classroom, and not just the students she was assigned, was greatly appreciated.

"We were better able to meet the children's needs," Rae said of co-teaching with the intervention specialist. "Sharing the workload and being in the same room at the same time allowed us to be equal in our roles. The students knew that we were a teaching team."

When creating lesson plans, Rae said they defined their overall roles and duties ahead of time. They often co-planned via Google Docs. Their plans, handouts, and activities could be printed out and modified as needed. Both were "owners" of a Google Classroom.

They were also eager to try implementing other co-teaching techniques involving different seating arrangements, teaching strategies, and were generally open to exploring new ideas.

But just as the intervention specialist was involved with the general class, so too was Rae involved with the students who were on an RTI plan. "Being able to provide daily documentation on student progress was much easier due to role sharing and working as a team," Rae noted.

Their duty sharing was especially important because it destigmatized the students who needed interventions. By working together to create a more inclusive classroom, Rae and the intervention specialist achieved an inclusivity that is especially important in the co-taught classroom.

Title One Specialists—Reading Specialist

Many educators view co-teaching as an equal parts arrangement. But this does not always have to be the case. In a variation of the Teaming approach, Susan, a reading specialist for grades K-8 in Canaan, New Hampshire, took a more backseat role in co-teaching as a resource for the general education teacher. She explained, "I had the time to research lessons online as well as textbook resources. I would then come in and teach that lesson for the day. Then I would leave the lesson for the teacher to keep in their file and use in subsequent years if they chose. I know many teachers did use the lessons again."

It is important to note that while Susan was not directly teaching for an equal amount of the time in the classroom, she was still highly involved with the daily activities of the general classroom, especially regarding the design of language arts and reading lesson plans. Her consistent involvement in the class ensured the needs of all the students were being met.

Before co-teaching, she described being a reading specialist as playing catch-up to the main lesson plan. While there were opportunities to insert strategies for her students within the lessons, those lessons were not planned out to consider their needs as struggling learners, nor were the students likely to take anything from the lesson that would help them in the future.

By inserting herself into the discussion and creation of those lesson plans as a co-teacher, Susan could better ensure the needs of struggling learners were met and add valuable input for the general classroom. Skills like reading comprehension, decoding, and fluency became more pronounced in the lesson plans and improved for ***all*** students.

"I have often found specialists are too far removed from the classroom," she said. For the specialist who wants to contribute to the classroom as a whole, but also wants to remain focused on the students who need him or her, this type of resource-driven co-teaching can be another way to utilize the skills and presence of both teachers.

Additionally, by teaching lessons to the general class every so often, Susan can better appreciate the daily challenges that general educators face, giving her better insight into their world additional strategies to use with other students. "Teaching a classroom filled with varied learners validated me," Susan noted, adding, "I think this made me seem more authentic to the teachers. Teachers are more likely to listen to a colleague who has walked, and is still capable of walking, in their shoes."

Speech and Language Pathologists

In one of my coaching experiences, I had the opportunity to work with a co-teaching pair that was a combination of a speech and language pathologist (SLP) and a seventh-grade English language arts (ELA) teacher at Lebanon Middle School. The first time I observed a lesson that the speech pathologist taught, I marveled at the difference in the way a speech pathologist approached teaching language, versus the way the language arts teacher teaches the same subject. There was a marked difference. Both instructional approaches were effective; however, when the lesson included both approaches to teaching a language based subject, the result was impressive.

Sara, the speech pathologist, was much more technical in the skills she was reinforcing and teaching with the students. Things like language retrieval and idea organization for essay writing are skills that are essential for any student. By comparison, the language arts teacher, Pam, had an approach that focused on the big picture—what those ideas were saying and how they related to the general curriculum.

After Sara experienced co-teaching, she found that her one-on-one sessions with students who needed speech intervention were more productive. It was easier to focus those sessions on targeted skills she and Pam co-taught. She could ensure that her speech interventions were more relevant to the grade level curriculum and, therefore, more beneficial for the students. Prior to co-teaching, she essentially worked in a bubble and would work on isolated skills that did not transfer as easily to what the students were doing in the classroom.

The combination of a speech pathologist and a language arts teacher is highly effective. The skills and goals they both aim to teach are inevitably intertwined—speech and language and language arts.

Sara contributed the following reflection on her experience:

An SLP's Thoughts on Co-Teaching

When I was first approached to co-teach an eighth grade English language arts class, I was both excited and afraid that there might be some resistance. The excitement came from my growing awareness that we, as SLPs, often operate in a bubble of therapy and have little to no sense of what is being taught or how it is being taught in the general education classroom. Sure, we are invited into special education pull-out sessions or resource room times to support students, but we do not see why they are missing the concepts in the first place.

I knew what vocabulary students were working on in therapy sessions, and the ways I was addressing figurative language, sentence and paragraph meaning and structure, executive functioning and problem-solving skills, but I had no concept of how or if these concepts that I incessantly emailed teachers about were being reinforced in the classroom.

The fact that I was being paired with a veteran English teacher was a bit intimidating since I was uncertain how to fit into the larger classroom. I was also unsure how much the teacher would be willing to let me speak in her classroom. I had heard that there were some special education teachers who felt like "glorified paraprofessionals" sitting in the classroom but not really teaching or participating. I did not want to do that; my schedule of students, testing, and meetings was far too busy to waste time sitting in a classroom.

In our first meeting, we were coached through sharing our hopes and concerns as well as discussing the importance of shared planning time. I was pleasantly surprised to have the classroom teacher share, with honesty, her concerns and hopes for the year. She was open to me jumping into the teaching and shared each week what needed to be taught. I shared what I wanted to do and what types of things I was seeing with students in therapy.

At the time, I was concerned that most of the students I was testing for speech and language disorders were scoring very low in relation to figurative language and that I might not be picking up a disorder but rather a widespread lack of direct teaching in the district. I was also running some groups using the Visualizing and Verbalizing Curriculum by Lindamood-Bell and was hoping to get that into the classroom.

One of the biggest challenges to navigate was the preset curriculum map. Each teacher needed to cover the same books and the classroom teacher had a variety of activities she needed her students to work through on a schedule. The number of books to be taught and the amount of writing that needed to happen was non-negotiable. I needed to find a way to fit into that timeline and not disrupt it while bringing in my expertise. This was further complicated by the number of days students would be missing class sessions to participate in state and national standardized testing.

The thing that set me at ease happened in our first class with the students. I was introduced as the co-teacher of the class, and the students were all told I would be teaching parts of the class and that I was available to answer questions in the same way she was. This was very important since this teacher also taught seventh grade ELA and some of the students had had her the previous year. Her introduction set the tone for the year and that was incredibly helpful.

In my opinion, the biggest success was the ability to provide scaffolds for the students related to language comprehension and expression. My training as a speech language pathologist makes me an expert in language, but not in literature or writing. I am able to pick apart the wording of a direction that a student did not understand. I often test for students' understanding of language comprehension and its use in isolation of content.

English teachers are experts in discussing the literary elements and the character perspectives across a book. They use the language structures that "my students" struggle with to teach new concepts and vocabulary, in rapid fire mode. They hand out vocabulary lists and expect students to look up definitions and memorize them.

While this is effective for students with average IQs and no learning disabilities, students with different learning needs often do not understand the language of directions. They often copy the definitions and turn in the paper without internalizing the meaning.

I was able to use my understanding of some assistive technology to support the students. I was able to take some class time to direct teach the use of features of the Text Help Read and Write Gold software to create visual vocabulary lists that included simplified definitions that could be shared with other students.

As an advocate of self-awareness and self-advocacy, I firmly believe that teaching students what to do when they do not understand something is key. The fact that the district was a "Google School" made it easy for the students to take turns creating the visual vocabulary lists and digitally share them with the students who asked for them. A small group of students were able to support each other in learning with grace.

Including language activities and metacognitive strategies into the lessons became easier as the semester went on. We pulled from the speech and language therapy toolbox and added those tools to the already created lessons. We added in Visualizing and Verbalizing strategies by Lindamood-Bell, executive functioning strategies, graphic organizers, goal setting templates, and vocabulary word acting into the lessons. We learned how to play with the ways things were taught while keeping the content and rigor consistent.

Some days we broke the class into ten minute mini-lessons, and sometimes I acted as a support, while other times the classroom teacher acted as a support while I ran a lesson. There was no hard division of roles and that is why it worked for us. Flexibility in planning and sharing the space is key.

The most important pieces for administration to understand are the fact that co-teaching impacts an SLP's schedule in a very significant way. Being in a classroom for five hours a week means that ten half-hour therapy sessions no longer fit into a schedule. Having a common planning period means that the time needs to be held as sacred time, because the weeks that co-teachers don't plan together are less successful in terms of the flow of the class and the ability for both teachers to jump in and not step on each other's toes. Just one week of having that planning period taken away for a meeting or testing can change the next few weeks of energy in the classroom. The two teachers need to have that time to go over the lessons and plan who will do what. They need to be able to say to each other that they want to be the only one instructing for a specific activity because there may be a reason they are allowing the students to struggle for a moment, and if the other jumps in to "help", without that communication, it can undermine the plan.

The biggest piece I would want new co-teaching SLPs to keep in mind is that it is okay not to know where to start; it will come with good communication. It will come. We are not trained to be classroom teachers. Running a whole class activity is very different from running a small group activity. Most importantly, if offered this opportunity, I would recommend taking it.

I have changed schools since this opportunity was given to me, but the lessons I learned permanently changed the way I conduct my therapy sessions, as well as the way I engage with teachers. I now write my IEPs to include individual and in-class treatment. I have a new awareness of the invaluable resource for therapeutic intervention that observing children in the classroom learning environment is.

Sara Lowe-Bouchard M.A., CCC-SLP

Teachers of English as a Second Language

For students who have English as a second language (ESL) and English language learners (ELL), it is critical for them to observe and learn English in a more natural setting. This is best done in the general classroom where interaction and comprehension can be emphasized. For example, the ESL teaching technique of Communicative Language, which emphasizes interaction as the goal of language learning, is highly effective when implemented in the general classroom.

Most general classroom interactions utilize a broader range of vocabulary and idioms than many non-native English speakers are familiar with. This issue often necessitates pulling ESL students aside to provide small group instruction and broaden their vocabulary.

Both goals of enhancing English language learning separately and including ELL students in the general classroom can easily be accomplished several of the co-teaching implementations offered in Chapter 2. In such an example, the general educator may be leading an activity about a particular lesson to enhance learning for one set of students while the ESL teacher may be leading a vocabulary workshop to improve background knowledge of key terms for ESL students. After a predetermined amount of time, the groups switch, and the teachers lead the same lessons at the appropriate pace for the next group.

Another often-employed solution to the problem of unfamiliar vocabulary is for the ESL teacher to read books aloud to students. Increasingly, many ESL teachers as well as general educators read from young-adult literature. Youth-oriented books tend to be more dialogue based, giving ESL teachers the opportunity to elaborate on different idioms and vocabulary not present in more formally written textbooks.

Additionally, there is a growing trend in many school districts to incorporate young-adult novels into curricula for their cultural relevance both independently and as a comparison to more classic genres. Including these types of novels into the general education lesson plans makes the lessons more relevant and easily relatable for the ESL students. It also gives the ESL teachers a sense of co-ownership over the general lesson plan.

Honigsfeld describes such a co-teaching arrangement between ESL teacher Barbara and general educator Vera. "Occasionally, Barbara will independently design an activity for the entire class related to what they are studying. She will choose books or projects that extend whatever topic Vera is working on, or she will help develop background information and vocabulary for all the students in the classroom. At other times, the two teachers will plan a whole class unit together, jointly deciding on activities, topics, materials, and schedules, and co-teach the unit" (Honigsfeld & Dove, 2010).

Such co-ownership of the lessons and overall flexibility in the co-teaching collaboration can be highly effective. Having co-teachers to support language development also allows for adaptability to the inevitable curveballs that come with teaching. Anne Beninghof and Mandy Leensvaart shared about their experience working with co-teaching teams supporting English Language Development (ELD), "Whether students were native English speakers or not, the ELD teachers could help; they had a valuable set of skills they used to provide explicit instruction in the language of reading, writing, and mathematics to decrease this gap. Once this role was explicitly defined and the rationale clear, teachers were able to move forward in implementing co-teaching" (Beninghof & Leensvaart, 2016).

ESL teachers fill many roles in the co-taught classroom, from providing instructional interventions to helping lead and create lessons with the general education teacher. The key is choosing co-teaching approaches that can be utilized to the benefit of all the students.

For example, many ESL teachers are apt technology users. This is because many ESL programs throughout the country incorporate online and virtual classrooms for their ESL students, to great success. Such technology skills make ESL teachers natural fits for co-teaching methods that require technology, namely One Guide Tech and One Facilitate Discussion. This co-teaching implementation is a perfect marriage of skills between the general educator and the ESL teacher and has the added benefit of more fully including ESL students into the general classroom.

According to Amanda, an ESL Department Head in Foxboro, Massachusetts, it is vital that the students and teachers all view each other as equal learners in the classroom, and not as separate groups, no matter what lesson plans they are following.

Finding that balance can be a difficult task. Honigsfeld describes the challenges of sharing classroom space between co-teachers. As she puts it, many teachers "are accustomed to having their classrooms as their sole domains and take comfort in the modicum of control they hold in their workspace." Learning to negotiate time and space with a co-teacher is a juggling act that requires compromise and respect from both educators. Depending on the co-teaching arrangement or even the requirements of the school district, a co-taught classroom could utilize pre-established pull-out programs, push-in programs, or a more flexible co-teaching method that is left to the teachers' discretion.

The ability of educators to negotiate a balance between push-in and pull-out methods, personal teaching space and group space, is vital to the educators' success as co-teachers.

Chapter 3 Review and Discussion Questions

Reflection Questions

- What specialist(s) do you co-teach with on a regular basis?
- What roles do those specialists usually fill when co-teaching with them?
- After reviewing Chapters 1-3, how might you better utilize the skills of those specialists?

Practical Application

With your specialist co-teacher, plan and implement a co-taught lesson using one of the implementations outlined in Chapter 2. Then reflect on the following questions:

- Did you feel successful/effective in what you wanted to accomplish? What worked? What did not work as planned? Why do you think that? What could you do differently next time?
- What is it that you have learned from your co-teacher and his or her style of teaching? About yourself? About your students?
- What is it that is wonderful in working with a variety of students?
- What is it that is frustrating or challenging in working with a variety of students in the classroom? What could you tell colleagues about the needs of students who learn differently?
- What are your next steps?

CHAPTER 4

The HOW of Fitting It All In: Chunking Lesson Plans®

A Lesson Planning Productivity Strategy

Chunking Lesson Plans®

I began to develop the concept of Chunking Lesson Plans® early in 2012 after working as a coach in classrooms with teachers and seeing how they struggled to do everything that needed to be done in the time they had available. To explain this lesson planning productivity and efficiency strategy, I'll use the concept of genre as a topic example and explain how Chunking Lesson Plans® works.

If I have five capable students, all on grade level, with no learning disabilities, in a focus group, and I want to teach them the concept of genre—not to be experts on it, but to know what genre is and be able to identify three types—most teachers would agree that I could teach the concept in about ten minutes to those five capable students.

But here is what I see happening in classrooms:

> You teach those ten minutes. Then you look around the room and you see a glazed look in Jessica's eyes, and David is kind of looking at you, puzzled, and you know that Rob (who is on an IEP) is just kind of "out there" at this point. You go through a few more examples. And you keep asking questions to try to pull information from your students to get them to participate. It's like pulling teeth because the same students are answering all the time, right?
>
> By now, twenty minutes of class time have gone by and you are still direct teaching. Maybe you have even included drama and visuals and you are doing outstanding direct teaching. Despite your best efforts, you realize that Rob might need a couple more examples before maybe, just maybe, he will get it. You go through another couple of examples that are easier and clearer, and you are hoping he will come along. Now you have spent twenty-five minutes in a direct teach. If you have a forty-five-minute class, that gives you only twenty minutes for practice activities or whatever else you must get done.

Now, what were those five capable students who got the information and understood it after the first ten minutes doing while you spent an additional fifteen minutes going over the material repeatedly for the rest of the class? Probably going, "Oh, geez. I'm bored." Who knows, they may have even begun to act out their boredom and frustration.

Most of us would agree that after twenty-five minutes, there's probably still a good number of the students who are going to need quite a bit more practice and, in most cases, there are probably still a handful of students who have no clue what genre is.

Weren't we there after ten minutes of direct teaching? Why did we spend twenty-five minutes only to be at the same place we were in ten minutes? What an epiphany this was for me!

What if we taught our core instruction—the concept of genre, for example—for ten minutes and then stopped? No matter how many glazed looks, we are done. What if we did something different? What if we chunked our lesson plans?

Let's say we have a forty-minute class:

Day 1:

- Five minutes of class is warm-up. After the warm-up, you take ten minutes and do your core teach. You teach genre, diffusion, FOIL method, whatever the topic, and you do it in ten minutes. Direct teach is a best practice technique, and ten minutes, done well, is powerful. You really zero in as if you were in a small group teaching those five capable students, but then you stop. Now you have twenty-five minutes left.
- For the next ten minutes, you put the students into mixed-ability groups: High-middle, middle-low, etc. In those mixed-ability groups, they are going to practice. Maybe you give them an activity; for instance, give them samples of different kinds of genres and have them use and implement the information you just shared. They practice what you just did for ten minutes, in a mixed-ability group, and then you stop.
- Now we have ten minutes left of class, so you take five minutes to pull the whole class back together.
- Once you get the class back together, you spend five minutes asking questions, clarifying, and addressing weaknesses ***based on what you observed while the class was in its groups***.

- You now have five minutes left to do a three-minute ticket to leave, exit card, or three-minute assessment (see Chapter 6: The HOW of Reaching All Learners, for details on exit cards) with just two or three questions that let students indicate whether they understand the information or not. With this information, you will know who needs a re-teach, who understands, and who does not.
- Finally, with two minutes left of class, you conclude your lesson and assign do-able homework.

Chunking Lesson Plans®
40 Minute Chunk of Time

40 min left	• 5 minutes - Warm up activity
35 min left	• 10 minutes - core teach (as if teaching five capable students in a small group)
25 min left	• 10 minutes - Mixed ability groups (High w/middle, middle w/low) practice, implementation, reinforcement in MIXED ability groups (group size maximum of 4)
15 min left	• 5 minutes - Pull class together - Direct Teach Q & A, clarify, reinforce key concepts, through essential questions determine level of understanding
10min left	• 5 minutes - Exit Card - Assess each student's understanding and identify those who need re-teaching, those who need practice and those who need enrichment.
5 min left	• 5 minutes - re-arrange desks for next class, verify homework, time for questions, etc.

Day 2:

- On day two, use those exit cards to determine three same-ability groups. Maybe the five-minute warm-up includes going over, in pairs, the do-able homework they did the night before.
- Next, take five minutes to break the class up into same-ability groups.
- Then take ten minutes and, depending on your goal and what you want to cover, do a core re-teach or reinforcement with the group who needs the extra time and attention, while the other groups work on review or challenge activities. The "expert" group might do an extension activity, enrichment, or a web quest. The goal is for the students in the expert group to go deeper or to have them come up with a skit, a chant, or a memory strategy, and then have them teach the rest of the class, because when they teach it, they learn it better. They will appreciate the memory strategies when they get to college.
- Spend ten minutes in same-ability groups, then pull the class back together for five minutes and do a direct teach Q & A or review of vocabulary—whatever you think that five minutes is best used for.
- Now you have ten minutes for core teaching, based upon your goals and what you need to accomplish.
- Finally, you do another ticket to leave followed by a couple of minutes assigning do-able homework and concluding the lesson. Why? Because you want to know whether there are still some students who need additional re-teach. There almost always will be, but now there should be fewer.
- And the students who needed acceleration? They accelerated. You are still covering the same core instruction you were supposed to cover; you are just doing it differently in a chunked lesson plan.

Chunking Lesson Plans®
40 Minute Chunk of Time

40 min left	•5 minutes - Warm up activity - Students pair up and share homework results
35 min left	•5 minutes - Provide instructions for group activity to follow - call out groups
30 min left	•10 minutes - 3 same ability groups based on Exit Cards: Group 1: Intervention/Reteach), Group 2: Practice, Group 3: Acceleration Activity
20 min left	•5 minutes - Pull class together - Direct Teach Q & A, clarify, reinforce key concepts, through essential questions determine level of understanding
15 min left	•10 minutes - core teach (as if teaching five capable students in a small group)
5 min left	•3 minutes - Exit Card - Assess each student's understanding and identify those who need re-teaching, those who need practice and those who need enrichment.
2 min left	•2 minutes - re-arrange desks for next class, verify homework, time for questions, etc.

On the following pages, I have provided samples of actual lesson plans that were chunked during a co-planning meeting. Co-teachers brought the lesson to the coaching session, and together, we adjusted the timing to enable each component of the lesson plan to be presented in a short chunk. The goal is to keep chunks under twelve minutes.

Part of the discussion included deciding which parts of the lesson were absolutely necessary and which parts could be replaced by a strategy or method that enhanced the lesson by differentiating instruction and the co-teacher's hope to support all students in reaching a higher level. Aspects of the lesson that did not provide the best use of instructional time were replaced with more effective methods.

I chose to include block scheduling lesson plans because they are longer than the forty minutes I described. In this way, you can see how lessons can be chunked for a very short amount of time as well as for longer class times, as available in a block schedule.

The challenge when working with block scheduling is figuring out when to include formative assessments and when to schedule same-ability groups for providing SDI, practice, and enrichment.

It's possible that the first forty minutes of an eighty-minute chunk could be "day one" and the second forty minutes of an eighty-minute chunk could be "day two." Teachers could take five minutes at the end of the first forty-minute chunk to review exit tickets and determine who would be in the three ability groups.

I recommend that teachers start with this structure just two days a week. It is preferable that they be consecutive days. Avoid a Friday and Monday scenario because too much time falls between the initial instruction and the group instruction.

The third day is perfect for a more fluid structure. In this way, teachers could teach the third day's objective, but also reinforce, supplement, and dig deeper into lesson objectives that were presented on the first two days. Then, if you find that this structure is beneficial, simply start the process over.

Chunking Lesson Plan Template™

Class/Period/Standard ______________________________

#Class Min	#Min Activity	Lesson Activity	Classroom Teacher	Specialist	Comment

Chunking Lesson Plan Sample Lesson™

Sample Lesson

Class/Period/Standard ______________________________

#Class Min	#Min Activity	Lesson Activity	Classroom Teacher	Intervention Specialist (if available)	Other
80	30	Intervention group Enrichment group	Enrichment	Intervention	
50 left	5	Transition – Students take out notes	Support	Support	
45 left	5	Review the parts of the body of an exam	Direct Teach	Support & Collect Data	
40 left	5	Students Highlight: 1) Hooks and Leads 2) Opinion Statements	Parallel teach. Guide students through activity – intense teach	Parallel teach. Guide students through activity – intense teach	Two groups – Mixed ability HML
35 left	5	Direct Teach (Whole class) Stuents share what they highlighted	Writing student input on board	Leading discussion	
30 left	12	Working on one to two paragraphs of the body	Floats between groups and asks essential questions – Documenting response.(Immediate feedback)	(Two paras in the room) plus intervention specialist – divide the class into small groups	Mixed ability
18 left	3	Whole class check-in – Depending on results of classroom teacher, teachers group assessments, either take lesson up a level, validate they are on the right track, or do a re-teach	Direct Teach	Support	

15	7	Working on one to two paragraphs of the body	Floats between groups and asks essential questions – documenting response. (Immediate feedback)	(Two paras in the room) plus intervention specialist – divide the class into small groups	
8	5	Power Grammar Power Vocabulary	Fun Activity/Video	Team teach	3x/week 2x/week
3	3	Exit Card – (Determine re-teach/accelerate)			

Chunking Lesson Plan Sample Lesson™

Class/Period/Standard ____________________

#Class Min	#Min Activity	Lesson Activity	Classroom Teacher	Additional Information	Other
80	10	Silent Reading	Support/Collect Data		
70	10	Reading log/check	Ditto		
60	7	Unit Opener – Introductin – goals, essential questions, setting expectations	Direct Teach		
53 left	3	Breaking students into 3 small groups	Direct Teach		
50	10	3 - each group has a poem to read – (adult read aloud) and determine meaning, pull out images, what is the story telling them about poetry	Ask essential questions, check for understaning – data collect		Mixed ability
40	10	Whole class report out – Discussion, sharing	Facilitator – use data from observation to drive discussion		
30	10	3-4 groups, second poem to read and discuss. Highlighting/ underlining key terms from questions that they should be looking for.	Ask essential questions, check for understaning – data collect		
20	10	Whole class report out – Discussion, sharing	Facilitator – use data from observation to drive discussion		
10		Exit Card			

Managing Lesson Chunks with Timer Apps

Using Timers in the Classroom

I received an unexpected answer from a co-teaching pair with whom I was working. I asked them, "Why do you use a timer? Do you do use it to motivate your students?"

Danna, the content specialist of the co-teaching team, answered, "Absolutely not."

She went on to explain, "We had a problem staying on schedule with our lesson plans. Brandi, my co-teacher, would start talking to elaborate on what I was teaching, but she would go on and on, and she would not stop talking. We were falling behind! We were not finishing our lesson plan. We talked about it and came up with a solution: We would set a timer for each chunk of our lesson plan. Then she knew, because she could see the timer, when she needed to stop talking."

Both Danna and Brandi laughed, acknowledging the challenge they faced and resolved.

Even though they started using a timer simply to keep the lesson on track, they found that using a timer was also incredibly effective for the students because they knew the timeframe for the activity. Additionally, the co-teachers found that they got a whole lot more done.

The most effective time managers of all among the co-teachers I have observed over the years are those who use visual timers for every chunk of their lesson plan. These teachers designated specific minutes to introduce material or practice a skill and varied activities to reach different learning styles.

To keep students on task during activities, use visual timers during class activities such as think-pair-shares, group work, timed individual assignments, etc. A visual timer is one that enables students to "see" time.

On-Screen Timer to Keep Students on Track!

During a recent seminar, Brenda expressed a need for an on-screen timer: something she could put on the desktop to "signal students that their time is up." We did a little research and found a solution to help you too!

- Interval Timer—Seconds: Amazing functionality, though it may be too complex for some classroom use.
- Timer + Touch HD: This is my favorite iPad timer app. It's so easy to use. Touch the app and move your fingers in clockwise direction to set time. Timer is shown in different colors for:
    - Minutes in Red
    - Hours in Blue
    - Seconds in Green
- PC Chrono has a timer, alarm, stopwatch, and countdown timer. It is an all-in-one program that is easy to configure and navigate through. It is a very basic, free app that comes with limited features; no sound settings.
- Online-Stopwatch.com: You will need to be online to use the browser app at Online-Stopwatch.com. It has a variety of different timer options, but you have to have an internet connection and your computer must be flash-enabled in order to use it.
- Use instrumental music clips or cell phone ring tones as timers: Sort them by how long they take to play and use them as auditory timers for students during transitions or non-reading activities—the music will cue students in to the "time" and keep them hopping. Avoid playing music while students are reading.

Chapter 4 Review and Discussion Questions

Reflection Questions

- After reviewing this chapter, how might you and your co-teacher use chunked lessons to maximize your time together with your students?
- How can you adapt this strategy for use in your classroom to increase learning, reach more learning styles, and enhance your teaching?
- For your subject area, how is chunking your lessons most likely to improve the acquisition of knowledge for all learners? How?

Practical Application

Using the information in this chapter for reference, adapt a co-taught lesson to the chunked lesson plan format and implement it in your classroom.

CHAPTER 5

THE HOW OF LOGISTICS & CO-PLANNING

Co-Planning Time

Co-planning has evolved over the past twenty-five years. Dr. Marilyn Friend refers to "A Contemporary Co-teaching Planning Model" that includes three components (Friend, 2014):

1. Periodic, intensive face-to-face macro planning
2. Ongoing electronic planning
3. On-the-spot fill-in planning strategies

Face-to-Face planning as a primary planning model is outdated and impractical. "Beyond spontaneous reflecting and planning, a successful co-teaching relationship requires a familiarity between teachers that goes beyond colleague status, and as such, co-teachers need to contact each other frequently" (S. M. Pratt, Imbody, Wolf, & Patterson, 2017).

Using both the opportunity to plan together at the same time, face-to-face, as well as the option of planning separately via available technology, provides a flexibility that enables the frequent communication that makes co-planning feasible for already busy educators. Current technology gives co-teachers the ability to work online, together, or separately as well as face-to-face. Consider the following insights and options for co-planning:

Co-Planning Time Is Sacred

Co-planning time is sacred. If it is built into your schedule, it is not a time for you to be pulled out to go to an IEP meeting, plan for your non-co-taught classes, correct tests, catch up on paperwork, or complain about Johnny. Co-planning time is time that, when used well, will transform co-teaching from difficult and challenging to manageable and fun.

Again, co-planning time is sacred. This means teachers need to push back on the people scheduling those meetings during co-planning time and say, "Do it another time." Tell the person in the hall demanding the special educator's time because of a student in crisis, "What would you do if I were out sick? Do what you would do then."

If you make the time and honor the time to plan together, when are you going to be able to make this co-teaching relationship work?

Minimum Co-Planning Time

I could plan with my co-teacher in one or two planning periods a week, and sometimes, if we really used our time well, we could do two weeks of lesson plans in forty-five minutes. How did we do that? We planned ahead. We came to the meeting with lesson plans sketched out and we used our time to determine accommodations and adaptations. We input activities and suggestions into the general plan for the curriculum. Then we arranged to meet again two or three days later for forty-five minutes to revisit the plan. We did some of the work outside of the planning period and came ready with an outline for changes. That made planning much more efficient.

Effective Use of Co-Planning Time

If your school provides you with co-planning time, stay focused on the task at hand. If possible, share information beforehand through your school's teacher mailboxes, email, or in the cloud via apps such as Google Drive or Dropbox, so your co-planning time can be used with maximum benefit.

Another time-saving option is to use sticky notes to make your changes, save your ideas, plan your interventions, or make enhancements to the lesson. Avoid using your precious planning time to scribe perfect lesson plans. Save that for later. If you must enter your plans into district lesson planning software, do that another time at your convenience.

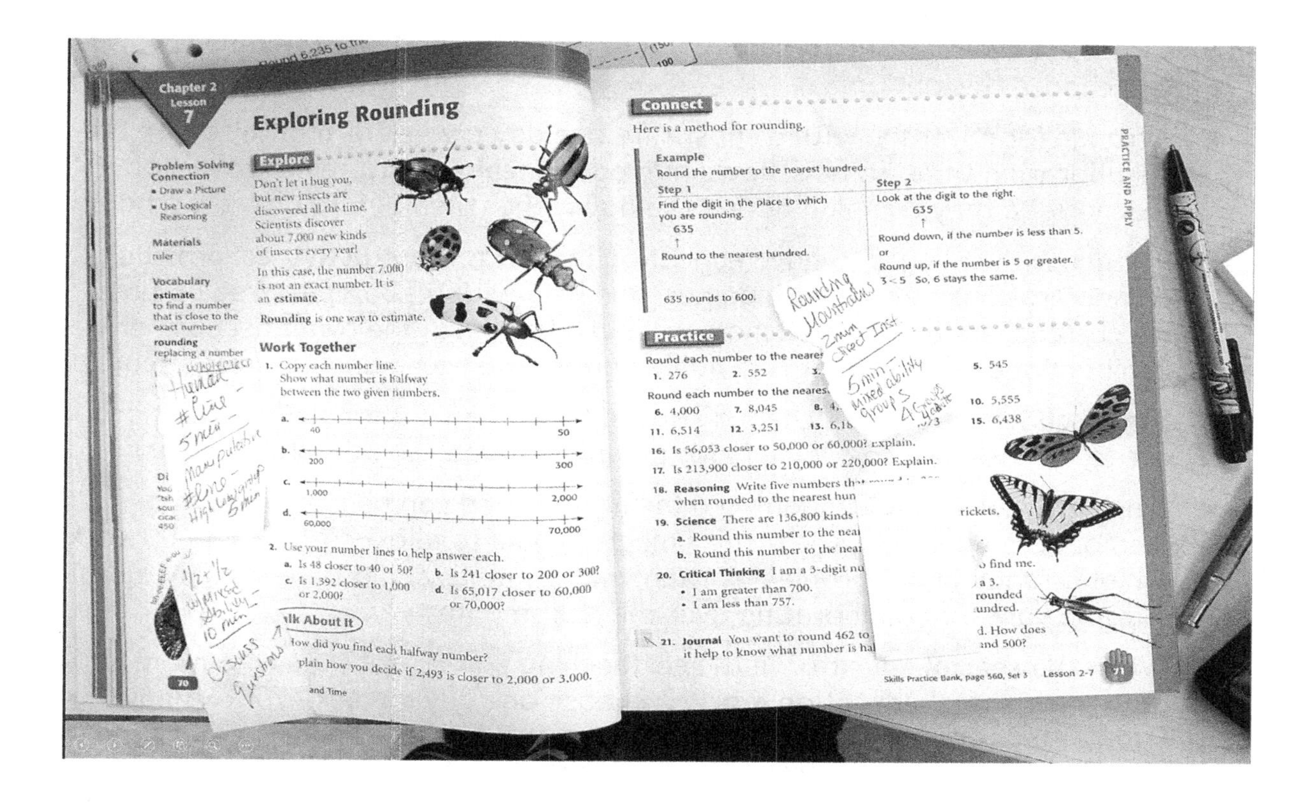

I Do Not Have Built-in Co-Planning Time!

How do you co-teach when you don't have conference or co-planning time together? Some of the co-teaching instructional approaches require minimal co-planning time. Some require extensive co-planning time. Choose the approach that you can support. Also, ask yourself, "How do I fit common co-planning time into my schedule?" Be creative. Is there a way?

If you do not have the time to discuss plans, review upcoming tests, and consider recommended modifications and the implementation of IEP goals, it will be difficult, if not impossible, to have a successful co-taught classroom implementing state standards (Ploessl, Rock, Schoenfeld, & Blanks, 2010).

Again, speak up if you are being asked to give up co-planning time for other duties. You need that time, and it is legitimate to require it. If your school does not provide co-planning time, it will probably make your life easier eventually if you can employ some of the following options:

- Use time before school, after school, or during common preps/specials to meet and plan. Remember, the goal is to make your job easier and more successful overall. It is a waste of your energy to begrudge the time spent if you choose this option.
- Arrange for coverage with a substitute one day a week or month to free up collaboration time. Some schools hire permanent substitutes to cover for co-teachers, so they can plan during the day rather than before or after school.
- Partner with colleges to have education majors present activities, provide demonstrations, review with games, and help with test prep to free up time for co-teachers to plan. Teachers will need to plan in the room because of liability issues; however, it is a viable option when co-planning time is scarce.
- Some schools pay co-teachers a stipend to plan after school. Other options are to compensate co-teachers for planning during the school vacations.
- Much of what is talked about in a faculty meeting can be presented in a memo. When possible, use faculty meeting time to allow co-teachers to work on long-range plans, problem solving, and future lesson outlines and establish a framework for collaborating over the next month.
- When the special educator in the co-teaching pair co-teaches with more than one general education teacher, choose one day a week—for example, Friday—to leave each class period fifteen minutes early. Then use that time to plan with one of the general education teachers who is free at that time. For example: first period of the day, James, a special education teacher, leaves Allen's math class fifteen minutes early and meets with Michael, the general education teacher he works with fourth period because it is Michael's prep period at that time.
- Some schools set up targeted activity periods for students to review for proficiency testing, cooperative learning groups, or peer tutoring to allow time for teachers to plan together. Support staff or school specialists can monitor these targeted activity periods.
- Substitutes often have free blocks of time when the teacher they are substituting for has prep periods. Schedule a substitute to cover your class during that free block of time.
- For information that must be communicated before the next school day, you might arrange to call each other after hours. At the least, communicate through the school mailbox or email.
- If the regular classroom teacher can provide the special education teacher with copies of lesson plans, tests, and projects ahead of time, it allows time for the specialist to assist with accommodations and make helpful recommendations. It also enables that person to go into the class prepared to help.

- Placing grade reports in the special education teacher's mailbox enables both the regular classroom teacher and the special education teacher to catch failures before they become quarterly or semester grades.
- Use email and Microsoft Word's "Insert Comments" and "Track Changes" features to collaborate on accommodations and adaptations.
- Use Google Drive, Google Docs, Google Slides, and Google Sheets to co-plan from anywhere at any time.

Co-Planning Meeting Agenda

It is important to have a plan as to how you will use your co-planning time. Without a plan, co-teachers run the risk of getting off track or bogged down in nonessential discussion or details, finding themselves at the end of the session with very little accomplished.

Who brings what to the meeting? Typically, the general education teacher would bring the standards-based lesson plans, sketched out but not carved in stone. The targets for the lesson may not change; co-planning time is primarily focused on discussing instructional delivery, individual adjustments, and SDI.

Consequently, the special education teacher brings knowledge of SDI, examples of ways to differentiate instruction, an understanding of how to reach all learners, and any materials that would support those aspects of the lesson planning session. It is not a bad idea to have access to a few books or resources to support your assertion that the strategies are based on research.

Fundamental Questions for Your Co-Planning Session

Guide your planning session with the following fundamental questions:

- What are our instructional goals?
- What are the characteristics of our learners?
- How can we meet the needs of all our students, including students with special needs, students with limited English proficiency, students with behavioral difficulties, gifted students, and everyone else?
- How will we chunk our lesson plan so that we maintain engagement and accomplish our goals?

- Who will lead each chunk of the lesson plan, and which chunks will be led by both teachers at the same time?
- What do we need to do outside of the planning session to find material, activities, videos, apps, etc., to implement our lesson plan?
- Who is responsible for what, and when is it due?

Co-Planning in the Cloud

Increasingly, co-teachers are planning in the cloud. Many use online portals specific to their district. Some plan using Google Drive and Google Apps such as Documents and Google Slides. My favorite and best solution is using a combination of Google Drive apps, Dropbox, and Trello!

- Co-plan your lessons using Google Docs, build PowerPoint presentations with Google Slides, and collect data on a Google Spreadsheet. Teachers are also using Dropbox to share files, Edmodo to plan and collaborate, and Evernote to collect and organize lesson plan ideas. All are web-based and cross-platform to allow you to plan anytime, from anywhere, with any device.

Google docs

Google Docs Home

- Create documents, spreadsheets and presentations online
- Share and collaborate in real time
- Safely store and organize your work
- Control who can see your documents
- Read user examples
- Get started

Share and collaborate in real time

2 of 6 

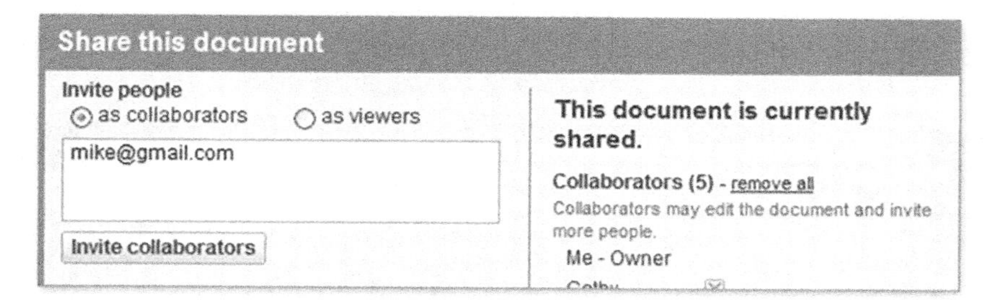

Choose who can access your documents.
Just enter the email addresses of the people with whom you want to share a given document and send them an invitation.

Share instantly.
Anyone you've invited to either edit or view your document, spreadsheet ... can access it as soon as they sign in.

Edit and present with others in real time.
Multiple people can view and make changes at the same tir... window for spreadsheets, and document revisions show you exactly wh... when. Viewing a presentation together is a breeze, as anyone joined in a pres... can automatically follow along with the presenter.

How To

Google docs

Google Docs Home

- Create documents, spreadsheets and presentations online
- Share and collaborate in real time
- Safely store and organize your work
- Control who can see your documents
- Read user examples
- Get started

Create documents, spreadsheets and presentations online

1 of 6 

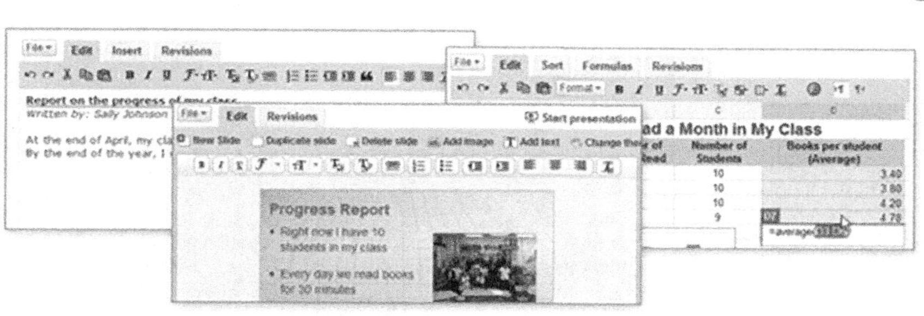

Create basic documents from scratch or start from a template.
You can easily do all the basics, including making bulleted lists, sorting by columns, adding tables, images, comments, formulas, changing fonts and more. And it's free.

Upload your existing files.
Google Docs accepts most popular file formats, including D... SV, PPT, etc. So go ahead and upload your existing files.

Familiar desktop feel makes editing a breeze.
Just click the toolbar buttons to bold, underline, indent, cha... format, change cell background color and so on.

How To

Trello

Sign up for Trello and create a free account. Here are a couple of examples that you can copy into your Trello account and use as a model. You'll be able to access them from Trello by searching for my name, or from the Bonus398.SusanFitzell.com

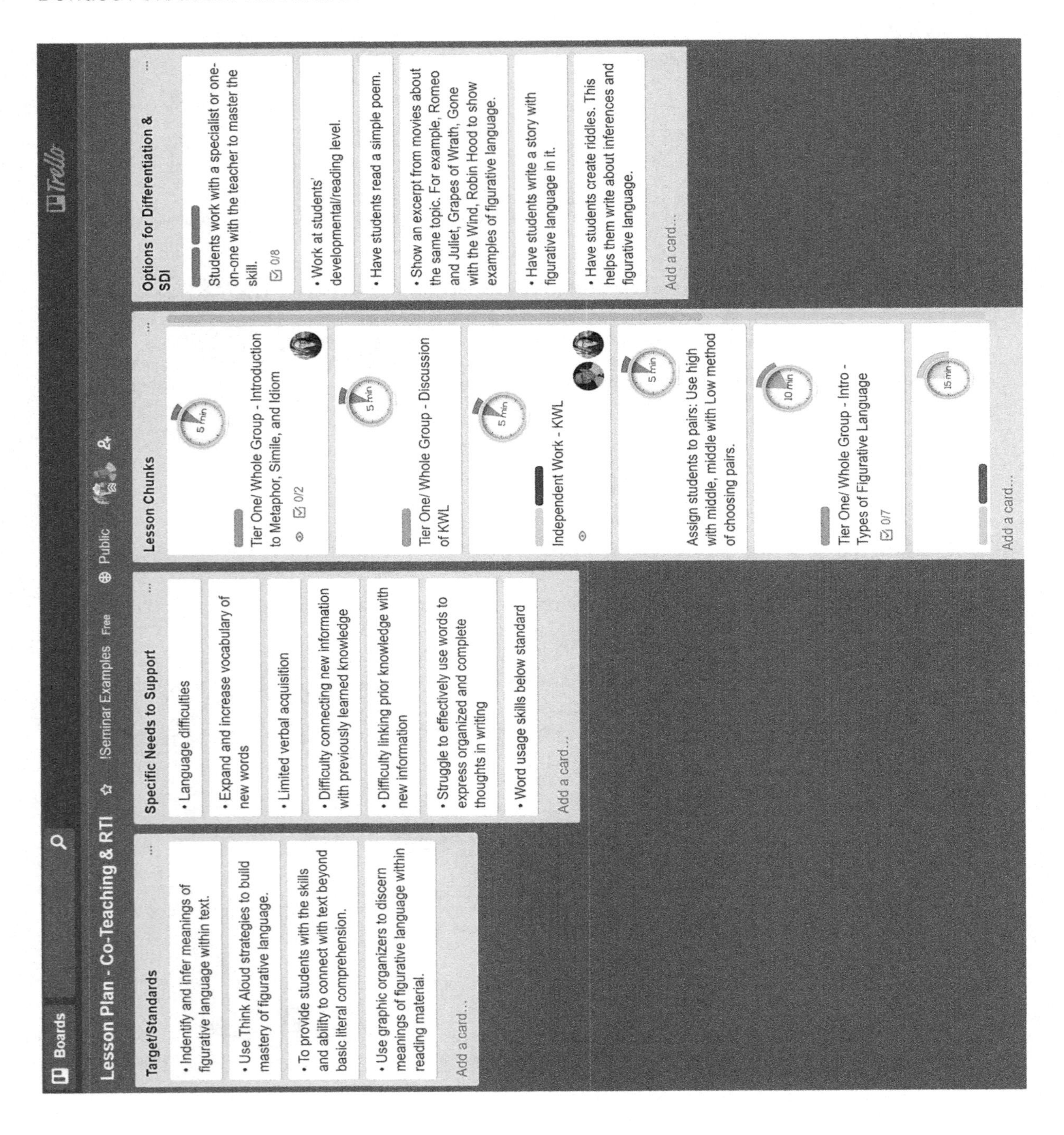

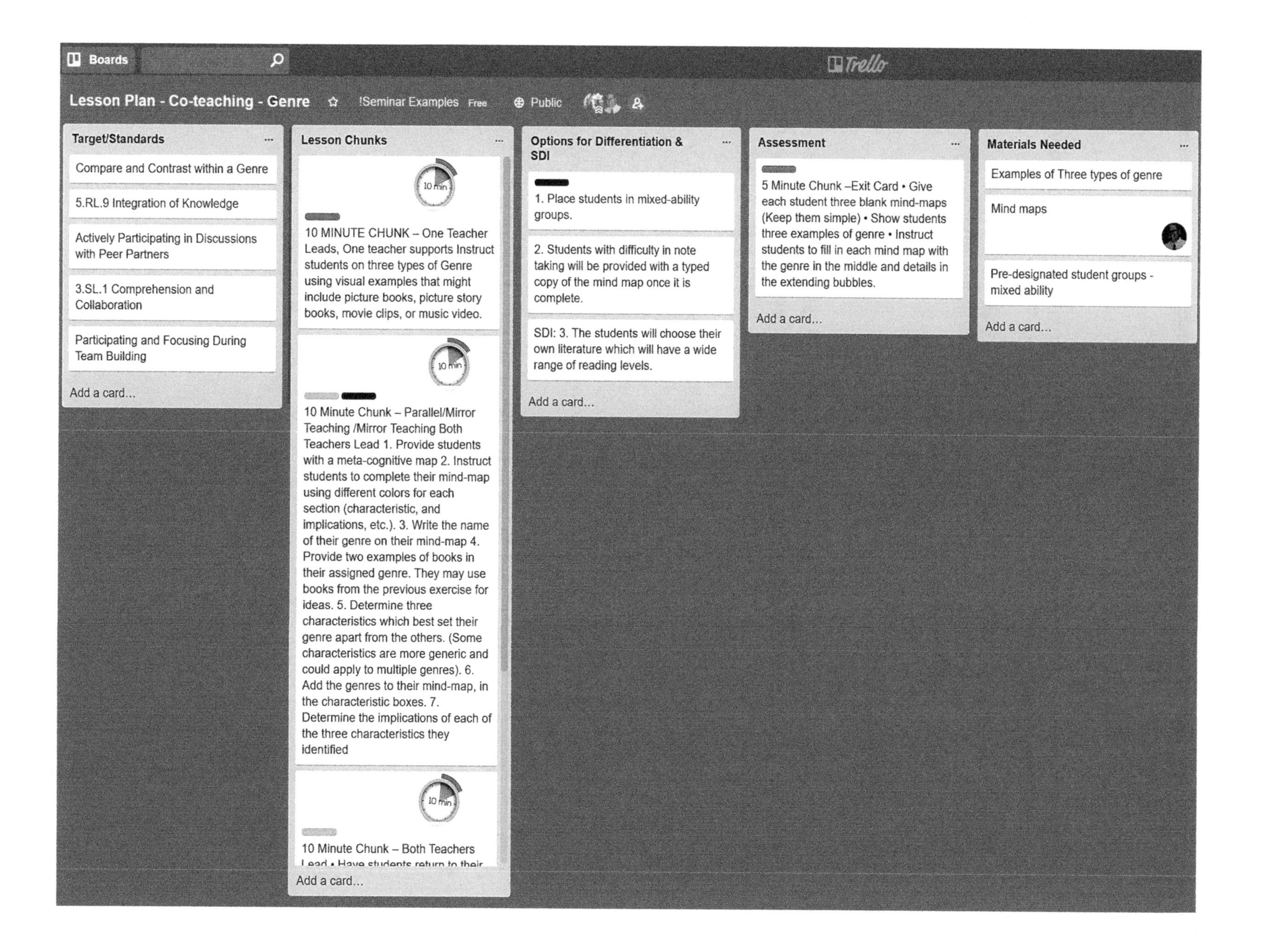
Boards
Trello
Lesson Plan - Co-teaching - Genre
!Seminar Examples Free
Public
Target/Standards
Compare and Contrast within a Genre
5.RL.9 Integration of Knowledge
Actively Participating in Discussions with Peer Partners
3.SL.1 Comprehension and Collaboration
Participating and Focusing During Team Building
Add a card...
Lesson Chunks
10 min
10 MINUTE CHUNK – One Teacher Leads, One teacher supports Instruct students on three types of Genre using visual examples that might include picture books, picture story books, movie clips, or music video.
10 min
10 Minute Chunk – Parallel/Mirror Teaching /Mirror Teaching Both Teachers Lead 1. Provide students with a meta-cognitive map 2. Instruct students to complete their mind-map using different colors for each section (characteristic, and implications, etc.). 3. Write the name of their genre on their mind-map 4. Provide two examples of books in their assigned genre. They may use books from the previous exercise for ideas. 5. Determine three characteristics which best set their genre apart from the others. (Some characteristics are more generic and could apply to multiple genres). 6. Add the genres to their mind-map, in the characteristic boxes. 7. Determine the implications of each of the three characteristics they identified
10 min
10 Minute Chunk – Both Teachers
Add a card...
Options for Differentiation & SDI
1. Place students in mixed-ability groups.
2. Students with difficulty in note taking will be provided with a typed copy of the mind map once it is complete.
SDI: 3. The students will choose their own literature which will have a wide range of reading levels.
Add a card...
Assessment
5 Minute Chunk –Exit Card • Give each student three blank mind-maps (Keep them simple) • Show students three examples of genre • Instruct students to fill in each mind map with the genre in the middle and details in the extending bubbles.
Add a card...
Materials Needed
Examples of Three types of genre
Mind maps
Pre-designated student groups - mixed ability
Add a card...

Chapter 5 Review and Discussion Questions

Reflection Questions

- After reviewing this chapter, what one planning strategy or tool did you find most likely to be beneficial to your planning efforts? Why?
- What tool or idea might you adapt for use with your co-teacher that may help to increase learning, reach more learning styles, and enhance your teaching? How will you employ this strategy?

Practical Application

With your co-teacher, plan and implement a co-taught lesson (or lessons) using the planning strategies outlined in this chapter. Then reflect on the following questions:

- What type of lesson or co-teaching model did you implement with your co-teacher? How did you communicate your plans before, during, and after the lesson?
- Did you feel successful/effective in what you wanted to accomplish? What worked? What did not work as planned? Why do you think that? What could you do differently next time?
- What is it that is frustrating or challenging in planning with your co-teacher? What would you do differently when planning future lessons?
- What are your next steps?

CHAPTER 6

The HOW of Healthy Collaboration

Looking at Personality Types

When I started working with other teachers in the classroom, I quickly discovered that understanding personality styles is critical. The first step was to understand my own personality and how my personality affected others.

When I spoke with my demonstrative body language, my extraversion emphasizing every aspect of who I was, I unintentionally overwhelmed people. It became clear that without an understanding of personality, I would continue to have relationships in the classroom that were not as productive as they could be. Too much time was spent misinterpreting one another.

Differences in personality—not just between teachers but also students—can lead to challenges and conflict. It is important to understand our students and how their personalities influence their learning styles.

When we understand learning style, we can be more helpful to our students by teaching them to identify how they learn and enabling them to learn at their maximum capability using strategies that fit their learning styles.

Most of us realize the importance of understanding student learning and personality styles. However, the importance of understanding adult personality styles is often glossed over in school environments.

In the business world, understanding your coworkers is emphasized in professional training. Managers, human resource workers, and team builders commonly realize the importance of understanding personality types.

Sometimes businesses will even group people based on the best fit between different personalities. Schools tend simply to throw people together and expect them to figure out how to work together, often with no training in personality theory, group process, or negotiation.

Everyone is different; some people approach the world from a logical standpoint, while some focus on values and harmony first. Some people think and then speak. Others speak and then think. Some need closure and make quick decisions. Other individuals want to keep their possibilities open.

Let's apply the adage, "Is your glass half-empty or half-full?" The image of a half-empty glass or a half-full glass represents personality types in terms of their attitude toward a task or concept. Personality types go beyond optimistic and pessimistic. There are countless nuances to the human personality, but we benefit when we try to understand basic personality types and how to address them.

Full Glass, Empty Glass Personality Types

Glass #1:

"You call that a glass of water? Well, back where I come from...."

OR

"It's half-empty now, and it wouldn't surprise me if it dried up completely."

OR

"Whose job is it to fill up this glass?"

If your co-teacher is this personality type, how might material be presented so she is comfortable with your approach? One method that might appeal is traditional outlining. Making an outline to present information is a very effective teaching strategy for verbal-linguistic and linear thinkers.

However, it is not the best approach for visual learners—who need to see information connected in terms of the whole to understand. What approach might you use when working with a co-teacher who not only values tradition, but also thinks in concrete, linear terms?

As a learning strategy specialist, I would add a graphic organizer to an outline. I would not expect my co-teacher to throw out the traditional outline and adopt my way of teaching. Rather, I understand the value of providing both tools in the classroom to reach more student learning styles.

What does this have to do with personality types? If someone has always done a task one way and you offer an alternative, you are going to have to do some convincing. Different personality types will respond in different ways to your efforts.

When she says, "Back where I come from..." what she really means is, "Where is the data? It always worked this way; why change it now?" When working with this personality type, present a strategy you know will work. Show your partner data that validates the use of strategies such as graphic organizers and nonlinguistic representation.

If your partner says, "It is half-empty now and it would not surprise me if it dried up completely," she needs you to demonstrate how your ideas benefit the students. She might ask, "What is the benefit in doing this? Where is the benefit in the graphic organizer? Why should I change what I'm doing to use that?" Tell her why. Show her the statistics to back up your suggestions and how results can be measured.

Do you think your co-teacher might respond to the glass half-full question with "Whose job is it to fill up this glass?" This personality type needs to ask questions. Answer them. If she has many questions, do not take offense. It is because this learning style makes it necessary for her to understand why she's using a given method. Once she understands, you can usually get her on board.

Glass #2:

"I cannot believe someone would leave that dirty glass out here! Clean this mess up right now!"

Do you work with this person? "Who left the mess in the classroom? Why do you keep your desk such a mess?" This person needs to have his ducks all in a row. Your mission with this co-teacher is to provide tools and forms that support the structure necessary for students to be successful in the classroom.

This personality type insists on practical, usable results. You'll need to show clearly how your method will benefit the teacher and students. Share approaches and techniques that provide immediate results.

Glass # 3

"Hmm...It is (ingeniously constructs a hacksaw from two straws and a shoelace and cuts the glass in half)...Ah...Now it is completely full!"

You may work with a teacher who goes hog-wild with solutions, mnemonics, and unique strategies.

This is the personality type that can do things no one else can.

When presenting options to this co-teacher, express how the teaching method you want to implement will increase the competency of the students in the classroom. This personality type is a problem-solver who values competence more than anything else. Make sure she understands that your intent is to help students grow and succeed on their tests. Make proficiency the criteria, and if it works, go for it!

Glass #4:

"Hey! I bet if we got a bunch of these glasses, we could make a waterslide! Or maybe a pool! Oh wait, we could freeze this water and make an ice sculpture! Or we could...."

Do you work with this person? He is always coming up with a new random idea and never knows what is going to be in the lesson plan that day.

Bruce was that kind of personality. The students loved him—science with Bruce was fun. I, however, was frustrated with the lack of discipline in the classroom. Students were all over the place, talking and not paying attention. I struggled because I felt the students did not show appropriate respect for Bruce or the classroom environment.

During one of our planning meetings, I suggested to Bruce that I might assist with discipline. He was perfectly fine with the idea. I played the disciplinarian while he remained the storyteller. I wrote the lecture structure on the whiteboard; I did the outlines and the graphic organizer; he told his stories. We worked well together that way.

This personality type develops relationships and fosters student growth. Bruce cared about the rapport with his students more than anything else. Yes, he wanted them to learn, but he believed they would learn best if they had a positive relationship with him. When working with a co-teacher who approaches teaching like Bruce, indicate how your teaching suggestions will promote student accomplishment.

How Can Understanding Personality Types Help Co-Teachers?

Think about your strengths and how they can complement your co-teacher's strengths. The first step is self-understanding. Assess your own instructional, management, and communication style. Do you describe things in pictures or focus on details? Do you talk first and listen later? Or do you listen and prefer not to talk until you've had time to reflect? Understanding and respecting one another's preferred approach fosters mutual respect, reduces misunderstandings, and maximizes collaboration. (Conderman, Johnston-Rodriguez, & Hartman, 2009; Keefe, Moore, & Duff, 2004)

I recommend you research personality styles further to gain a deeper understanding. My efforts to understand personality types have made a huge difference in my teaching relationships and have benefited my personal relationships. It's a worthwhile time investment.

When we understand our personality type and communication preferences, we can strategize to communicate more effectively with other personality types. For example, if I, an extrovert, want to communicate effectively with a quiet and thoughtful introvert, I will be more successful if I use communication strategies that are more readily received by my introvert co-teacher. I'll deliberately speak more quietly. I'll respect his or her wider circle of personal space. I won't expect an immediate response. I'll exercise patience and allow my co-teacher time to reflect and get back to me.

Be assured I am not changing my personality. Rather, I'm choosing to use strategies that are more effective with a different personality type. That is the real advantage of understanding personality preferences. We become more skilled at communicating with a variety of personalities because we have a greater understanding of communication dynamics.

Collaboration Challenges and Solutions

First Five Minutes of Class

A few years ago, I worked with an unhappy co-teaching pair. Doris, a young high school science teacher, was logical, lecture-based, and needing full control; Johanna, a seasoned special educator, was creative, flexible, and motherly. They were in crisis mode.

The tension between the teachers was intense. Their co-teaching relationship was conflictual, and students were not gaining much benefit from having co-teachers.

They assigned student seating so that all the students with special needs were in the back and side rows. While this allowed Johanna easy access to students with an IEP, they were completely segregated from the other students.

During coaching, I suggested that Johanna open class with a review activity. She would design, prepare, and deliver the activity during the first five minutes of class.

The logic behind this suggested implementation of One Teach, One Assist was:

- It supports parity: Students would view the co-teacher as more than a helper because she would be leading students in an activity.
- Because the activity was a review activity from the prior day's lesson, it would accelerate the special education teacher's understanding of the prescribed content.
- The general education teacher had five minutes to observe and collect data, gaining an opportunity to see students differently from how he did while lecturing.
- Students would be exposed to a review using an instructional approach other than verbal-linguistic lecture.
- Both teachers' talents were honored and utilized to benefit student learning and growth.

They agreed to try the suggestion.

Six weeks later, I revisited the same classroom. Johanna told me she had been planning and delivering the first five minutes of class. She shared that the approach was going well. She explained that based on the prior day's lesson, she had planned a creative, fun, engaging activity to reinforce the objective.

They went one step further, integrating the students with an IEP into a more inclusive seating plan. No longer were the students segregated.

Both Doris and Johanna started to see each other's value despite their different teaching approaches. Consequently, their relationship improved. It was one little change—having the co-teacher open class—that created a positive dynamic. Students saw both teachers as credible leaders of the class.

One way to establish parity and implement One Teach, One Assist is for the specialist to start the class by leading a review.

Potential Roadblocks: Challenges

Compatibility is at the heart of the obstacles that come up between co-teachers. In their meta-analysis of thirty-two qualitative studies, Scruggs, Mastropieri, & McDuffie (2007) found that compatibility among professionals was the most important element in successful co-teaching relationships. What are some things that can impact compatibility?

Teaching Methodology

Sometimes conflict evolves from a difference in methodology. When personalities clash in the way a classroom is run, or if one teacher's approach is very different than the other teacher's methods, it may cause issues.

One or both teachers may come to the class with specific expectations. However, a lack of communication—especially prior to the first day of class—often results in misperceptions about how the class will proceed. This leads to frustration and conflict.

Personality Differences

Personality differences can be a big problem. For example:

Bob, an elementary special education teacher, was exasperated. He felt that one of the classrooms he was working with was out of control. Bob preferred a more orderly classroom, where students worked quietly and did not speak out. In contrast, his co-teacher, Takesha, had an approach to class management that was very loosely structured. It drove Bob crazy. It created stress and conflict because he felt powerless in his position to do anything about it.

Another example of potential discord is when a classroom teacher with very strict standards is paired with a special education teacher who will try anything—including cajoling, bribery, or doing half the work for them—to try to motivate students to do the work. Either scenario results in conflict.

When teaching styles are drastically different, it can be difficult to find common ground. Both teachers are responsible for the class and should be committed to making it work. Communication is the best solution.

Comfort Zones

Comfort zones are a significant factor in compatibility. In a co-teaching situation, some expectations may be beyond the comfort zone of either the teacher or the special education teacher. Sometimes an IEP requires one or both to use unfamiliar strategies. Other times, a teacher may not be comfortable sharing a classroom. People struggle when they are out of their comfort zones.

Credibility

Credibility can often become a roadblock when co-teaching, particularly when the special education teacher is not familiar with the class content. Sometimes, the general education teacher may be unaware of the co-teacher's familiarity with the subject, area of expertise, or background. This can lead to conflict.

Both teachers should take the time to get to know each other, share their expectations for the classroom, and explain their preferred teaching methods. This enables co-teachers to rally their strengths, be it content expertise or knowledge of learning strategy.

Insufficient Time

We have all heard it before: There is simply not enough time to prepare materials for students, meet with other teachers, and get everything done for the classroom. Often, special education teachers are sent from room to room, with barely enough time to eat or take care of themselves. They are also expected to attend team meetings, complete paperwork, and be available for crisis interventions and questions about student issues.

To help ensure co-teacher success, the paradigms of planning and prep time need to change. School districts should consider how much time is necessary for co-teachers to work effectively together.

Lack of Administrative Support

Lack of administrative support can also inhibit a successful co-teaching situation. Sometimes, administrators are unable to allow teachers the communication time, training, or even prep materials necessary to plan properly. Funding can be a problem, particularly regarding quality training and follow-up.

At times, there is a lack of support for inclusion efforts as well as implementation of the differentiated instruction required by current federal and state mandates. Other times, an administrator may simply have no voice among the teachers to say, "This is a legal requirement. We need to do it and you are accountable."

Legal Worries

Often, the general education teacher is concerned about not meeting the IEP requirements of students with disabilities. This situation can create issues because the special education teacher may become the only source of assistance for a given student.

Sometimes the classroom teacher will feel more comfortable saying, "You take care of Johnny because you know how to deal with him and I don't." This is caused by a concern that the classroom teacher cannot meet the student's needs, or the fear that the teacher could be liable if he or she takes responsibility and then cannot meet that responsibility according to the standards of the law.

The general education teacher is ultimately responsible for the education of the child.

Other Practicalities

- It can be difficult to see lesson plans before class.
- There is often a lack of training in a problem-solving approach to collaboration.
- Cost of training and staffing minimizes available opportunities for professional development.

Overcoming Roadblocks: Solutions

Be Flexible

Co-teachers must be flexible. This can be a difficult requirement. Some people can go with the flow, while others cannot. However, without flexibility there is only rigidity. This creates a strained relationship. Be flexible and life will be easier, and your students will be better served.

Identify and Focus on Your Special Education Teacher's Strengths

The general education teacher has strengths in the classroom. The special education teacher also has strengths. Find those strengths and celebrate them. This allows you to maximize the benefit of co-teaching.

Deborah, a middle school co-teacher, brought up the merits of being seen as a teacher in her own right, and not an accessory to the learning of only a handful of students. "What has helped in co-teaching is letting the students know I am an actual teacher and treating me like an actual teacher," she said. "What has not helped was when they expect me to sit in the back of the classroom and wait for students who need help. Being seen as an equal is vital to co-teaching."

Being seen as an equal is vital to co-teaching.

Adopt a "They Are All Our Students" Attitude

An "They are all our students" attitude is not only critical for the special education teacher, but also extremely important for students with an IEP. It is critical that general education teachers work with students in such a way that students with special needs are not stigmatized. Stigmatization as a "sped kid" leaves scars that can last a lifetime.

When the special education teacher is the primary interaction for an IEP student, everyone loses. The classroom teacher misses the chance to develop a potentially rewarding relationship with the student, and the student with special needs knows he or she is being ignored by the classroom teacher, which reinforces feelings of inferiority.

Make Time for Communication a Priority

Similarly, good communication is essential to any co-teaching arrangement. Heather, a teacher at Woodstock Elementary School in Bryant Pond, Maine, talked about the importance of going through lesson plans and scripting things out. "Co-teaching is like learning a dance with a new partner," she said. "You have to practice, practice, practice, and then you can learn to ad-lib together."

Judy, a language arts teacher from North Royalton, Ohio, noted that, "The key for me is knowing that in front of the students, we [my co-teacher and I] are always on the same page." Communication is key to being on the same page in the co-taught classroom.

Stop Trying to Be Perfect!

Some of the most successful co-teaching arrangements Heather has been involved in were those where she and her co-teacher acknowledged they did not have all the answers. These acknowledgments first happened privately, but they soon migrated to the classroom where the students could be shown that you never stop learning and you can learn from others by admitting what you do not know and asking for help. As Heather put it, "With some teachers I worked with, we stopped 'rehearsing' those conversations and allowed them to happen organically in front of the students. This was done when we really trusted each other and had worked together for a few years."

Make Choices that Build Trust and Respect

That trust is another important part of co-teaching. A productive co-teaching relationship is built on mutual respect and trust, which can be developed when co-teachers share responsibility in the classroom.

Ten Tips that Foster Positive Co-Teaching and Collaboration

At its best, co-teaching offers support to both teachers. A pair of experienced, successful co-teachers is like a finely tuned machine—every piece works together smoothly. The teachers support each other in everything they do. Here are twelve ways teachers can support each other in a co-teaching classroom.

1. There are many ways to implement co-teaching. Communicate with your co-teacher and your administrators to determine what will work best in your classroom. Finding an arrangement that works for everyone is a good first step in a successful co-teaching relationship.
2. Even if your co-teaching approach is One Teach, One Assist, always emphasize to your students that you are both "the teacher." It is not one teacher, one less-important teacher.
3. When co-teaching, we must make decisions that are in the best interest of our students. Over the years, traditional practice has reinforced the myth that special education teachers should be with the students who need basic skills while the general education teacher teaches the whole class. That is not necessarily true. Let the situation dictate the response.
4. Know your strengths and weaknesses. As a part of your planning together, communicate with each other about where you feel you do well and in what areas you feel you are not as strong. You may find that you can fill each other's gaps, so to speak. Together, two great teachers can make a spectacular co-teaching team.
5. You must plan. It is unavoidable—to be a good team, you must spend time working together to create and refine your classroom plans. Administrations do not always allow prep periods where both teachers are free, or they may only leave one or two periods a week free for planning. Make the most of the time you have and be creative in finding any extra time you may need.
6. Plan for your planning. As much as possible, get your lesson plans and weekly goals set before you meet with each other. Then you will be

free to work strictly on the parts of the lesson plan for which you need one another. Efficient use of your time is essential.

7. Do not isolate anyone. When you lean on the One Teach, One Assist approach as your main approach, it is easy to slip into a pattern where the specialist is focused on only a few students, while the general education teacher works with the rest of class. This establishes a negative "otherness" for the small group, including the teacher. Small groups can be extremely effective; just be sure that they are not isolating the same group of students all the time.
8. When co-teachers only use a One Teach, One Assist approach, students can frequently get the picture that one teacher is the "real" teacher while the other teacher is someone secondary. A good way to avoid this is to have the support teacher teach the general classroom a subject or topic in which he or she is particularly proficient, rather than having him or her constantly relegated to typical "support" tasks.
9. If you will be working with a Parallel Teaching or Alternative Teaching approach, set aside a prep period for the two of you to sketch out an arrangement that works in your classroom. You may need to move things around to find a setup that allows you both to be teaching simultaneously without distracting students or each other. Careful planning of your shared space will pay off.
10. If you are part of a new co-teaching pair—and especially if co-teaching is new to your school—be patient with the process. It will take time for you both to adjust to each other's personalities and teaching styles.

The Essential Ingredients for Effective Collaboration

One of the most important aspects of an effective working relationship between professionals is clear and consistent communication. It is critical to communicate frequently and use organizing tools that can help define roles, clarify expectations, and set parameters for class norms as part of the communication process.

Why is structure and time to talk so important? Because without having a system in place to discuss issues, organize information, and handle variables, too much is subject to guesswork. This inevitably causes problems and communication breakdown. It's essential for co-teachers to share their thoughts, feelings, and plans for co-teaching with each other to provide effective instruction for all students. (Conderman et al., 2009)

As Ploessl and Rock conclude in "On the Same Page—Practical Techniques to Enhance Co-Teaching Interactions," "If co-teaching partners are willing to invest time and effort in enhancing communications skills, finding regular planning time, improving instructional approaches, and resolving conflicts, they not only can reverse unproductive interactions but can even prevent them entirely" (Ploessl et al., 2010).

How to Woo Your Co-Teacher

When I started working in classrooms, I worked with some very resistant teachers. Some did not want me teaching at all, or they did not see any value in my working with ***their*** students. Some of my co-teachers preferred that I sit in the background and only step in if one of ***my*** students with an IEP needed help. I often felt like all I was doing was holding up the wall. I did not have much input in lesson planning. But I knew I had more to contribute to the classroom than just blending in with the wallpaper. I had ideas and plans for lessons that would greatly benefit the students.

Back then, mind mapping—a visual way to represent ideas and concepts—was relatively new. The general education teacher I worked with at the time, Nicole, was skeptical about the value of mind mapping as a teaching method. Still, I was confident that mind mapping would increase student comprehension of the linear notes being delivered via lecture.

I observed the lessons as they happened in class. Afterwards, I asked for the teacher's overhead notes so I could copy them. After creating mind maps of the day's notes, I added icons and clip-art that enhanced visual comprehension. I also changed the font color to white and printed it again so that the mind map was visible, but the labels were not. This process created "mind map skeleton notes." I printed a master copy. I wouldn't woo my co-teacher with chocolate or flowers; I'd woo her with cool strategies that she didn't have to create!

Before class, I showed Nicole my creation. I exclaimed, "Look what I did! I made this last night to help reinforce yesterday's lesson. It will take just two minutes of class time to review this with the students. I am positive it will help everyone understand the content, but it will really help the students who struggle. I know we have a lot to cover today, so I promise it will only take a few minutes."

I presented the mind maps to her with all the excitement and exuberance I felt about the tool. Admittedly, I did not ask permission to use the maps with the students. Rather, with the confidence of the certified teacher that I was, I approached it from a "let's use this and see how it works" standpoint. I assured her it would not take much time nor set her behind in her lesson plan. I was a salesperson selling her on the idea.

Nicole was receptive to using the mind maps, especially when she saw how quickly they could be incorporated and just how well the students took to them. Making the mind maps from her outlines was a baby step. It was a way to get my foot in the door as an equal in the co-taught classroom. Seeing how it helped all the students made her more receptive to other suggestions I made in the future. Eventually, we developed a rapport and a level of parity where co-teaching was reaping positive results with the students.

The day arrived when my co-teacher approached me. She shoved a paper in front of me and proudly said, "I wanted to show you what I created for the class! Look! What do you think?" What an amazing feeling it was to see that she had created a mind map activity for the students. We had come full circle.

Before any type of co-teaching arrangement can be used, it is important to establish a good working relationship with your co-teacher. Whether you are the general education teacher or a special educator, understanding each other's teaching preferences and comfort zones is essential to effective co-teaching. However, this type of understanding requires that both teachers are interested in making the co-teaching relationship work.

When one teacher wants to co-teach but the other is resistant, it poses a significant challenge. Developing a positive relationship when working under duress takes time. Sometimes, it helps to woo your co-teacher. Often, an educator who is hesitant to try co-teaching can be won over with a certain amount of wooing and positive persistence.

The key, I have found, is taking baby steps to try new things along the co-teaching journey. Often, educators who are hesitant to co-teach either do not want to lose their already limited teaching time, or do not know how to incorporate a second teacher into lessons they have likely been teaching for years. By offering small changes and suggestions, you can ease accommodations, adaptations, and differentiated instruction into the lesson plan without being intrusive.

When the Special Education Teacher Isn't Sold on Co-Teaching

At times, it may be the special educator who is hesitant to try co-teaching. The specialist may be unsure of his or her knowledge of the subject or the ability to hold the attention of so many more students at one time. Often, special educators are accustomed to teaching one-on-one, or in small groups. Tackling a class of thirty students is a very different challenge!

A Possible Solution to Engage Your Special Ed Co-Teacher

In this situation, the classroom teacher might use similar incremental changes to ease the special educator into a growing co-teacher role. Start out small: Ask for input on lesson plans. Work up to asking the specialist to summarize information for the class, as in One Teach, One Summarize. Possibly, start the first five minutes of class with the specialist leading an activity he or she planned. As we saw with Doris and Johanna, having the special educator do the introduction of a lesson establishes parity in the eyes of the students and builds confidence in the co-teaching relationship. Begin with baby steps, and the possibilities are endless.

Co-Teaching and Parity

One of the biggest issues schools face when instituting a co-teaching initiative is the challenge of establishing parity for both teachers. Parity is a critical ingredient in co-teaching. It is important that both teachers feel respected and valued for their contributions and that students perceive each teacher as an active participant in their education.

Moving from Inequality to Parity in the Co-Taught Classroom

Chris and Katelyn, co-teachers at Frink Middle School, had been co-teaching together for five years. Their first year together was the year the middle school initiated co-teaching and inclusion. The school used a model for implementing co-teaching that I call the "dumped-in method of co-teaching." Teachers were simply dumped into it without supports or training. Consequently, Chris and Katelyn struggled significantly during that first year to sort out their co-teaching relationship. It did not go well.

When asked how their relationship evolved, Chris replied, "When we started out, I was viewed as a teacher's assistant in the classroom. It brought my morale down as a teacher, even though I had been teaching for five years."

"And that was my first year of teaching," Katelyn added.

Chris continued to explain, "It brought my morale down because the students looked at her as the teacher and at me as the assistant."

Elaborating, Katelyn said, "We did not know the different co-teaching approaches. We did not know that both our names should be on the door and that we both should have a desk in the room. We did not realize we should be doing everything together because both of us were certified teachers. As hard as we tried to explain to the students, every day, that Chris was also a teacher so the students needed to respect her as much as they would respect any other teacher, it was difficult for the students to understand because we did not know what we were supposed to do. Neither we, nor the students, understood the concept."

Chris added, "Now, the students understand it, and they view both of us as teachers. We had some training from you on co-teaching and learned how it should be implemented. We used the training that we attended to plan over the summer for this year. Now both our names are on the door; we both have a desk in the classroom; we plan together; and we started out teaching together on the same day."

What Made Co-Teaching Work?

Chris and Katelyn's co-teaching relationship improved because they made the effort to get training together on what co-teaching looks like. They discussed what they learned and used their time in the summer to plan for the following school year, beginning the year on the same page.

The key here is that they made a commitment to each other to make it work. Then they followed through on that commitment. They also made the decision to treat each other as equals in the classroom—a conscious commitment to be successful as co-teachers. This was a significant factor in their success.

People often ask, "Do co-teachers need to have two desks in the room?" The answer to that question is no. Some co-teaching pairs with two desks in the classroom have noted a significant difference in students' perception regarding the teacher's roles. However, many co-teaching pairs have been very successful with establishing parity in the classroom without having two desks.

At the elementary level, the collaborating co-teacher is usually in the classroom for only a portion of the day. Having a desk in the room or his or her name on the door isn't always feasible. However, the collaborating co-teacher should be introduced as a teacher. He or she should have a spot in the room to call his or her own and have his or her name on the board or flipchart.

At the high school and middle school level, one option is to have a hook on the wall next to the classroom door with a clear sleeve, hung at eye level. This hook can be used to display a chart that includes each class period, the name of each class, and both co-teachers' names listed during the period they are in the room together. If there is a schedule change, the chart can be quickly changed and replaced.

Other Ways to Establish Clear Parity:

- Both teachers' names are on any paperwork related to that subject or class.
- Both teachers call a student's home—based on their availability or knowledge of a situation—regardless of whether the student is on an individualized education plan or not.
- Both teachers have a key to the classroom.
- Materials are shared between both teachers, including answer keys.
- Both teachers have access to the grade book.

Use Language That Clearly Establishes Parity to Students and Others

- Use phrases such as "our students" rather than "your students."
- Say "we" rather than "I" when speaking to the class.
- Never identify students as special education students in front of the class.
- Encourage groups to work together in mixed-ability groups so that expectations conveyed are spoken using the same language for all students.

Maintaining Trust in the Co-Taught Classroom

Suppose Ellen is a general education teacher who has committed to co-planning with Martina, her special education co-teacher. Their lesson plan involves different activities, including Alternative Teaching strategies. Consequently, both teachers would have groups simultaneously and be teaching those groups different material. Then Martina gets pulled from the room to deal with a student crisis and Ellen is left to figure out an emergency lesson plan on the spot.

How many times do you think Ellen will be willing to plan a lesson Martina—and continue to treat Martina as an equal—when she cannot trust that her special education teacher will be there to follow through?

Administrators and special educators need to understand that pulling a special education teacher from a co-taught classroom is a violation of trust. Once trust is broken, it is very difficult to get it back. Without trust there is little parity.

Another trust issue between co-teachers is punctuality. Teachers who teach alone cannot be late to class, lest chaos ensue with unattended students. Co-teachers cannot be late either because being present together at the beginning of class sets the tone of parity.

Trust and Respect:

Two teachers in the classroom can be good for ***all*** the students in a classroom—when both co-teachers respect each other. Most of us teach because we want to make a difference. Consider how much more impact you can make with access to another teacher's skillset to collaborate with and capitalize upon.

One co-teacher summed it up with, "If you have a trusting relationship, you can say almost anything because your co-teacher trusts you." Yet we know that the words we choose can make or break that relationship.

Collaboration Tips that Foster Trust and Respect

- Approach from a position of care.
- Be clear about what you want to say.
- Operate from a belief that encourages taking risks.
- Listen to understand, not to judge.
- Make positive statements that are specific and reflect what is valued by the other person.
- Look for success not only in academic areas.
- Discuss problems only with each other.

Pick-Me-Ups, Pick-You-Ups

- Compliment your colleague where all can see.
- Send a letter of appreciation; cc the principal.
- Remember special days with cards.

Questions to Consider When Preparing to Teach Together

Co-Planning Time

Although many of the co-teaching implementations described in Chapter 2 require minimal planning time, it's critical that co-teachers communicate. When co-teachers don't carve out some time to review, reflect, and plan, their relationship suffers. Consequently, their instructional effectiveness is minimized.

- How much time do we need to plan?
- When will we make the time to plan?
- What checks can we put in place to ensure we use our time effectively?
- What materials should we bring to the planning meeting with us?
- Are we comfortable planning in the cloud? What planning apps can we utilize? How can planning virtually maximize our effectiveness and efficiency?

Instruction

Co-teaching appears to be more successful when both teachers utilize agreed-upon strategies. These include providing "structure, clarity, enthusiasm, maximizing student engagement, and motivational strategies. Not only did effective teaching behaviors lead to increased academic achievement, it also led to a greater degree of effective collaboration between the two co-teachers" (Mastropieri et al., 2005). Given the importance of being on the same page regarding instruction, consider discussing these questions with your co-teacher.

- How will we determine the content to be taught? Will we use curriculum compacting, curriculum mapping data, or state standards to target the most critical content?
- Who will plan what?
- When will the special education co-teacher implement instruction to students with disabilities, without disabilities, both?
- How will the co-teacher implement instruction?
- How will we decide who teaches what?
- Who creates curriculum adaptations, accommodations, and modifications?
- Who adapts the tests?

- How will we use our strengths in the classroom when planning instruction?
- How will we present the content? Will one person do all the direct teaching, or will both share responsibility for teaching the lesson?
- Should we rotate responsibilities?
- If working with a paraprofessional, who will train the paraprofessional to use the specific instruction strategies?
- Who will evaluate the effectiveness of the instruction provided by the paraprofessional?

Student Behavior

- What are the classroom expectations for students and adults?
- How are class expectations communicated to the students?
- What is the plan to address unacceptable student behavior in a timely manner?
- What are the specific roles of the adults in the room in supporting positive student behavior?
- How will we be consistent in managing behavior and supporting each other's authority?
- What are our pet peeves? What student behavior pushes our buttons? What can we not tolerate in the classroom?
- If our discipline style is very different, where can we find common ground?

Communication

- How will we ensure regular communication with each other?
- How will we address communication needs with each other?
- Who will communicate with the parents of students on an IEP? What about the parents of students not on an IEP? Do we share the responsibility for communication equally?
- How should we handle conflict or concern with each other to preserve the harmony of our relationship?
- Who will communicate with parents about routine daily occurrences, unusual situations, other?
- What do we need to know about each other?
- What do I need to work effectively in my classroom?
- What can I not tolerate in my co-teacher?

- What am I looking forward to in co-teaching?
- What are my non-negotiables?
- The most important thing to me in our co-teaching relationship is...
- What are our expectations of each other?
- How do we react to unexpected changes in plans?
- What are our expectations regarding:
    - Class work and homework being done on time, or independently?
    - Grading?
    - Noise level?
    - Small-group work?
    - Differentiating instruction?
    - Giving or receiving feedback?
    - Dividing the workload?

Co-Teaching Preparation Questionnaire

____
____
____

Are we comfortable planning in the cloud? ______________________
What planning apps can we utilize? ______________________
How can planning virtually maximize our ability to plan effectively and efficiently? ______________________

Instruction:
What will we teach? ______________________
Who will plan what? ______________________
What approach will we use? ______________________
Who will teach what? ______________________
Who will create curriculum adaptations, accommodations, modifications, and test adaptations?
____

Student behavior:
Are the ground rules clearly defined and understood by the class? __________
How will we address behavior issues and support each other's authority?
____
____
What pet peeves or student behaviors can you not tolerate in the classroom?
____
____

Communication:
How can we ensure regular communication and address our needs with each other?
____
____
Who will be responsible for interacting with the parent of students on an IEP?
____
Who will be responsible for interacting with parents on routine issues?
____
What's the best way for others to share new ideas with you? __________
____

How should we handle issues or concerns with each other to minimize conflict?
____
____

Personal:
What do we need to know about each other to work effectively together?
____
____
What are you looking forward to and what can you not tolerate in your co-teacher?
____
____
What are your non-negotiable issues? ______________________________
____
What is the most important thing to you in a co-teaching relationship?
____
____

Expectations:
Timeliness of class work and homework ___________________________
____
Students working independently or collaboratively ___________________
____
Grading ____
Noise level in the classroom
____
Small group work
____
Differentiating
instruction____
Giving & receiving feedback ______________________________________
Dividing the work load ____

<u>**Notes:**</u>

Scripts for Effective Communication

Things Never to Say to Your Co-Teacher

I was co-teaching biology with a teacher who could say the meanest things with a smile on his face. One day, I was teaching the parts of the heart. When I finished explaining the difference between the inferior vena cava and the superior vena cava, he (who will remain nameless) told the class, "Yes, it is just like Mrs. Fitzell and I. She's the inferior vena cava, and I'm the superior vena cava."

The class laughed. I felt humiliated, diminished, and betrayed.

Months later, when we were reviewing the eye, which has an inferior oblique and superior oblique, he repeated the analogy again. He thought it was funny. I thought it was mean. These were two of the most humiliating experiences I had while co-teaching because he said these things in front of the entire class.

Co-teaching and collaboration are challenging. They require educators to stretch beyond their comfort zones. Many teachers are forced into co-teaching. They find themselves paired with another adult in the classroom—without any training to navigate the situation. They don't know what to do or say. Yet, what we ***say*** to each other can make or break a relationship.

If you asked me, "What is one thing you should never say to your co-teacher?", my reply would be, "Don't announce to the class that you are superior, and your co-teacher is inferior." But not everyone is me. So, I asked my teaching colleagues the same question.

Here is what they said:

> **"Mrs./Ms./Mr. will be assisting me today," said in front of the class.**
>
> Your co-teacher hears: I do not respect you or your teaching skills.
>
> Your students hear: The special ed. teacher is not my/a real teacher.
>
> **"We don't do it that way!"**

Your co-teacher hears: Your expertise does not matter.

"Thank you but I don't need your help, I can handle this myself."

OR

"I didn't like your lesson, so I had *my* students do it *my* way."

OR

"Your input isn't needed. You have nothing to offer."

OR

"That's not right. You are wrong. My way is better."

Your co-teacher hears: I do not respect you or your teaching skills.

"That student isn't one of *mine* so I won't work with him."

OR

"I'll do my thing; you do yours."

Your co-teacher hears: I'm not interested in being collaborative.

"This is my classroom. Take care of your students. I am the real teacher."

Your co-teacher hears: I not only do not respect you or your teaching skills, but I have no interest in being collaborative.

"You take your students and I'll take my students," within student earshot.

Your co-teacher hears: I am not interested in being collaborative.

Your students hear: That teacher does not care about me.

"You are the content specialist, I'm just here for special ed. support."

Your co-teacher hears: I am not interested in working harder than necessary.

"You can't see the answer key."

Your co-teacher hears: You are going to help the students cheat. I do not trust you.

"Are you sure you get this?"

Your co-teacher hears: I am the one with the _______________ (fill in the blank) degree. You are not smart enough to do this job.

"I can't plan with you during our planning time. I have to write IEPs."

Your co-teacher hears: Planning with you to benefit our students is not a priority of mine. You and the students are not important.

"I can't teach your special ed. students unless you're physically present in the classroom."

Your co-teacher hears: Your special ed. students are not my problem. I only teach students who are not on an IEP.

"This is an Advanced Placement class. We don't make accommodations in this class!"

Your co-teacher hears: It does not matter how smart your students are, I am not willing to teach them if they do not learn the way I teach.

"I don't know why they are in this class. Those special ed. students can't do this."

Your co-teacher hears: I have made up my mind that the special ed. students cannot learn and that they do not belong in this class.

"Anything you need from me today?"

Your co-teacher hears: Being in class with you to benefit our students is not a priority of mine. You and the students are not important.

"I am so lucky I don't have your class this year!"

Your ex-co-teacher hears: I hated working with you.

Choose Words Strategically

Notice "all," "never" and "always." Ask to get more specificity. Often these words are arbitrary limits on behavior. Be specific. Avoid general comments and clarify pronouns such as "it," "that," etc. Be very careful with advice.

Also, any statement with the phrase, "I know..." followed by "but..." typically triggers a negative response. For example, "I know you worked hard on that lesson, but some students seemed confused."

Susanne Gaddis, PhD, the Communications Doctor, writes:

"Adopting, the "words to use...words to lose" philosophy can work miracles for improving one's interpersonal communication. The basic idea behind this philosophy is that some words and phrases build relationships up, and some words and phrases tear relationships down. Since effective communication is about building and maintaining relationships, we need to choose our words wisely. "Words to use...words to lose" simply facilitates a stronger, more positive emotional vocabulary.

Words to Lose:	***Words to Use:***
• But • Should • Must • Cannot • Do not • Never	• And • Next Time • Please • Can • Do • Specifics

Denotations Versus Connotations

As we carefully choose words and phrases, it is a good idea to keep in mind that words have both denotations as well as connotations—which is their emotional impact.

For example, have you ever noticed that successful real estate agents sell homes rather than houses? By nature, a house has no personality and is devoid of love. Conversely, a home is a warm and loving place. "Home" gathers its considerable emotional power for the simple reason that it is inhabited in a way that a house is not.

Similarly, the phrases you use can provoke certain feelings.

Prepare for Communication

When communicating, always be prepared.

- Learn skills and strategies for positive communication.
- Have a game plan so your emotions do not get the best of you.
- Never address a difficulty with your colleague in front of a group. It should always be one-to-one.
- Focus on success, not your fears.

Incorporate Active Listening Practices

Active listening, as the name suggests, is an active process. As you listen to a person speaking, watch his or her facial expressions and body language. You are actively asking yourself the following three questions:

- What is this person feeling?
- What exactly did this person experience?
- What did this person do?

Periodically, you are asking yourself a fourth question that integrates these:

- What is it like to be in his or her shoes? What is happening to this person?

Active listening can increase a person's comfort, interest, and motivation. It can communicate to the speaker that you value him or her as a person. It also helps us to gain an understanding of the speaker's experience by asking thoughtful questions. Most importantly, it communicates that understanding to the speaker so he or she feels heard.

What to Do When in Conflict

In the classroom, conflicts will sometimes happen. How can we handle conflict in a constructive way? When situations get tough, remember that most conflicts stem from differences in personality. That other person is not ***trying*** to upset you.

How do we respond when something happens in the classroom that triggers frustration or anger? Often, we think thoughts like, "That person should know better," or "I told her she should do such-and-such but she didn't listen to me!"

Or maybe it's closer to: "She's an idiot" or "He's a control freak—I cannot stand him" or "He thinks he knows everything!"

Every one of these types of statements that we think to ourselves in times of conflict is negative self-talk. Negative self-talk begets more negativity.

What if we change our self-talk?

Instead of: "This person is doing this to annoy me...."

Replace that thought with: "She is trying her best. This is just her personality. How might I approach this personality that is so different from mine?"

We could say: "I can handle this."

Or: "This isn't about me; this is about him, and I need to know how to approach him."

Instead of taking things personally, we understand it is simply about personality.

Once you have your positive self-talk, start considering solutions to the problem. Consult a respected colleague; request the aid of someone who seems to be able to work with just about anyone. Seek that person out and ask how you might approach the problem. Ideally, you would do this without naming the person with whom you are in conflict.

Many resources are available to help people figure out what to say. In a difficult situation, use those resources. Albert Ellis has written several books that share strategies for how to handle difficult situations. These suggest ways to keep our minds in a rational and positive place. For example, just the title of his book, ***How to Stubbornly Refuse to Make Yourself Miserable About Anything—Yes, Anything*** (Paperback - July 1988) encourages a smile.

If your shared planning sessions always seem to go awry, possibly audiotape some of those interactions and listen for communication that might be sabotaging your co-teaching relationship (Ploessl et al., 2010).

Consider using "I" statements. Avoid using the word "you" when communicating how you feel. Be careful to avoid blaming language. Even if you believe the other person is wrong, find a way to approach the conversation from a positive perspective.

Once you figure out how you want to handle the problem, role-play the conversation with a friend. Visualize the interaction in your mind. Practice what you will say until you feel confident.

At times, it is best to say nothing. That choice is more difficult for some personalities than for others. Sometimes it is important to speak up about our concerns, and that is easy for some personalities and more difficult for others. The most critical factor is that—whatever we choose to do—we try to frame our actions, words, and thoughts in positive ways.

Stopping Conflict in Its Tracks!

Have you ever found yourself in a conversation with a colleague that left you shaking your head and wondering what that was all about? Sometimes, we leave conversations feeling defeated, and strangely so, because we are not always sure what happened.

Is there someone in your life who seems to have an answer for everything? What about someone who is overly critical? How do we handle these types of conversations and the characters in our lives who challenge us with their words?

Consider learning words and phrases that stop conflict in its tracks.

I remember a colleague of mine who worked in the business world. He loved to jibe me about being a teacher. Every time we got together, he would disparage the teaching profession. He loved to see my reaction. Of course, I always reacted in passionate defense. Over the years, this became a tiresome tradition between us.

Finally, one day, he started in with his usual tirade. I simply looked at him with a smile on my face and said, "You have an interesting perspective. I will have to give that more thought." Then I changed the subject. Much to my amazement, his jaw dropped. He seemed to have to search for what to say next. It took the wind out of his sails, and it was done so nicely.

Knowing phrases that stop conflict in its tracks is just one piece of the conflict-avoidance puzzle. The words we speak are less than 10 percent of our total communication. Body language and tone of voice are critical factors in how we communicate. It's often not what we say, but how we say it that determines whether our interactions will be positive or negative.

We Convey More Than Our Words

Don't Use That Tone With Me!

Tone of voice communicates more than the words we speak. A calm tone of voice and relaxed body language will be the key factors as to whether your words stop conflict in its tracks. When practicing these scripts, be certain there is no sarcasm in your tone. Try to be calm, cool, and collected. Avoid moving into the other person's personal space.

Body Language Sends a Loud Message

Body language communicates a significant amount of what we are trying to express. Our body language sends a message to those we interact with and those who observe us. Make sure your body language is consistent with the verbal message you want to send. If it is inconsistent, you could be sending mixed messages. Mixed messages can cause the listener to doubt the sincerity of what is being said. Sometimes, this can even lead to confusion between enthusiasm and aggressiveness (Conderman et al., 2009).

Body Language Activity: Aggressive, Neutral, or Assertive?

Some body language is aggressive, and some is assertive; body language may send a negative message, a neutral message, or a positive message. Consider the following list of body language behaviors.

- Finger pointing
- Shuffling from foot to foot
- Wringing of hands
- Blushing
- Nose-to-nose
- Hands at sides
- Hands-on hips
- Nervous cough
- Looking in the eyes
- Looking down and around
- Straightening clothes
- Arms crossed across chest
- Slumped shoulders

"What Do I Say When My Colleague Says..."

Phrases That Shift the Dynamic Without Escalating Conflict

- What can I do to support you?
- Can we talk about something I think might help us work together better?
- I would like to talk about ______________, but first I would like to get your point of view.
- I think we may have different ideas about ______________. I would really like to hear your thoughts and share my perspective as well.

Comebacks That Don't Escalate the Conflict

When using the following statements, be careful that your tone of voice is calm and without any hint of sarcasm.

- I see.
- Thank you for letting me know how you feel.
- Perhaps you are right.
- I hear you.
- Ouch! (This cues in the other person that he or she is being hurtful.)
- I can see this upset you.
- I am sorry you were hurt. That was not my intent.
- I should not have to defend myself, and I will not.
- Excuse me; I am not finished.
- You have an interesting perspective.
- I will have to give that some thought.
- I will talk to you when you are calm.
- I will talk to you when I am calm.
- Agree with some of the statement but not all. Example: "You have a chip on your shoulder because you are short." Agree. Say, "Yes, I am short."

Ask a Question

- Why does that bother you?
- How so?
- What makes you say that?
- I know you would not have said that unless you had a good reason. Could you tell me what it was?

Offline Coping Techniques

- Do not take their behavior personally.
- Write down details of what annoys you.
- Think about why it annoys you.
- Which of your buttons does this person push?
- Why do you respond to him or her in the way you do?

It's Working!

Not Working as Well

Let's Try ...

What's Working? Card

Improving collaboration in the classroom improves the overall experience for teachers, paraprofessionals, and students—and it may be accomplished by something as simple as a 3x5 card.

As professionals, we try to phrase our words in a way that will get a positive response. For example, saying, "I would really like to hear your thinking on this and share my perspective as well," is a positive way to open a potentially conflictual conversation.

Sometimes, however, we do not really hear what the other person is saying. Our fears, agendas, and even enthusiasm get in the way of the kind of listening necessary to foster good communication. Without effective communication, we make many assumptions about the people with whom we interact. Those assumptions might be very inaccurate and create tremendous conflict, rather than promoting inclusion.

This is where the index card comes into play. The card is a simple way to give feedback to individual members of the teaching team. I found it useful for reinforcing the positives. It can be delivered in person or placed in a teacher mailbox.

What should you say on these cards? Here are some tips for using index cards to communicate clearly:

- Be as careful with your written phrasing as you are with spoken words.
- Do not use red ink when writing the card.
- If you feel the person receiving the feedback may not understand why you are communicating with a card, consider delivering it in person.

Phrase your concerns in a positive way. The primary difference with writing it down is you are giving the other person a chance to see what you are trying to communicate, without the filter mechanisms of a face-to-face conversation.

As always, be flexible when trying to improve collaboration with others. Keep conversations professional. Try to compliment your colleague frequently, especially when others are around.

How Is Co-Teaching Going?

"The importance of a shared vision on the part of members of co-teaching teams as to what they consider as good education for students is not mentioned in definitions of co-teaching." After an extensive literature review on co-teaching practice, authors Fluijt, Bakker, and Struyf argue that "sense-making by reflection about what can be considered as good education—good teaching and good learning—is essential when co-teachers want to understand or change their practice or relationship with their partner" (Fluijt, Bakker, & Struyf, 2016).

Following is a list of questions to ask yourselves when trying to evaluate your co-teaching process. Ideally, co-teachers should meet to discuss progress twice a month. Make a date to have this conversation and stick to it!

- Are students with an IEP reaching higher standards?
- Are general education students reaching higher standards?
- Are you teaching to the middle or lower achievers?
- Are you using Station Teaching and flexible grouping to accelerate learning?
- Do students know who is designated as special education?
- Do they feel both teachers are there to help all students?
- Do they see both teachers as equals?
- Are there social and behavioral benefits?
- How will you determine students' perceptions of your co-taught class?
- Are you communicating?
- Are you feeling fulfilled in your co-teaching experience?
- Do both teachers believe their skills are valued and used to maximize student success in the classroom?
- Are you differentiating instruction?
- Do you feel the workload division is fair and consistent?
- What are you doing well?
- What needs to change?
- Are you making time to plan together?
- Is planning time being used effectively?

- Is administration aware of how the co-taught process is going in your classroom?
- How will you keep administration informed?

When students succeed as the result of co-teaching, be sure administration is aware. Provide documentation and feedback.

More than one successful co-teaching pair has lamented that their co-taught class was reassigned because of an administrative decision. Sometimes, that decision is made because school administrators are unaware of how the relationship is contributing to student success and higher state test scores.

Additionally, administrators cannot support resolutions to obstacles in the co-teaching process if they are unaware of those obstacles. When presenting concerns to an administrator, be sure to present possible solutions. When administrators do not see the successes or problems in a co-teaching situation, they are unable to support the process.

Co-Teaching Observation Form

The following form is a tool for observing the co-teaching process. Provide the tool to a trusted peer and ask for objective feedback on how the co-teaching process is going in your classroom. It is difficult to assess how well we are doing from the "inside." Objective feedback can be invaluable to improving your process.

CO-TEACHING OBSERVATION FORM

CO-TEACHER NAMES: Content_______________ SpEd _______________ Subject: __________ Date:________

Start time:________ End time:__________ Debrief time:__________ Other:________________________

TIME	INSTRUCTIONAL MATERIALS	INSTRUCTIONAL METHODS/CO-TEACH IMPLEMENTATION	STUDENT SKILL REQUEST	CO-TEACHER SKILLS BEING MAXIMIZED – (Who is doing what?)	STUDENT BEHAVIOR & # ENGAGED	COMMENTS

Questions:

Suggestions are on reverse side.
Suggestions are options – NOT should haves!

Use space to diagram classroom to provide feedback on structure/engagement.

Chapter 6 Review and Discussion Questions

Reflection Questions

- When you think about teaching, and your students, what are your three most important beliefs?
- When you think about classroom climate, what are your three most important beliefs? What might happen if your beliefs are significantly different from your co-teacher's?
- When considering your personality and communication style, what are your strengths and weaknesses? Do you meet problems head-on, or do you avoid? Do you speak up or remain silent?
- Within your own discipline (for example, general education, special education, speech/language therapy, reading instruction), what are your areas of strength and weakness? What do you do best? Why are your students fortunate to have you as their teacher? What do you give them?
- How are your strengths and weaknesses likely to affect a co-teaching relationship?
- Based upon the "Glass Analogy" personality examples in this section, how would you describe your personality?
- Based on your responses, what are three important things a co-teacher should keep in mind when working with you?
- How would you describe your co-teacher's personality?
- What do you do when one teacher perceives a problem but is uncomfortable raising the matter with the other teacher?

Practical Application

Determine the three most difficult challenges you face when working with your co-teaching partner. Journal your thoughts for future discussion.

Compare your list of challenges with your co-teaching partner and discuss strategies to overcome the challenges you face, together. Develop and document a plan for overcoming the roadblocks you face, together.

What steps might you need to take to achieve a more productive and understanding relationship with your co-teacher?

CHAPTER 7

EFFECTIVE SMALL GROUPS AND STATIONS

What Constitutes Effective Small-Group Instruction?

Effective Small-Group Instruction

- Uses assessment data to create lesson plans and determine the groups.
- Keeps groups small, preferably three to four students to a group. Sometimes it might even be appropriate to have pairs.
- Groups are flexible. This means groups change as students grow, test out of a curriculum section, choose activities based on the type of activity required, etc.
- Learning profile instructional materials are geared toward student ability levels when activities are not based on differentiating by process or student.
- Small-group activities are tailored to address student needs.

Ineffective Small-Group Instruction

- Has students in groups, but all activity is directed by the teacher.
- Keeps students in the same groups continually, usually in same-ability groups. This is tracking within a class.
- Uses the same materials with all students in all groups.
- Uses the same independent-state work assignments for the entire class.
- Uses small groups to complete worksheets, and more worksheets, and more worksheets.

Some Effective Flexible Grouping Options

- Students might be grouped by readiness, interest in the topic or a learning process, or their student learning profile.
- Students might be grouped by student similarities or dissimilarities, ability levels or same-ability levels, using strategic behavioral grouping, self-starters with students who need support to get started, etc.
- Students might be grouped by the teacher planning the group, by students choosing their partners, or through random group generation.

If you were a fly on the wall in a classroom that is fully engaged in flexible grouping, you might see small groups of the same ability working together, mixed-ability groups, pairs, and partners, and even some one-on-one interaction.

Strategies for Effective Group Processes

Establish ground rules. According to a study by Janice Whately on ground rules in team projects, "agreeing [to] ground rules seems to contribute to improved team spirit or cohesion. Using the ground rules suggestions as a basis for preparing a contract for all team members to sign is a means of formalising agreement to ground rules" (Whatley, 2009). For students to behave appropriately and stay on task during small group work, they must be taught how to work in a group.

Students have been trained over the years to sit at desks lined up in rows and passively receive information. Many, if not most, students have no idea how to work in a group. If they have experience with group work, it might be quite limited because schools still teach primarily through a direct teaching, whole class model. When students are suddenly asked to work in a group, they often misbehave and mismanage their time. They simply do not know how to do small group work.

Consequently, teachers need to teach students how to work in a group. The first step in the process is to establish ground rules and norms for interaction. These guidelines must be enforced by teachers and students themselves for group work to be effective. Ground rules should encourage positive collaborative behaviors among all students. In my experience, students abide by rules best when they have a part in making them. Guidelines/ground rules need to be posted in the classroom, so students can readily refer to them. If students or teachers believe additional rules are needed, they can be added later.

Class Plan for Differentiating Within Groups

- Decide on a physical classroom desk and table arrangement.
- Will one room arrangement work, or will teachers need to have options for multiple arrangements depending on the group activity required?
- How will the class be rearranged when necessary? What will be required to accomplish rearranging the classroom?
- What routines and skills are necessary for students to learn to have the class run smoothly when deviating from the traditional row arrangement? Have students practice moving from one room arrangement to another.
- Use a signal, either a hand gesture or a sound, to notify students of time remaining until a transition; then use the signal again when the transition needs to occur. Before any transition, remind students of behavioral expectations.
- The goal in designing the classroom to be conducive to small group work is to design a structure that allows the teacher or co-teachers to interact quickly and easily with all students.

Train Student Experts

Suppose I have ten minutes to focus on coaching. I want that time to be uninterrupted. The last thing in the world I want during a coaching session is to be bombarded by students asking, "What do I do next, Mrs. Fitzell?" "Now what do I do, Mrs. Fitzell?" "Mrs. Fitzell, will you check this for me?"

A significant benefit to Station Teaching is having the time to work closely with students one-on-one or in small groups. Keeping that benefit in the face of interruptions requires that we spend time at the beginning of the process teaching students how to use centers and training student experts who can help you manage your centers.

Student experts are not experts on the content. They are experts on how the station works, how to check activities in and out (including taking inventory of materials), and what to do after completing an activity.

The student expert is trained to answer questions from other students like, "I don't understand what the teacher wants me to do." "Who is my partner supposed to be?" "What do I do next?" "What do I do if I'm finished?" so students in centers do not need to interrupt the teacher.

You might even consider training your biggest, baddest, most difficult student to be your expert because that student is going to think, "Oh, I'm an expert!" I have seen some of the most difficult-to-manage ADHD students become the most amazing peer leaders when given the opportunity. You will be amazed how well this approach can work.

Practice the Station Teaching Process

Practice behavioral expectations for the Station Teaching approach. Students know how to do a worksheet, and they know how to pretend they are following along, but they do not necessarily know how to get out of their seats, go sit with partners, get to work, and stay on task without disrupting other students along the way. We have to teach them these skills.

I have been asked, "How can I make centers work in a forty-five-minute class period? There isn't enough time." My first answer is always to use timers. As teachers today, we need to be very efficient with our use of time. Teach students how to move in the classroom, from one activity or station to another, quickly and quietly. Train them. Make it a contest or a game and reward them for transitioning between activities very quickly.

I have seen middle school classrooms with gifted students, students with ADHD, students in the spectrum, and even students with Tourette's syndrome successfully manage these movement challenges. The teachers in these classrooms have drilled the students to practice how to move the desks and regroup. The students are successful. They do it silently, they move quickly, and they finish within fifteen to twenty seconds. Seconds! I have been in awe of that.

The teachers make it a contest. They train their students to meet the expectations and periodically give incentives: "Gosh, you guys did so well today when moving into groups that I am going to give you..." some incentive. The students just love it.

In high school, teachers will say, "All right, the whole class transitioned into groups in ten seconds. None of my other classes have done it that fast." Then, in the next class, the teacher says, "Hey, my last class did it in ten seconds—do you think you can beat them?" Students love to meet that challenge and earn bragging rights for their class. This stuff is straight out of Dale Carnegie, but so what? It works!

Options for Determining Which Students Should Be in Which Groups

Teachers can use several methods to form groups. One way is to use assessment data to group students. For example, teachers might use standardized test scores, CBM, progress monitoring, informal assessments such as classroom observations, exit cards, action research, observation, and student self-assessment.

Group students based on targeted areas of instruction. If students did poorly on a specific state standard or are struggling to understand a curriculum concept, those students might be grouped together to accelerate growth.

Students might also be grouped in mixed-ability groups so every group has peer tutors and supports in place for students who are struggling. In a study by Mastropieri et al. (2005), results indicated that peer tutoring intervention was associated with improvements in student performance, and students in co-teaching settings perform better than those in non-co-teaching settings when instruction included peer tutoring.

In "Lessons from the Best and Worst Student Team Experiences: How a Teacher Can Make the Difference," authors Bacon, Stewart, and Silver concluded their research "admonishes us as teachers to place students in team situations that have the greatest chance for success. Although we cannot ensure the success of every team, by offering written instructions for the teams, maximizing team longevity, giving students a say in team assignments, avoiding the traditional peer evaluation process, matching the team size to the pedagogical objectives, and finding ways to improve team training, we can establish an environment that is most likely to lead to good team experiences"(Bacon et al., 1999).

Implementing Ongoing Assessment Within a Classroom as a Means to Defining Groups

Here are some options to provide a healthy team and small group work environment Use student data sources as a guide for grouping students. Some sources include:

- A student's journal entries.
- Short answer test responses.
- Open response test results.
- Homework completion.
- Notebook checks.
- Class participation.
- Previously completed projects.
- Problem-solving skills.

Teacher generated data:

- Anecdotal records.
- Teacher observation.
- Class discussion.
- Rubrics.
- Exit cards.
- Individualized assessment.
- Student-teacher conferencing.
- Observation of small group interaction.
- Data collected during class discussion (one teacher leads discussion while the other teacher takes notes on student responses and behavior).

Use the data to create triads: one high achiever, one midrange achiever, and one low achiever.

Use Student Talent and Interest to Define Groups

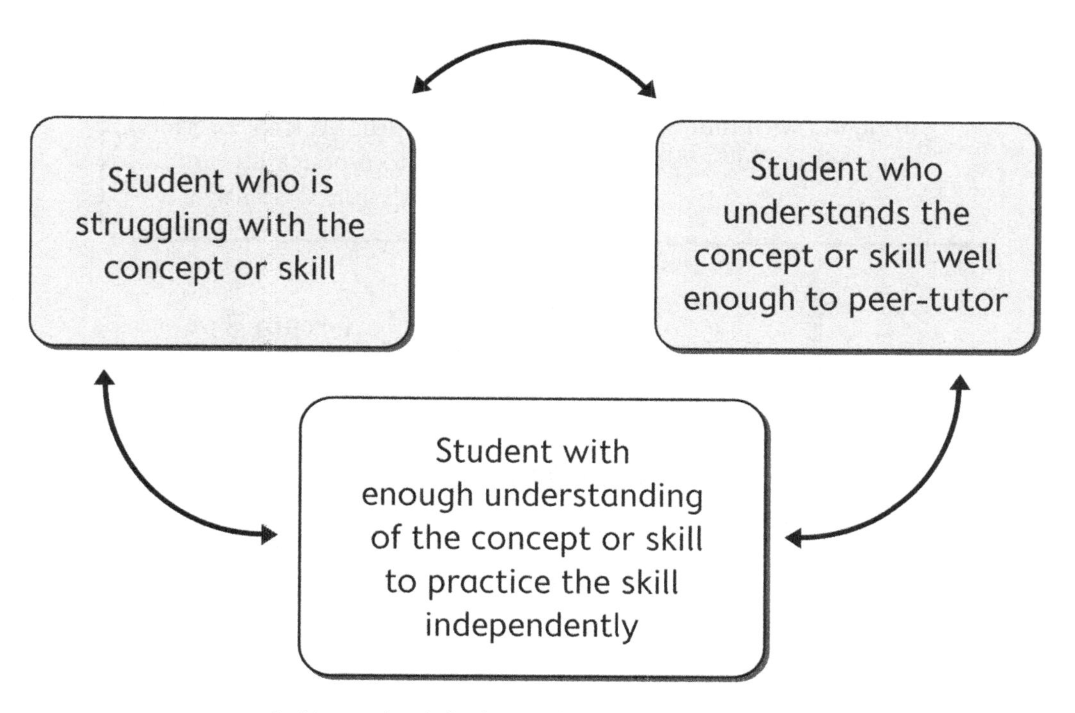

EXIT CARD GROUPINGS – Small Groups Version 1

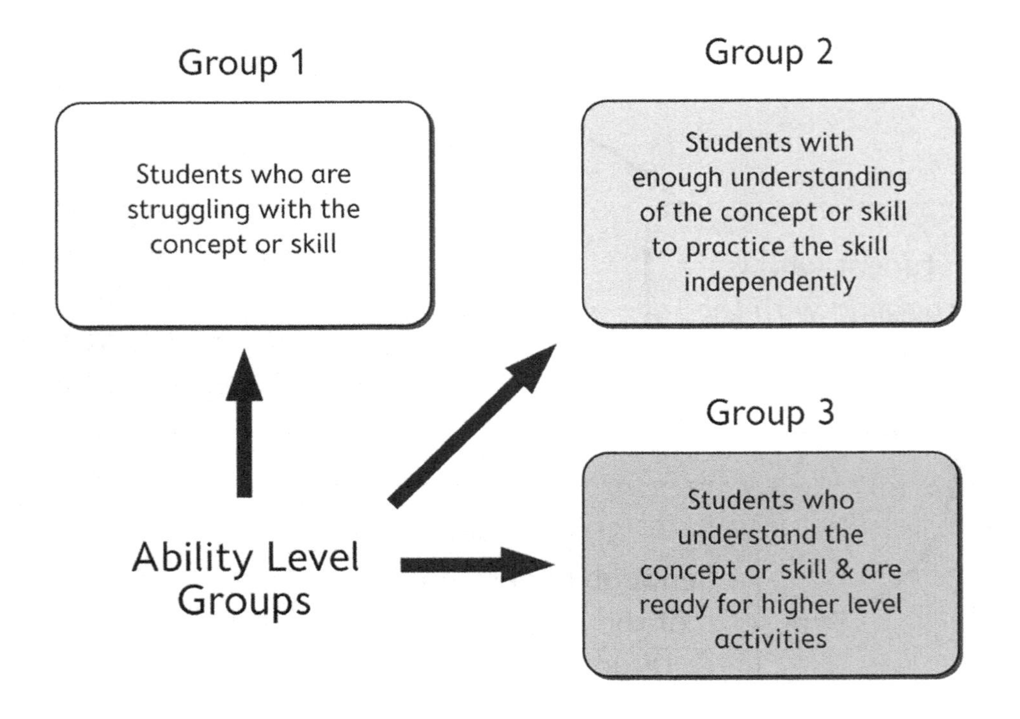

EXIT CARD GROUPINGS – Small Groups Version 2

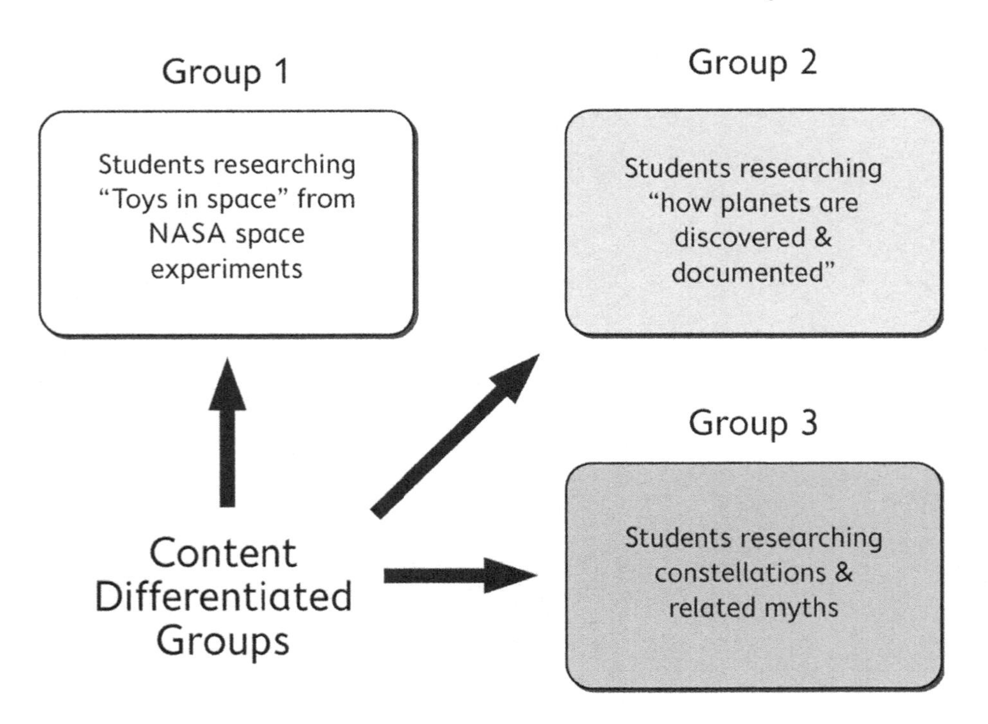

EXIT CARD GROUPINGS – Small Groups Version 3

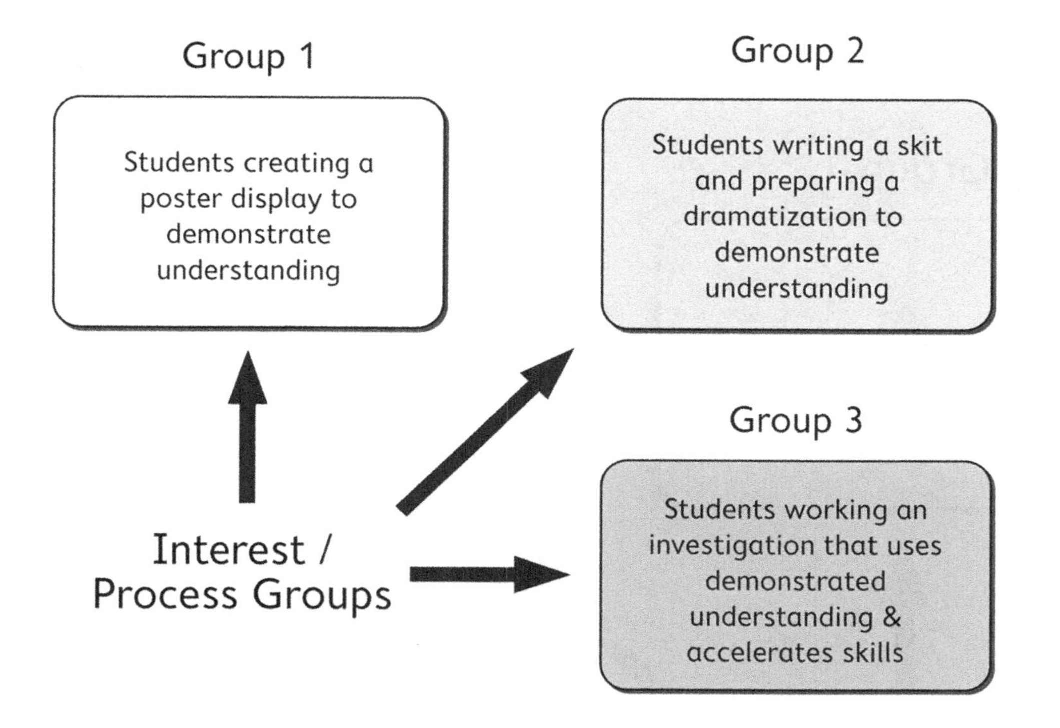

EXIT CARD GROUPINGS – Small Groups

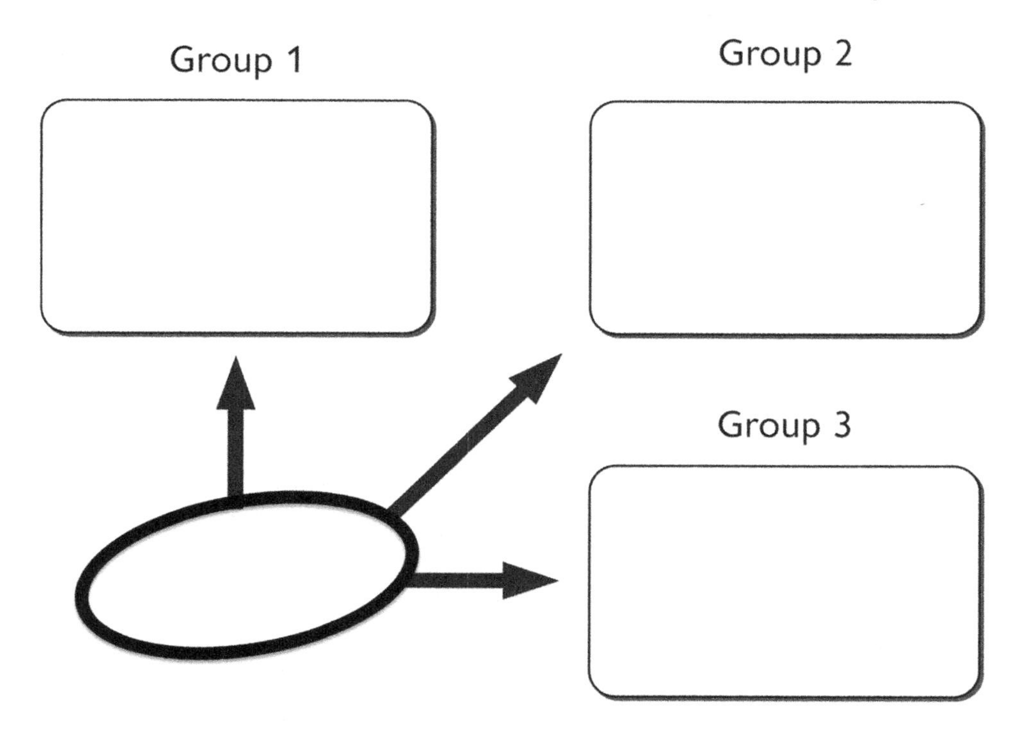

EXIT CARD GROUPINGS – Small Groups Template

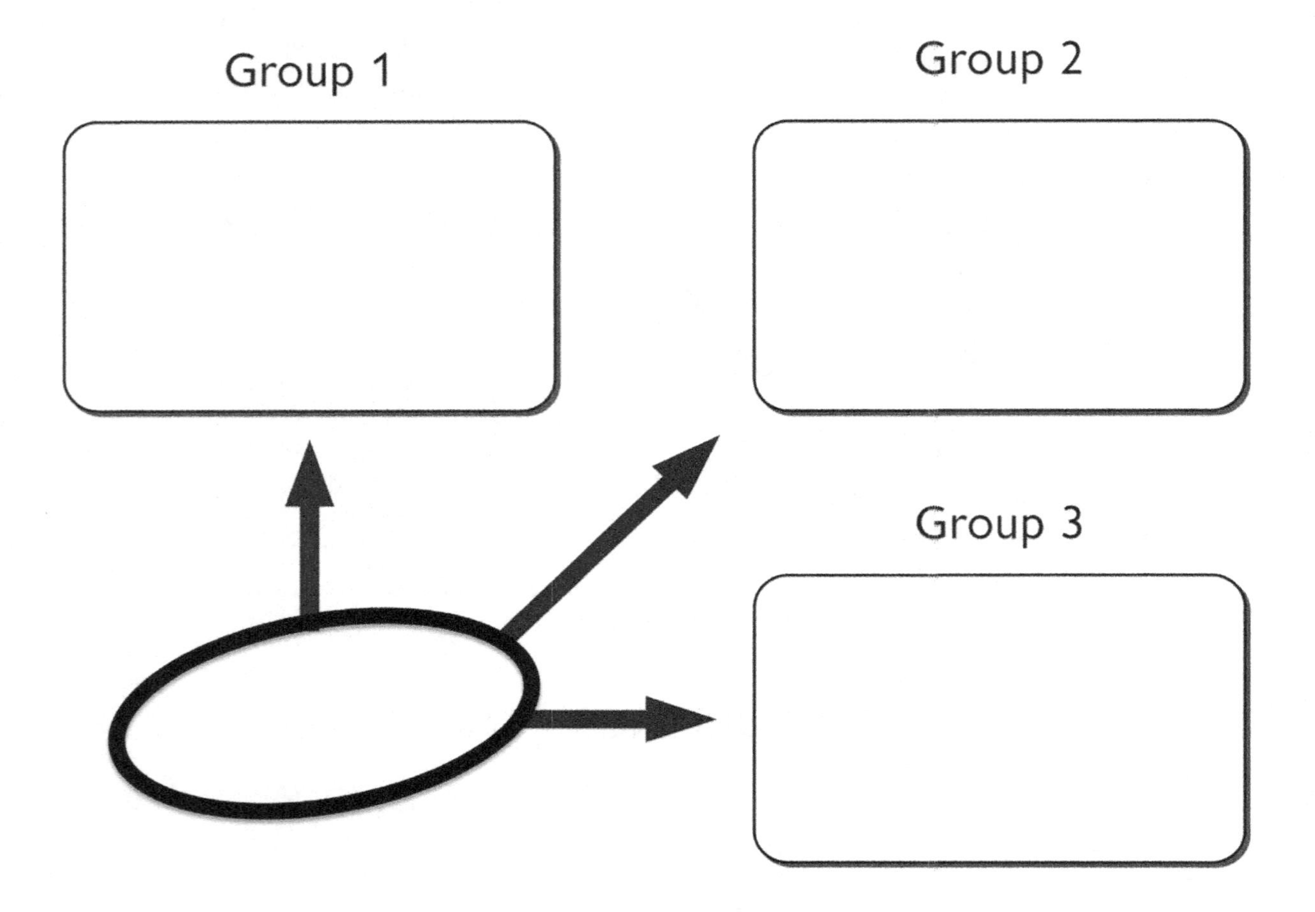

Use Grade Book to Determine High-Low Partners

Pairs:

- Partners have different learning styles.
- Ability-based pair.
- One high achiever with one low achiever (but not the lowest).

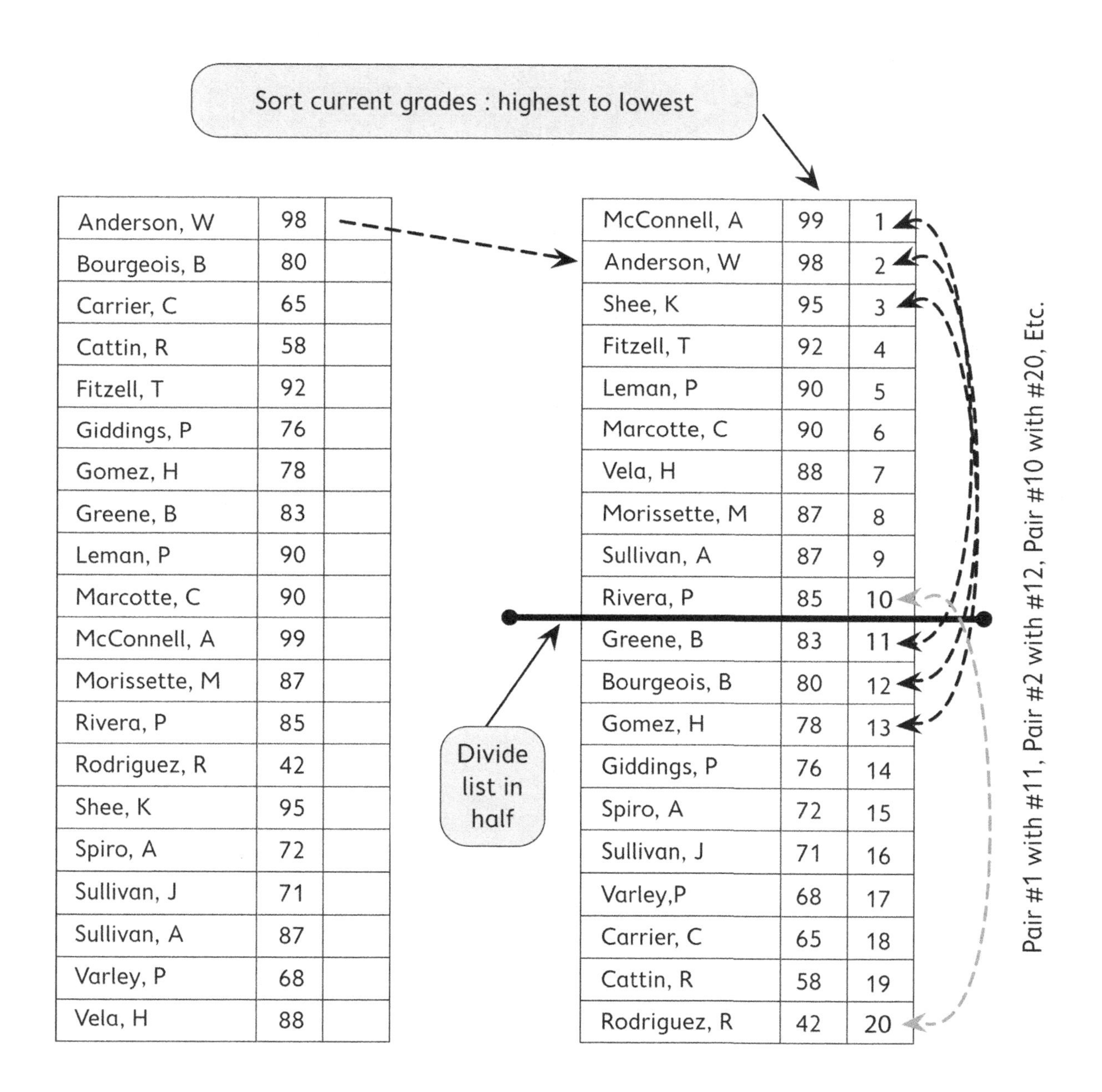

Anderson, W	98	
Bourgeois, B	80	
Carrier, C	65	
Cattin, R	58	
Fitzell, T	92	
Giddings, P	76	
Gomez, H	78	
Greene, B	83	
Leman, P	90	
Marcotte, C	90	
McConnell, A	99	
Morissette, M	87	
Rivera, P	85	
Rodriguez, R	42	
Shee, K	95	
Spiro, A	72	
Sullivan, J	71	
Sullivan, A	87	
Varley, P	68	
Vela, H	88	

McConnell, A	99	1
Anderson, W	98	2
Shee, K	95	3
Fitzell, T	92	4
Leman, P	90	5
Marcotte, C	90	6
Vela, H	88	7
Morissette, M	87	8
Sullivan, A	87	9
Rivera, P	85	10
Greene, B	83	11
Bourgeois, B	80	12
Gomez, H	78	13
Giddings, P	76	14
Spiro, A	72	15
Sullivan, J	71	16
Varley,P	68	17
Carrier, C	65	18
Cattin, R	58	19
Rodriguez, R	42	20

High-Middle-Middle-Low

Use the same process as you do for High-Low, but instead, divide the gradebook into quarters and choose one student from each quarter for a group of four.

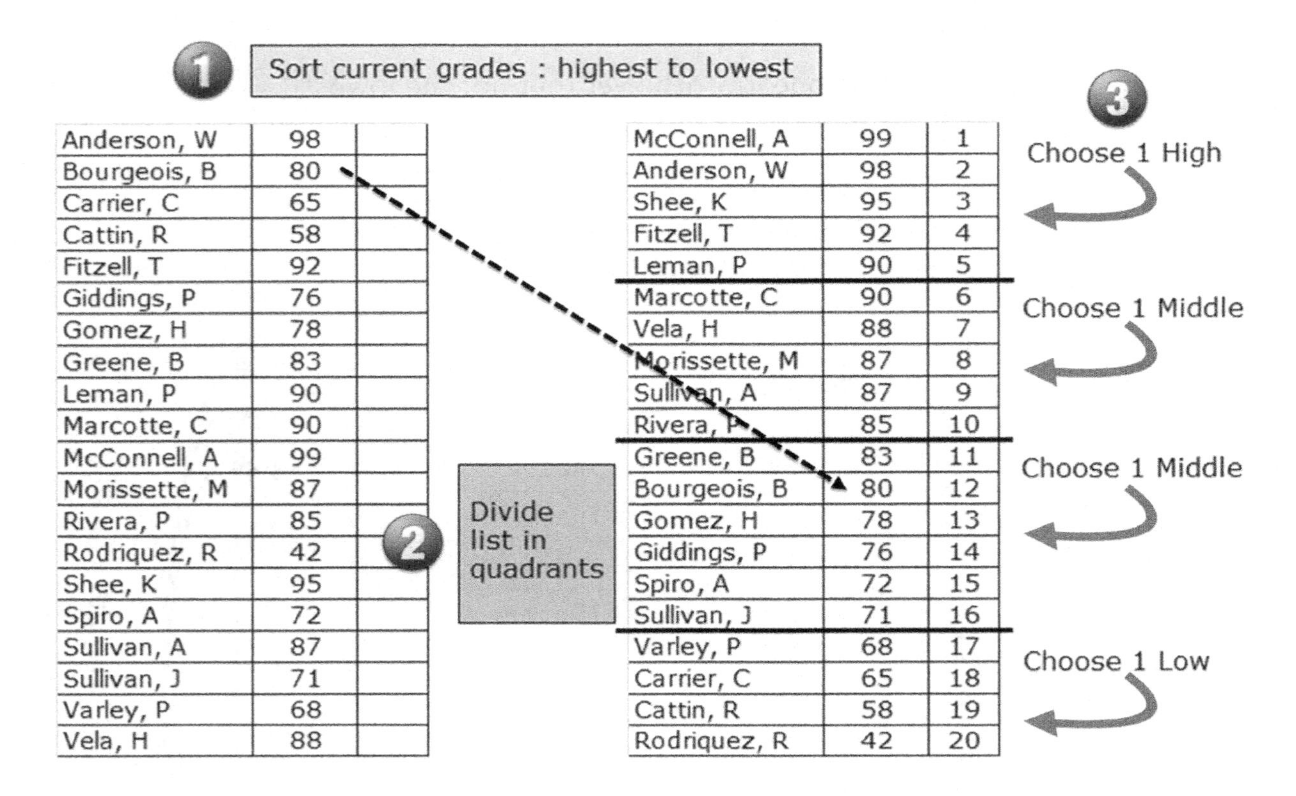

Anderson, W	98	
Bourgeois, B	80	
Carrier, C	65	
Cattin, R	58	
Fitzell, T	92	
Giddings, P	76	
Gomez, H	78	
Greene, B	83	
Leman, P	90	
Marcotte, C	90	
McConnell, A	99	
Morissette, M	87	
Rivera, P	85	
Rodriquez, R	42	
Shee, K	95	
Spiro, A	72	
Sullivan, A	87	
Sullivan, J	71	
Varley, P	68	
Vela, H	88	

McConnell, A	99	1
Anderson, W	98	2
Shee, K	95	3
Fitzell, T	92	4
Leman, P	90	5
Marcotte, C	90	6
Vela, H	88	7
Morissette, M	87	8
Sullivan, A	87	9
Rivera, P	85	10
Greene, B	83	11
Bourgeois, B	80	12
Gomez, H	78	13
Giddings, P	76	14
Spiro, A	72	15
Sullivan, J	71	16
Varley, P	68	17
Carrier, C	65	18
Cattin, R	58	19
Rodriquez, R	42	20

Arrange Your Classroom Environment for Success

Once you have identified your students' needs and settled on a co-teaching implementation, it is time to set up the classroom.

Remember our co-teachers in Kinston, North Carolina, whom I mentioned earlier in the book? Working in a small classroom, they had divided their class in half and implemented Teach Half Then Switch—Skills and Rigor by arranging the desks into two makeshift "conference tables." The two teachers were at either end, so as not to drown each other out. Because each conference table put the students in each group close together with the teacher right there, they had complete behavioral control. It was one of the most effective uses of small space I have ever seen.

Sometimes, the challenge to implementing co-teaching approaches is physical classroom size and arrangement. Too often, I have heard co-teachers lament, "We do not have a way to move the desks around to do the groupings you are suggesting." In my role as a coach, I have observed proof of this issue. Here are some of the challenges I have observed:

- Technology in the classroom was installed over decades, resulting in an inefficient and/or inflexible classroom set up. For example, a computer lab where wires hang down from the ceilings to power workstations; or, an interactive whiteboard placed near the door instead of in the middle of the wall; or insufficient power outlets to use tech devices.
- Immovable science lab stations or heavy tables that are impossible to move to accommodate groupings as designed.
- Overcrowded classrooms that have so many desks it is difficult to create multiple groupings.
- Classroom furniture that is not conducive to cooperative learning approaches.

One option is to problem-solve groupings on graph paper just as an interior designer might present options for remodeling a kitchen. Formulate possibilities on paper before moving desks.

When you and your co-teachers find two to three possible alternatives, create 8.5" X 11" diagrams of the designs, color code them, and hang them by the door.

Then, as students enter the room for the class period, ask them to start arranging desks based on the seating chart of the day. This option works well with students fifth grade and up.

Often, teachers resist changing the seating arrangements in their classrooms because it is time consuming for teachers to move desks between class periods to set up the room. That time may be necessary to monitor students, gather lesson props, respond to student needs, or take care of one's own personal needs.

Yet, if you have the students' help with the rearrangement, the process moves more quickly and gets students involved before the lesson even begins. Co-teachers can have them helping out like this as early as fourth or fifth grade. With the younger students, it is important to teach them how to read the diagrams ahead of time, so they know how to set up the room appropriately. Do a few drills and practice so students are successful. Overall, it saves a lot of time.

Co-teachers can even make a game of moving desks into specific arrangement. At the end of the lesson, if you want to move the desks back the way they were, split the students into teams and time them. Make it a contest.

Assign team names and put the winning team's name on the board. Students of all ages like having their team name on the board and knowing their class was faster than the previous period. This mini-competition makes moving your desks around a whole lot easier.

Develop a Class Plan for Differentiating Within Groups

- Decide on a physical classroom desk and table arrangement.
- Will one room arrangement work, or will teachers need to have options for multiple arrangements depending on the group activity required?
- How will the class be rearranged when necessary? What will be required to accomplish rearranging the classroom?
- What routines and skills are necessary for students to learn to have the class run smoothly when we deviate from the traditional row arrangement? Have students practice moving from one room arrangement to another.
- Use a signal, either a hand gesture or a sound, to notify students of time remaining until a transition; then use the signal again when the transition needs to occur. Before any transition, remind students of behavioral expectations.

Desk Arrangements

Flexible Group Classroom Option 1

Lab Station File Crates
Bulletin Board with file folders
White Board
Text resources at varied reading levels
Projects Table
Conference Chair
Desk
Chalkboard
Computers

24 Students - Groups of 4 + small group option for projects & computer work

Flexible Group Classroom Option 2

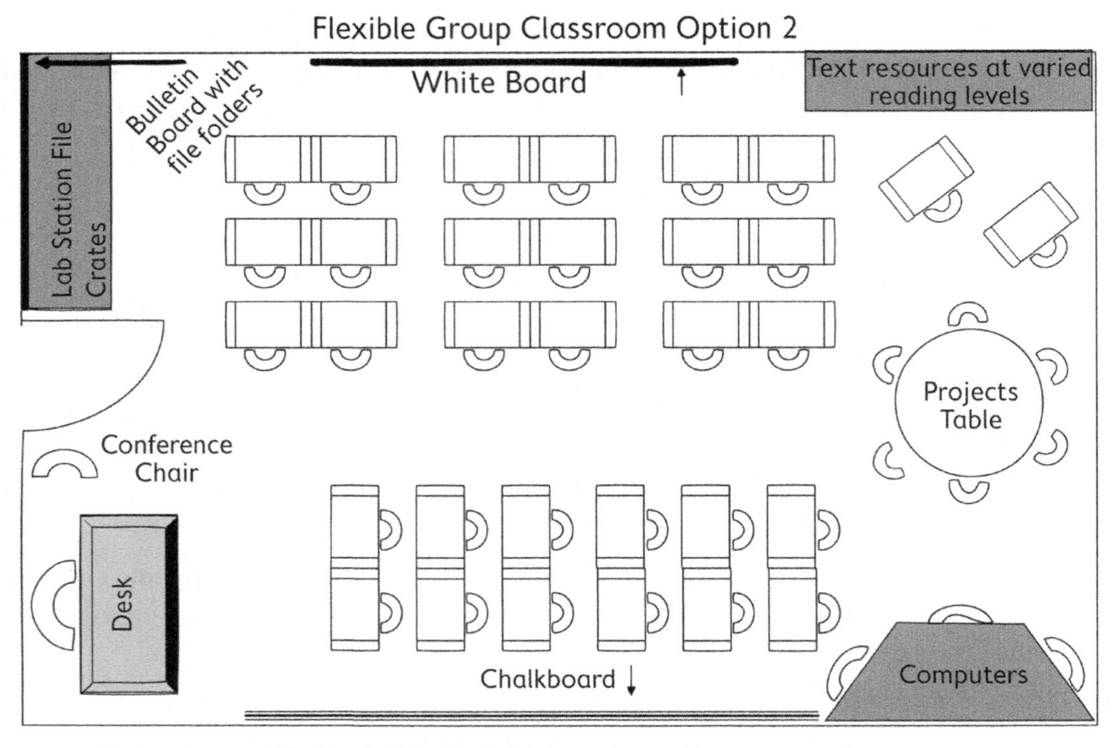

32 Students - Pairs & Divided Class w/ small group options

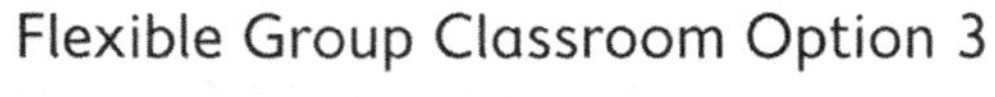
Flexible Group Classroom Option 3

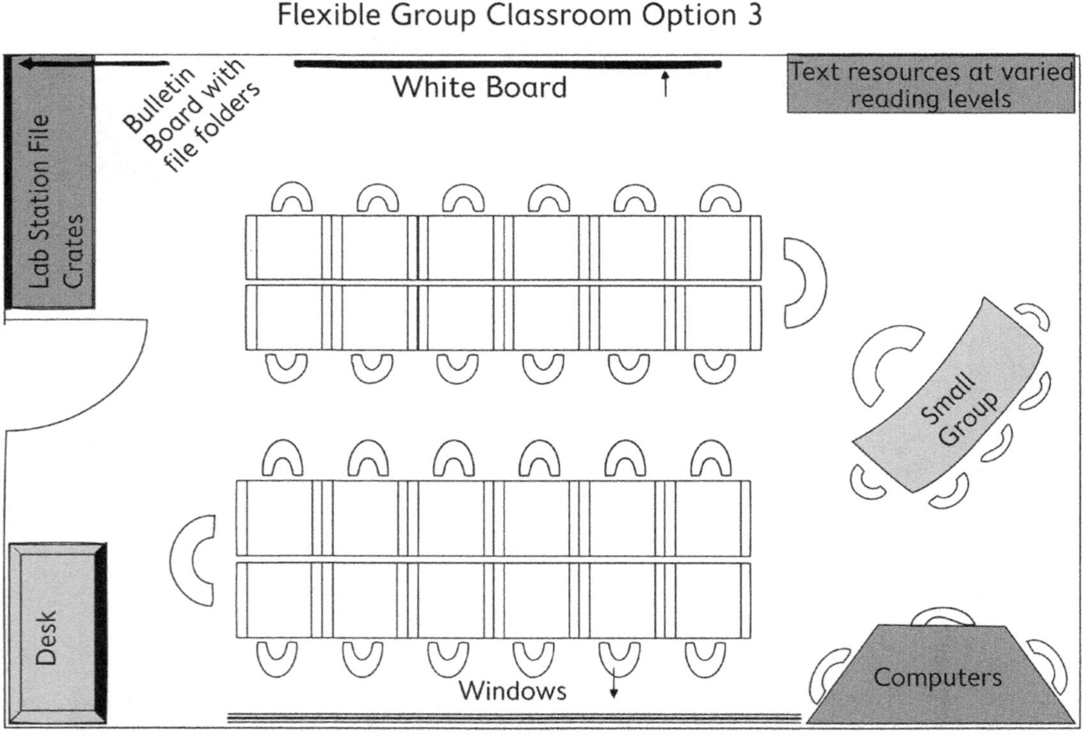

29 Students - Divided Class w/ small group options

Conference Table Style

In terms of desk arrangements, conference table style is a favorite of mine. It is flexible for different lessons and can be very minimalist in that it does not take a lot of space. You have the proximity for Parallel Teaching, pre-separation for smaller group teaching, and you have the students close together so they can hear you without needing to speak loudly. It is also a great way to maximize space with a large class size. When you put eight students on each side of four rows, you suddenly have two groups of sixteen students. That is thirty-two students if you can get the rows that close.

One teacher I worked with had his high school biology students sit on the floor instead of at desks to work around fixed, heavy lab tables!

Additional Resources

Video Bonus

Navigate to EduVideo.SusanFitzell.com

Take a few moments to watch the video about standing stations on the Bonus Materials webpage titled, "Fidgety Students and Overcrowded Classrooms."

Standing Stations in Your Classroom!

Do you have students who cannot sit still in class or cannot sit to do homework? I had students who struggled to sit still in the classroom, until I realized one day that if I allowed them to stand and work on a raised platform like a bookcase, they were more focused. When my son was little, he would eat better if he could stand at the dining room table. It also minimized trips to the hospital because he no longer fell out of his chair.

And as for myself, I cannot sit to focus. I create a standing station in my office and in my hotel rooms with a lap desk on top of the desk or by placing an upside-down drawer on the desk. I put my laptop on top of the drawer.

Another reason to use standing stations is to provide a solution that not only meets students' needs for movement, but also opens up some space and creates a variety of options for Station Teaching.

This student had the option of standing or sitting on a high stool. She used both options during this class period.

Behavior Management for Small Groups & Acceleration Centers

Avoiding difficult tasks is one of the most common reasons for student behavior problems. When planning activities that students must do either independently or in small groups, it is important to assign activities within the student's range of ability. Some things to consider when setting up and implementing independent and small-group activities are:

- Provide instruction and activities that match students of varying skill levels.
- Assess student progress frequently by monitoring student work and error patterns to identify what needs to be re-taught.
- Provide a means for co-teachers and support staff to scan student work so errors can be caught early, hopefully avoiding student frustration and misbehavior.
- Avoid using worksheets as the primary focus of small-group work and Acceleration Centers. Worksheets should be kept to a minimum, if not eliminated altogether.
- Establish nonverbal signals or cues to redirect students to return to task or improve behavior.

- Establish clear routines for students to follow. Model and practice these routines.
- Notice positive behavior. Research indicates that teachers should give students more positive than negative comments.
- Use proximity control. The co-teaching environment makes this much more do-able.
- Ignore misbehavior that is rewarded by teacher attention.
- Have students owe time if they waste time. Making restitution in this manner is quite effective.

Introducing the Group Activity

- Arrange tasks so all students are within the teacher's view.
- Be thorough when explaining instructions and giving directions.
- Make sure students understand what they are going to do and why they are going to do it.
- Be clear in stating teacher expectations.
- Establish time limits and provide checkpoints within those time limits. For example, if students are going to work in small groups for fifteen minutes, check in with students as a whole class to make sure they are on track every three to four minutes.
- Describe and model the final product.
- Monitor small groups and provide guidance as needed.

Establishing Group Ground Rules

A very effective technique for teaching students appropriate small group behavior is to have students take an active role in identifying what appropriate behavior looks like. It is worth taking the time to do some role-play with the students to show the difference between an ineffective group and an effective group. Another very effective strategy is to have students give their input on inappropriate behavior—for example, putting other students down in the group or laughing at group members' ideas. Students are more likely to comply if they have agreed with reasonable behavior and consequences.

Here Are Some Suggested Ground Rules:

- Start on time.
- Practice respect for yourself and others.
- Come prepared to do your part.
- Be a good listener.
- No putdowns.
- Make sure everyone gets a chance to contribute.
- Accept constructive criticism gracefully.
- Critique ideas, not people.
- No interruptions; let people finish talking.
- Ask for help when you are confused about what to do.
- Help others when you can.
- Do your fair share of the work.

Establish Teacher Expectations for Small-Group Work

- Describe or model the expectations for activities.
- Provide models and examples of what the outcome should, and should not, look like.
- Rehearse the expectations.
- Notice positive group behavior.
- Correct misbehavior and teach appropriate behavior. (We cannot assume that students know what to do.)
- Review expectations frequently.

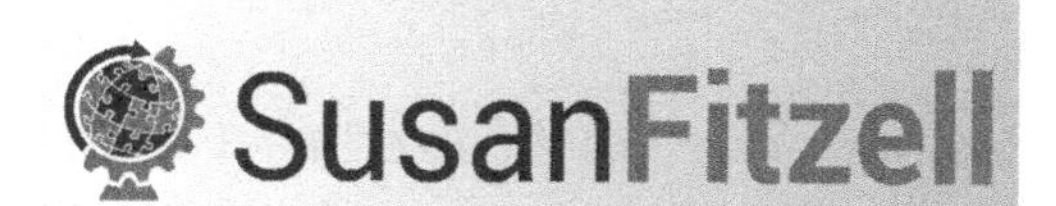

Additional Resources

This chapter provides many strategies that motivate students to choose success.

For a more complete and detailed support, get Susan's Solution Series book, ***Motivating Students to Choose Success: Proven Strategies to Lend a Helping Hand.***

Go to Shop.SusanFitzell.com

Also, navigate to SusanFitzell.com for helpful articles on behavior management, conflict resolution, bullying prevention, and motivation.

For program handouts:

Bonus398.susanfitzell.com

For professional development options:

SusanFitzell.com/Teachers/

Behavior Management Cue Card

Using a cue card to redirect students can go a long way toward minimizing power struggles. Calmly, quietly, and quickly approach and redirect students who are off-task.

Instructions:

- Print out this card or your own version of the card.
- Choose your display method:
- Tape a card on the upper right corner of each student desk.
- Laminate the card.
- Use clear shipping tape to secure it to the desk.
- Hang it from a lanyard around your neck or keep it in your pocket.
- Laminate the card.
- Punch a hole in the top of the card to hang from a lanyard.
- Explain the card to the students:
- You might say, "I want to use a system to help the class stay on track without embarrassing anyone by saying something out loud. I also want a way to praise you and let you know I am pleased with good behavior and choices without causing embarrassment. I am going to use this card to let you know my expectations or give kudos—quietly. Here is an example of the card and what the pictures mean."
- Explain what each picture means.
- Explain that you do not expect students to say anything in response.
- Explain how you will use the card.
- When a student needs to be redirected, simply walk quietly up to the student.
- Make eye contact—and preferably smile. The point is to minimize the possibility that a power struggle will ensue.
- After eye contact is made with the student, point to the picture that sends the message you need to deliver.
- Do not wait for a response.
- Turn around and walk away.
- If a student chooses to say something in response to a redirection, he or she is inviting a power struggle.
- Avoid taking the bait if possible. Turn and walk away and wait to see whether the student complies.

- When a student earns praise, simply walk up to the student, make eye contact, smile, and point to the "praise" picture.
- Do not wait for a response.
- Turn around and walk away.
- Be generous with your praise. Students should receive five to seven positive statements from the teacher in ratio to each negative comment.

Develop a Positive Reinforcement System for Small Group and Fitzell Acceleration Centers™ Work

Depending on the grade you are teaching, the type of positive reinforcement you might choose will be different. Sixth-graders might respond well to earning points or tickets for positive behavior. You might also try having a bar graph for each group on the table that can be filled in as students progress toward completion of an assignment. Once the bar graph is filled in, students earn a reward.

Older students also respond well to earning points or even stickers for positive behavior. I have seen high school students compete aggressively with each other to see who could earn the most stickers. Points or stickers can be traded in for a free homework pass for everyone in the group, or students can put their names in a bucket for a raffle and the prize could be a free homework pass or extra time on the computer or some other privilege that motivates your students.

The essential point: The most important factor in managing behavior is responding to problem behavior consistently.

Work Quietly

Get to work!

Take out your pencil.

Open your book.

High five!

You should be reading.

Show Respect.

You're doing Great!

Thank you for doing the right thing.

Grading Small Group Work

A common complaint from parents, students, and some teachers about small group work is: "One or two students do all the work while the other students are slackers." This issue is a valid complaint when teachers grade the small group with one grade for the whole group. There are other options. Below is one way to grade small group work:

# Points Possible	Item Graded
This is an individual grade.	Each student in the group chooses their 'part' of the process or project. That student is responsible for his or her part and is graded on how well that part is completed. Teachers must sign off on each student's part and ensure the assignment is within that student's capabilities.

20	Each student completes a self-evaluation. Students will score their own efforts toward the success of the group project.
20	Each student evaluates his or her group. See the handout "Group Processing: How did we do?"
60	Teacher evaluates the group's completed assignment based on teamwork and final product.
100	Total possible points for "group grade"

This is an individual grade	Optional based on the maturity and trustworthiness of the group: Each student evaluates every other student in the group. They MUST explain in detail why they scored each student as they did.
	This grade may be combined with each student's individual grade, or be a separate grade altogether.

With this model, each student earns two or three grades for a group assignment. Each student gets one or two individual grades and a group grade. This model rewards students who work as a team and take responsibility for their part of the process, and it provides a logical consequence for students who do the minimum.

Group Process Observation – Data Collection Chart

Directions: List skills to be observed on slanted lines. Rate student success on a scale of 1–5.

Date: Subject: Section:

Scale: 1–5
1 = Not observed
5 = Consistently demonstrated

Student Name							Notes

Collect Data – Carry a Clipboard Chart

Formative Assessment: Classroom Observation

Student Name	Off task	Needs support w/notes	Check for understanding	Book open, materials ready	Affect positive or negative +/-						Comments

Group Processing: How Did We Do?

On a scale of 1–7, rate your group performance	1	2	3	4	5	6	7
Staying on task							
Respectful listening							
Encouraging each other							
Starting on time							
Coming to the session prepared							

Summarize progress made during this group session

Chapter 7 Review and Discussion Questions

Reflection Questions

- What do you feel are the benefits of the Fitzell Acceleration Center™ implementation?
- If Acceleration Centers allowed you to meet your students' needs better by providing not only intervention for students who need re-teaching, but to advance students who are already successful, how might you address the challenges of implementing Fitzell Acceleration Centers?
- Can Fitzell Acceleration Centers respond to all learners in your school environment? How might co-teaching make Acceleration Centers more do-able for your school or classroom?

Practical Application

Experiment with the Fitzell Acceleration Centers and set up one center you can use in your curriculum. Be prepared to discuss your thoughts on this process. If completing this course individually, journal your thoughts and experiences on this application.

- What differentiated instructional strategies did you use when planning your station activities to ensure each of you addressed all learners in the class?
- What types of resource materials are available in the lesson to support your students' diverse learning needs?
- How will you and your co-teacher collaborate on developing these materials?

Reflection Questions

- Will the desk arrangements discussed in this chapter work for all activities or will they need to be rearranged for certain things?
- If rearrangement will be needed, how will that be accomplished? Can the students do it quickly and safely?
- Will co-teachers be able to see each other clearly to coordinate activities and communicate?
- When setting up your seating arrangements, it is important to remember that students with disabilities need to be seated among their classmates in a way that integrates them naturally without creating stigma.
- How did you decide how to seat students within the classroom?
- How have cooperative learning team structures been incorporated in the classroom organization?
- How do you know students with disabilities feel included in the classroom?

CHAPTER 8

SCHOOL LEADERS AND THEIR ROLE IN COLLABORATION SUCCESS

Considerations for School Administrators Implementing Co-Teaching Initiatives

Should Co-Teaching Be Voluntary?

Implementing a Co-Teaching Initiative? Start Small with Willing Teachers

Some teachers and school administrators believe co-teaching should be voluntary. We have learned that when a new co-teaching initiative begins in a district, it is best to start small (Dove & Honigsfeld, 2010) and with teachers who are willing to experiment, if possible. By using this approach, a school can work out any major issues before implementing the co-teaching initiative school or district-wide.

This strategy works well because the anxiety teachers may have before implementation of a co-teaching program will only be exacerbated if the program is started too quickly, by doing too much, and without proper preparation or training with unwilling or reluctant teachers. Any problems that occur become fuel for the argument that co-teaching does not work.

Ideally, school districts should start their co-teaching initiative with teachers who are willing to take on the challenge and immerse themselves in professional development geared toward making co-teaching a success.

How to Match Co-Teachers for Success

Sometimes, schools have no choice but to assign teachers to a co-teaching role, even the unwilling, because of the need to meet IEP requirements or state standards. In this situation, carefully try to match up personalities for the best possible success. Co-teaching is like an arranged marriage, and the personalities sharing a classroom can make or break the co-teaching relationship. All the conflict resolution or professionalism in the world cannot compensate for two seriously mismatched personalities.

When beginning a co-teaching initiative, district administrators may find themselves struggling to find appropriate co-teaching matches. When setting up teams for an idea this big, it is important to think outside-the-box; teachers may need to be moved to different grade levels or courses, schedules may need to be changed or adjusted, etc., so that teachers who are willing to co-teach can work together.

Most importantly, ask for and consider teacher input. Survey teachers to determine their preferences for grade level, subjects, and preferred partners. If possible, allow teachers to choose their partners (Wendy W. Murawski, 2008).

A School Principal's Role in a Successful Co-Teaching Initiative

Just like the classroom teacher, administrators may be nervous about their roles in the co-teaching initiative and how to best support their staff. It is imperative that administrators understand what co-teaching is, what it is not, and that they coach and mentor their staff in a positive, productive way to achieve the best possible results.

Co-Teaching Initiatives: The Bottom Line

My experience has shown me that the best way to implement a successful co-teaching program, on any campus or in any district, is to start small with a few teams of dedicated, professional educators who are willing to collaborate, with training and coaching. Both training in the form of in-service, as well long-term embedded coaching are key to the success of co-teaching initiatives. Walsh (2012) states:

> *"Moreover, it was found that effective professional development facilitated at the school level by professional learning communities was key to the positive effect of co-teaching and that these results were sustained by system-level parameters that reinforced factors supportive of co-teaching within the annual school improvement planning process. It was also found that providing guidance for administrators to look for and reinforce factors critical to successful co-teaching could ensure that strategies emphasized in professional development were implemented in co-taught classrooms."*

Walsh goes on to say that the instruction that was a direct result of the coaching provided to co-teachers resulted in accelerated outcomes for students with disabilities.

In their research study, "Teachers' experiences with co-teaching as a model for inclusive education," Pancsofar & Petroff (2016) conclude:

> *"...results highlight the role that professional development and careful attention to the structure of teachers' experiences with co-teaching may play in teachers' use of different co-teaching approaches and the ways in which roles and responsibilities are distributed across co-teachers. While these empirical findings are exploratory, they are consistent with previous literature that has heralded the need for ongoing, intensive, and high-quality pre-service and in-service training around co-teaching in optimising collaborative teaming within co-teaching practice."*

And authors Sweigart and Landrum (2015) state:

> *"Thus, if we cannot trust that both general educators and special educators are well-trained and highly skilled at implementing effective practices and differentiating instruction, merely putting the two types of teachers together in heterogeneous classes, including students with disabilities, may not have the desired effect. Qualitative studies have found that co-taught classrooms with special education teachers relegated to the role of the assistant (which is often the case), have often been shaped by general education teachers' tendency to gravitate toward large group, undifferentiated instruction."*

When the data collected from well-trained and supported "model" teams shows gains in student performance, other teachers will be motivated to participate, and motivated teachers will always be more successful than coerced teachers.

In this age of testing, fear, and reprisal, teachers need to be motivated and taught how to best utilize their time and efforts to help students succeed. Co-teaching, done well, is one of the surest ways to make a difference for students.

Speaking of High-Stakes Testing

According to Mastropieri et al. (2005):

> *"High-stakes testing, where it existed, exerted a strong influence on how content was covered and how co-teachers collaborated. In sites where high-stakes testing was not a factor, teachers were freer to determine what content to cover and the best way to cover it. However, where high stakes testing was a factor, classroom instructions and collaborative efforts were much different. In some situations, specific guidelines were provided that recommended initiating and ending dates for all content within particular grade levels, irrespective of whether students were ready to move on or not. Such guidelines directly influence the pace of instruction that teachers maintain. Further, this rapid pace minimizes the amount of extra practice or supplemental review activities that can be inserted in the curriculum, which directly influences the role of the special educator in modifying content for students with disabilities in inclusive classes."*

For co-teaching to be successful in a high-stakes test environment, school administrators need to foster a culture that supports co-teaching by entrusting teachers to make necessary adjustments, enhancements, and non-critical changes to their lesson plans to support student learning. These do not need to require reducing rigor. However, it may require analyzing lesson plans to take out the less effective teaching strategies, incorporate instruction that aligns with UDL and differentiated instruction, and slow down the pace.

Where Does Co-Teaching Take Place?

If students with special needs are included in the general classroom but go with the special education teacher to a different room for instruction on a regular basis, this is not co-teaching. This is a pull-out program. Although this may seem to be a sensible approach to managing wide gaps and ability levels in the classroom, the benefits of a co-teaching environment are lost. When students with special needs are not in the classroom, they are missing out on the opportunity to interact with positive peer role models, higher-order thinking from group discussion, and interaction between their teachers. They may also miss out on instruction they will need for classroom assessments or their state tests.

Co-teaching usually takes place in one classroom. Different ability levels can be addressed through flexible grouping, Acceleration Centers, tiered lesson plans, mixed-ability groups, and occasional same-ability groups. Only in very specific situations, is it appropriate to take some students out of the room. Examples of when it may be appropriate and/or necessary to take students out of the general classroom may include: oral testing, Teach Half Then Switch implementations where one group will be very actively engaged in a lab or physical activity while the other group needs a quiet environment, or One Silent and One Oral implementations. The key component in these scenarios is that they are infrequent short chunks of time. If students are pulled out frequently for a large chunk of the class, that's not co-teaching. That's divide and conquer.

When students with special needs are pulled out for specific instruction, a RTI action, or for skill-building, be cautious about regularly including students without an IEP in the pull-out group. It is important not to give the impression that general education students are receiving special education without proper assessment, documentation, eligibility determination, and placement procedures being followed. It is critical that students are not denied a "least restrictive environment" by being pulled out of the general classroom unnecessarily.

How Many Days a Week Should We Co-Teach?

Daily co-teaching is the ideal co-teaching situation. Co-teaching on a daily basis provides consistency, an understanding of day-to-day classroom dynamics, the ability for teachers to follow through with lesson plans and necessary supports together, and a thorough knowledge of what is happening with each student on a day-to-day basis. Most schools, however, because of shortages in staffing, numbers of students with special needs, and limited or restrictive schedules, find it difficult to assign teachers to a classroom every day. Consequently, special education teachers are often spread between several classes over the course of two or three days.

When co-teaching is not feasible on a daily basis, it can still be successful if teachers plan carefully for the days that the co-teacher is present and use strategies such as Acceleration Centers or Station Teaching Implementations on those days. Teachers should try to plan activities for the days the co-teacher is present that take full advantage of having another certified teacher in the room.

One consequence of having a special education teacher assigned to many classrooms is often a lack of time to plan with the co-teacher. As I said in Chapter 6, the time a special education teacher is assigned to a classroom should be held sacred. Special educators should not be pulled away from the general education classroom for crises, IEP meetings, or other duties. If time to meet for IEPs is an issue, or the special educator needs time for assessments and other professional responsibilities, it might be best to schedule him or her in the classroom four days a week and allow one day a week for work outside the classroom.

Co-Teaching, Inclusion, and Student Numbers

A common question asked when a district puts inclusion and co-teaching into place is, "How many students with special needs should be placed in the general education classroom?" There is no black-and-white answer to this question; however, it is important to first clarify terms and then address the issue.

Usually, the question of how many students with special needs to include in the general education classroom is more a function of the inclusion process than the co-teaching process. Remember that co-teaching is not inclusion, and inclusion is not co-teaching. First, let's define inclusion.

> *Inclusion is a concept whereby students with disabilities should be participants in the educational life of the regular classroom. The concept claims inclusion is an inherent right of the student and values this participation as a foundation of the educational experience for all students.*

In 1993, IDEA findings and current research forced a push toward inclusion.

Types of Inclusion

Full Inclusion	Responsible Inclusion
• Placement takes precedence over individual needs • Placement in regular classrooms is an end in itself • Recommends one type of placement for all children and downplays the use of any alternative settings for instructional purposes	• Placement is individualized and needs-based • Placement is a means to an end: appropriate educational program • Emotionally and behaviorally disordered students are only placed in a regular classroom when appropriate support is in place.

While there is no explicit percentage or ratio that defines the ideal inclusion classroom, typically one would want less than 33 percent of the students on an IEP as part of the general education classroom roster. More ideally, the percentage might be 25 percent of students on an IEP and 75 percent average to gifted.

After an extensive literature review on the topic of co-teaching, Hannover Research (2012) states:

> Student placement is a central concern when designing a co-teaching model. The Council for Exceptional Children notes that no more than one third of the class should be students with IEPs; the rest should be a mix of high-achieving, average achieving, and low-achieving students. This balance ensures that the presence of two teachers (one of them likely a special education teacher) is justified, and that students without disabilities are benefiting from the arrangement—which may not be the case if the proportion of disabled students is much higher.

The difficulty is that school districts rarely have enough staffing and/or funding to provide adequate support of the ideal inclusion environment. Because of these issues and scheduling concerns, schools often struggle with the following:

- Placing all students on an IEP and all students at risk in the same classroom.

  This does not result in inclusion. Rather, it is another form of a self-contained class and segregating the lowest-level students out of the general population. While this may seem to make sense because students are all of similar academic level and the classroom could be well staffed, it creates a class where there are fewer positive role models for behavior, where there are fewer students thinking on the higher levels of Bloom's taxonomy participating in discussions, where self-esteem and morale are lower because students know they are in the "dummy class," and finally, where test scores remain low because of typically lower standards in the classroom. According to research, when we put low-level students together in the same classroom they achieve a percentile gain of -23 percent (Marzano, 2001).

- Spreading students with special needs evenly between all classroom teachers

  Some districts attempt to distribute students among the classes in a "one-for-you, one-for-you" approach. The difficulty that arises from this approach is that schools rarely have enough staffing to have every class co-taught. Consequently, general classroom teachers are under-supported in this approach. Special education teachers are spread too thin and services to students with special needs end up lacking.

When a district I was teaching in first instituted inclusion in the high school, two to three classrooms in every core subject area were chosen to be co-taught. Students with special needs were then placed into each of these co-taught classrooms. English, math, social studies, and science had specific classrooms designated as inclusion co-taught classrooms. Because there was a high percentage of students with special needs in the district, each of these classrooms had between ten and thirteen students on an IEP. Class sizes ranged from twenty-seven to thirty-three students. What this meant was that some classrooms had almost 50 percent of the population with special needs. Classroom teachers felt that the numbers of students on an IEP in the classroom were too high.

After two years of lobbying that students with special needs should be spread out among more classrooms, the administrators chose to add more inclusion classrooms for each subject area. However, the district budget did not allow for additional special education staff. Consequently, there was not enough staff to co-teach in all the classrooms designated as inclusion classrooms. Classroom teachers, however, still required support for students with special needs.

To deal with minimal staffing, the special education staff ended up being scheduled so they might be in one classroom three days a week and another classroom two days a week. Co-teachers quickly realized that this situation made it much more difficult to co-teach effectively because planning time was reduced, consistency was lacking, specialists did not know what was happening in the classroom from one day to the next, and student follow-up suffered. Some teachers decided they would prefer to have a larger percentage of students on an IEP in the classroom and have a co-teacher always there. Unfortunately, that sentiment came too late.

Eventually, the demands placed on special education staff made their placement in the co-teaching environment even more difficult so, rather than co-teach, the school moved to a consult model. Each department was assigned one special educator to cover all the classes. Paraprofessionals were placed in some classrooms for support, and all teachers had fully-included classrooms. This model was the least desirable because classroom teachers did not feel adequately supported. Students were less able to have their needs met because there was not a certified special education teacher in the room to assist in planning, differentiating instruction, and adapting and modifying curriculum.

The moral of the story is: Be careful what you wish for.

Effective Methods of Distributing Students in Co-Taught Classrooms

Clearly, depending on many variables, including school size, grade level, staffing, and budgets, some of these recommendations may seem daunting, if not impossible. That said, they are valid considerations. Just do the best you can to implement as many of these ideas as possible given your school or district's circumstances.

- Avoid putting students who "feed off" each other together (these are often students who have been in the same self-contained classroom over the years).
- When placing students in a classroom, consider the other services they might need and how service providers might need to coordinate to provide those services. Generally, it may not be wise to put all the students who need speech therapy in the same classroom; however, you must consider specialist schedules and how class placement affects the ability of the specialists to provide services.

- It is better to have more students (not to exceed 33 percent special needs) in a class than to spread students out so that teachers only have two or three students with special needs in the class. Why? There's rarely enough special education staff to manage this setup, and students get short-changed.
- Avoid the current misguided trend to load general education classrooms with students with special needs as well as the lowest performing students. Inclusion means including students with special needs in a heterogeneous group. It does not mean we track students by taking out the top performers and putting those top performers in other classes. That is simply tracking by another name. Statistics show tracking does not work. (See the research study in the appendix for more information.) How are students going to be exposed to higher-level thinking, positive peer role models, and opportunities to learn from peers if we create one big class that will be prone to behavior problems? High school is a bit different in that there are honors classes. However, when I see honors classes in fifth and sixth grade, I question the practice on multiple levels, including ethical standards. Remember, the decisions we make for students at this stage of their lives affects the rest of their lives!
- Just because a student is on an IEP does not mean he or she needs to be in ***all*** co-taught classes. A student may need co-taught math, yet do fine in language arts with no co-teacher. Carefully make these determinations at the IEP meeting. (ARD meeting if you are from Texas.)
- Hand-schedule all students with special needs before the computer creates the master schedule. Hand scheduling is the only way to be certain students are in the right classes and no one teacher is loaded with 50 percent students on an IEP in his or her class.
- There are varied opinions as to whether special education teachers or intervention specialists should be "grade level" and covering multiple subjects or "content experts" and covering one subject over multiple grades. Of course, depending on staffing, it might be two subjects or two grade levels.
- At the elementary level, there are usually so many variables that it is best to use common sense when scheduling. At the secondary level, it has been my experience—both as someone who co-taught and as a teacher's coach exposed to many different approaches to co-teaching over the past two decades—that content area expertise at the secondary level is usually more successful for all involved than grade level co-teaching. Here is why:
- If special education teachers are focused on one or two subjects over a few grade levels, they have the focus and time to become experts on that subject. The sooner they become content area competent, the sooner they are truly ready to co-teach, support students at a variety of levels of ability, and feel comfortable with the subject themselves.

- It avoids the stigma that follows students when the grade level special educator follows the same group of students from class to class every day. Those students become "the sped students with the grownup."
- General education teachers are more apt to plan with a co-teacher whom they see multiple periods of the day, or who is knowledgeable about the subject, or whom they know they will be working with for more than one year.
- Students with special needs do not become as dependent on a special educator when they see more than one during the school day as they might when they have the same adult following them to each co-taught class every day. They have to become more independent.
- I have seen grade level teams work well. They can be the perfect solution for transition years: sixth and ninth grades. Grade level teams allow the special educator to get to know students well. The school staff needs to determine what will work best for students given its staffing, schedule, and district requirements.

Scheduling Co-Teaching

Scheduling co-teaching can be extremely difficult, especially at the secondary level. At the elementary level, the challenge is usually a lack of special education staff to co-teach daily at each academic grade level where inclusion is the desired approach. At the secondary school level, school schedules provide challenges because of requirements for qualified teachers at each grade level to be comfortable with the content that may need co-teaching support.

Hand-schedule all students on an IEP into co-taught classes based on level of need—in fact, schedule students ***not*** in co-taught classes by hand, too. Only those needing the most support need to be in co-taught classes. Just because a student is in an IEP does not mean that student needs to be in a co-taught class.

One high school I was working with in Texas only hand-scheduled students on an IEP that needed co-taught classes. All other students were randomly scheduled into classes. One of my co-teaching pairs ended up with a class composition of 50 percent on an IEP. The rest of the mix was comprised of ELL and students on a 504 plan. The teachers were overwhelmed and dealing with substantial behavior issues. "Allowing computers to randomly populate classes for the master schedule is not the best approach to take when first establishing co-teaching at a school" (Wendy W. Murawski, 2008).

Following are some examples of how co-teaching might be scheduled from a teacher and staffing perspective. The examples vary to address staffing levels and scheduling challenges.

Co-Teaching Scheduling Option 1

Teacher	Period A	Period B	Period C	Period D	Period E	Period F	Period G
	Co-taught Social Studies	Co-taught Social Studies	Resource	Lunch	Prep & Co-Plan	Co-taught Social Studies	Co-taught Social Studies
	Co-taught Math	Resource	Co-taught Math	Co-taught Math	Lunch	Prep & Co-plan	Co-taught Math
	Resource	Co-taught English	Co-taught English	Prep & Co-plan	Co-taught English	Lunch	Co-taught English
	Co-taught Science	Co-taught Science	Prep & Co-plan	Resource	Lunch	Co-taught Science	Co-taught Science

Co-Teaching Scheduling Option 2

Teacher	Period A	Period B	Period C	Period D	Period E	Period F	Period G
	Co-taught Social Studies	Co-taught Math	Resource	Lunch	Prep & Co-Plan	Co-taught Social Studies	Co-taught Math
	Co-taught English	Resource	Co-taught English	Co-taught Science	Lunch	Prep & Co-plan	Co-taught Science

Scheduling options 1 and 2 are the most effective co-teaching options if and when administration can prevent the co-taught classes from becoming disproportionately filled with students with special needs. Being in the classroom five days per week provides the most consistency. The maximum percentage of students with special needs in a co-taught or inclusion class is approximately 30 percent. Even 30 percent can be too high a percentage if that 30 percent is significantly disabled.

Preferably, that 30 percent is a mix of students with mild to moderate learning disabilities. When too many students have significant needs or are highly involved, the inclusion model becomes strained and potentially ineffective.

That 30 percent is based on my professional experience with co-teaching and inclusion. Presently, no specific data exists on the ideal percentage. If schools had plentiful budgets and enough special education staff was available, I would aim for a maximum of 25 percent of students with special needs in the inclusion or co-taught classroom and the rest of the students heterogeneously grouped.

Co-Teaching Scheduling Option 3

Teacher	Period A	Period B	Period C	Period D	Period E	Period F	Period G
	(M,W) Co-taught Social Studies (T,TH) Co-taught Math	(M,W) Co-taught Social Studies (T,TH) Co-taught Math	Resource	Lunch	Prep & Co-Plan	(M,W) Co-taught Social Studies (T,TH) Co-taught Math	(M,W) Co-taught Social Studies (T,TH) Co-taught Math
	Friday CMD*	Friday CMD*	Resource	Friday CMD*	Friday CMD*	Friday CMD*	Friday CMD*
	(W,F) Co-taught English (T,TH) Co-taught Science	Resource	W,F) Co-taught English (T,TH) Co-taught Science	W,F) Co-taught English (T,TH) Co-taught Science	Lunch	Prep & Co-Plan	W,F) Co-taught English (T,TH) Co-taught Science
	Monday CMD*	Resource	Monday CMD*	Monday CMD*	Monday CMD*	Monday CMD*	Monday CMD*

* Case Management Day

Lack of common planning time as well as pulling special educators out of co-taught classes for meetings, student crises, and testing are issues known to destroy co-teaching relationships. If the special educator is continually pulled out of class to address other issues, the general education teacher feels abandoned and is often stuck having to quickly come up with a different lesson plan. Over time, the general education teacher realizes he or she cannot depend on the co-teacher and gradually assigns that person less and less responsibility for the class, which defeats the purpose of co-teaching.

One solution to address this pervasive problem is to provide each special educator, when possible, a case management day (or most of a day): one day a week dedicated exclusively to special education duties such as IEP meetings, caseloads, or individual student problems. ***This way, the general education teacher can rely on the co-teacher to be in class all period with no interruptions,*** and the special education teacher can better plan his or her schedule.

On a case management day, special education teachers have the time to consult, attend meetings, and plan with co-teachers as necessary. Teachers choose when to have lunch and prep based on their co-teacher's prep period and any other meetings they have scheduled.

When there is more than one special education teacher on staff, the one-day assignment can be given on a rotating basis so that each day one teacher is available exclusively for special education duties.

Caution: A case management day should not be used as a once-a-week full day prep.

If this model is to be implemented, some legalities must be considered:

- Legally, this model cannot be called a program. Instead, it must be called a *service delivery model.*
- It must be flexible so that if any student needs five days of co-teaching a week, it can be provided. Parents cannot be told, "Sorry, we only offer co-teaching four days per week."
- Teachers must be available to provide co-teaching support five days per week if the team determines that is what the child needs.
- A red flag would go up if absolutely no students in the school ever needed five days of special instruction. Legally, it could be said that the case management model is a "program" and not necessarily individualized. It is impossible or at best highly unlikely, for ***all*** students to need only four days of co-teaching support.

Co-Teaching Scheduling Option 4

Teacher	Period A	Period B	Period C	Period D	Period E	Period F	Period G
	(M,W) Co-taught Social Studies (T,TH) Co-taught Math	(M,W) Co-taught Social Studies (T,TH) Co-taught Math	Resource	Lunch	Prep & Co-Plan	(M,W) Co-taught Social Studies (T,TH) Co-taught Math	(M,W) Co-taught Social Studies (T,TH) Co-taught Math
	Friday In class consult	Friday In class consult	Resource	Lunch	Prep & Co-plan	Friday In class consult	Friday In class consult
	(W,F) Co-taught English (T,TH) Co-taught Science	Resource	W,F) Co-taught English (T,TH) Co-taught Science	W,F) Co-taught English (T,TH) Co-taught Science	Lunch	Prep & Co-Plan	W,F) Co-taught English (T,TH) Co-taught Science
	Monday In class consult	Resource	Monday In class consult	Monday In class consult	Lunch	Prep & Co-plan	Monday In class consult

In class consult: Teachers are assigned to a specific class that needs support yet does not require full time co-teaching. For example: a special education teacher consults with a general education teacher who has a small number of students with special needs in class whereas those students do not need daily support.

Co-teaching is possible during 'in class consult' periods if the general education teacher sets up Acceleration Centers™ and uses that time for center work. Acceleration Centers™ are ideal for this situation. See the section on academic strategies for instructions on how to implement Acceleration Centers™. Acceleration Centers™ also work well for the two-day-per-week co-teach model.

Remember: Co-Teaching Time Is Sacred—Don't Break Trust

Administrators must respect that co-teachers are in a classroom together because they are collaborating to meet the needs of all students. Consequently, special education teachers should not be pulled out of class:

- for emergency meetings
- to help with behavior problems
- to talk to a parent
- to cover another teacher
- to participate on committees
- to test students
- or for any reason barring an emergency, where there are no other options

If co-teachers plan a lesson together with both teachers implementing critical elements of a lesson plan, to pull the special education teacher or specialist out of the classroom breaks trust. The general education teacher trusted that her co-teacher would be present for the instruction that they planned to implement together. When the specialist is absent, the general education teacher is put in a position to recreate a new lesson on her own on the fly. For most teachers, that is highly stressful and often feels like a betrayal.

Administrators need to view co-taught classes as classes taught by two essential teachers working as one team. Pulling the special educator out of the class not only damages the co-teaching relationship; it may be a violation of the students' IEP.

How Do We Measure the Success of a Co-Teaching Initiative?

To implement a co-teaching model that takes these challenges into account and facilitates effective instruction, some researchers have encouraged districts to perform *internal evaluations of co-teaching effectiveness.* In such scenarios, individual teachers may take on the responsibility of data collection to contribute to a broader research effort. In this vein, Wendy Murawski and Lisa A. Dieker have noted that:

Co-teachers could have students participate in content-driven pre-post assessments, complete questionnaires or surveys about their experiences in a co-taught class, or collect curriculum-based assessments over time to demonstrate student achievement. This data should be compared to student outcomes in classes in which co-teaching is not occurring. In addition, students' progress toward their IEP goals (for students with disabilities) is another method by which co-teaching's effectiveness should be assessed.

What Should a Co-Taught Class Look Like?

School administrators often ask what co-teaching looks like. This is especially challenging to assess for administrators who are new to the concept of co-teaching. An excellent article that includes the background and tools to help administrators know what to look for in a co-taught classroom is "Observing Co-Teaching: What to Ask For, Look For, and Listen For," by Wendy Murawski and Wendy Lochner (W. W. Murawski & Lochner, 2011). I have not found a better resource that clearly defines what administrators should see in a co-taught classroom.

Chapter 8 Review and Discussion Questions

Reflection Questions

- Based on the information provided in this chapter, how would you describe the level of responsibility with which inclusion is being applied on your campus?
- What suggestions might you make to distribute students more effectively within the co-taught classrooms on your campus?
- If you can't do much about how students are assigned to classes, how might you apply the classroom management techniques discussed here to better distribute students within the available classrooms?
- Determine which co-teaching scheduling option most closely matches how you are currently scheduling time with the co-teachers on your campus. Discuss or consider whether this process is working effectively.
- What co-teaching scheduling option do you feel would best serve your co-teaching teams? Why? How would you implement this option?

BIBLIOGRAPHY

Almon, Sheanoka, and Jay Feng. 2012. "Co-Teaching vs. Solo-Teaching: Effect on Fourth Graders' Math Achievement." ***Mid-South Educational Research Association Annual Conference***, 1–33.

Bacon, Donald R., Kim A. Stewart, and William S. Silver. 1999. "Lessons from the Best and Worst Student Team Experiences: How a Teacher Can Make the Difference." ***Journal of Management Education*** 23 (5): 467–88. doi:10.1177/105256299902300503.

Beninghof, Anne, and Mandy Leensvaart. 2016. "Co-Teaching to Support ELLs." ***Educational Leadership*** 73 (5): 70–73.

Boaler, Jo. 2006. "How a Detracked Mathematics Approach Promoted Respect, Responsibility, and High Achievement." ***Theory into Practice***. doi:10.1207/s15430421tip4501_6.

Booker, K., B. Gill, R. Zimmer, and T. R Sass. 2009. "Achievement and Attainment in Chicago Charter Schools. Technical Report." ***Rand Corporation***.

Burris, C. C., J P Heubert, and H. M. Levin. 2006. "Accelerating Mathematics Achievement Using Heterogeneous Grouping." ***American Educational Research Journal*** 43 (1): 137–54. doi:10.3102/00028312043001105.

Conderman, Greg, Sarah Johnston-Rodriguez, and Paula Hartman. 2009. "Communicating and Collaborating in Co-Taught Classrooms." In ***Teaching Exceptional Children Plus***, 5:2–17.

Dove, Maria, and Andrea Honigsfeld. 2010. "ESL Coteaching and Collaboration: Opportunities to Develop Teacher Leadership and Enhance Student Learning." ***TESOL Journal*** 1 (1): 3–22. doi:10.5054/tj.2010.214879.

Duke, Nell K., and P. David Pearson. 2002. "Effective Practices for Developing Reading Comprehension." ***What Research Has to Say about Reading Instruction***, 205–42. doi:10.1598/0872071774.10.

Florian, Lani. 2014. "What Counts as Evidence of Inclusive Education?" ***European Journal of Special Needs Education*** 29 (3): 286–94. doi:10.1080/08856257.2014.933551.

Fluijt, D., C. Bakker, and E. Struyf. 2016. "Team-Reflection: The Missing Link in Co-Teaching Teams." ***European Journal of Special Needs Education*** 31 (2). doi:10.1080/08856257.2015.1125690.

Friend, Marilyn. 2014. "IL Council for Exceptional Children." In ***Co-Teach 2.0: Mistakes of the Past, Solutions for the Future***. Chicag: Council for Exceptional Children. 1110 North Glebe Road Suite 300, Arlington, VA 22201. Tel: 888-232-7733; Fax: 703-264-9494; e-mail: cecpubs@ cec. sped. org; Web site: http:// www. cec. sped. org/AM/Template. cfm? Section= Publications1. doi:10.12968/ bjhc.2014.20.3.144.

Friend, Marilyn, Lynne Cook, DeAnna Hurley-Chamberlain, and Cynthia Shamberger. 2010. "Co-Teaching: An Illustration of the Complexity of Collaboration in Special Education." ***Journal of Educational and Psychological Consultation*** 20 (1): 9–27. doi:10.1080/10474410903535380.

Haghighi, Jaber Khales, and Khadijeh Abdollahi. 2014. "On the Efficacy of Team Teaching and Station Teaching in the Enhancement of Students' Reading Comprehension in an EAP Situation." ***Procedia—Social and Behavioral Sciences 98 882 – 890*** 98: 882–90.

Hannover Research. 2012. "The Effectiveness of the Co-Teaching Model." ***Hannover Research—District Administration Practice***. Washington, DC.

Honigsfeld, Andrea, and Maria G. Dove. 2010. ***Collaboration and Co-Teaching: Strategies for English Learners***. 1 Edition. Thousand Oaks, CA: Corwin.

Horn, Ilana Seidel. 2006. "Lessons Learned from Detracked Mathematics Departments." ***Theory into Practice***. doi:10.1207/s15430421tip4501_10.

Individuals with Disabilities Education Act (IDEA). 2017. "[USC03] 20 USC CHAPTER 33, SUBCHAPTER I: GENERAL PROVISIONS." ***Individuals with Disabilities Education Act*** . http://uscode.house.gov/view.xhtml?path=/prelim@title20/chapter33/subchapter1&edition=prelim.

Keefe, Elizabeth B., Veronica Moore, and Frances Duff. 2004. "' The Four Knows ' of Collaborative Teaching." ***Teaching Exceptional Children*** 36 (5): 36–42.

Kelly, S., and H. Price. 2011. "The Correlates of Tracking Policy: Opportunity Hoarding, Status Competition, or a Technical-Functional Explanation?" ***American Educational Research Journal***. doi:10.3102/0002831210395927.

Kelly, Sean. 2007. "The Contours of Tracking in North Carolina." ***High School Journal***. doi:10.1353/hsj.2007.0016.

Learned, Julie E., Michael V. Dowd, and Joseph R. Jenkins. 2009. "Instructional Conferencing." ***Teaching Exceptional Children*** 41 (5): 46–51.

Loveless, T., Steve Farkas, and Ann Duffett. 2008. "High-Achieving Students in the Era of NCLB." ***Thomas B. Fordham Institute***.

Loveless, Tom. 1999. "Will Tracking Reform Promote Social Equity?" ***Educational Leadership***.

Lucas. 1999. ***Tracking Inequality: Stratification and Mobility in American High Schools. Sociology of Education. Teachers College Press***.

Mastropieri, M. A., T. E. Scruggs, J. Graetz, J. Norland, W. Gardizi, and K. Mcduffie. 2005. "Case Studies in Co-Teaching in the Content Areas: Successes, Failures, and Challenges." ***Intervention in School and Clinic***.

McCoach, D. Betsy, Ann A. O'Connell, and Heather Levitt. 2006. "Ability Grouping Across Kindergarten Using an Early Childhood Longitudinal Study." ***The Journal of Educational Research***. doi:10.3200/JOER.99.6.339-346.

Mckenna, John William, Colin Muething, Andrea Flower, Diane Pedrotty Bryant, and Brian Bryant. 2015. "Use and Relationships among Effective Practices in Co-Taught Inclusive High School Classrooms." ***International Journal of Inclusive Education*** 19 (1): 53–70. doi:10.1080/13603116.2014.906665.

Murawski, W. W., and H. Lee Swanson. 2001. "A Meta-Analysis of Co-Teaching Research: Where Are the Data?" ***Remedial and Special Education***.

Murawski, W. W., and W. W. Lochner. 2011. "Observing Co-Teaching: What to Ask For, Look For, and Listen For." ***Intervention in School and Clinic*** 46 (3): 174–83.

Murawski, Wendy W. 2008. "Five Keys to Co-Teaching in Inclusive Classrooms." ***School Administrator*** 65 (8). American Association of School Administrators. 801 North Quincy Street Suite 700, Arlington, VA 22203-1730. Tel: 703-528-0700; Fax: 703-841-1543; e-mail: info@aasa.org; Web site: http://www.aasa.org: 29.

Murawski, Wendy W, and Lisa Dieker. 2004. "50 Ways to Keep Your Co-Teacher Strategies for Before, During, and After Co-Teaching." ***Teaching Exceptional Children*** 40 (4): 40–48.

Oh-Young, Conrad, and John Filler. 2015. "A Meta-Analysis of the Effects of Placement on Academic and Social Skill Outcome Measures of Students with Disabilities." ***Research in Developmental Disabilities*** 47: 80–92. doi:10.1016/j.ridd.2015.08.014.

Pancsofar, Nadya, and Jerry G. Petroff. 2016. "Teachers' Experiences with Co-Teaching as a Model for Inclusive Education." ***International Journal of Inclusive Education*** 20 (10): 1043–53. doi:10.1080/13603116.2016.1145264.

Partnership, Idea. 2013. "Common Core State Standards," no. June.

Peng, Peng, and Douglas Fuchs. 2015. "A Randomized Control Trial of Working Memory Training With and Without Strategy Instruction Effects on Young Children's Working Memory and Comprehension." ***Journal of Learning Disabilities***, 22219415594609. doi:10.1177/0022219415594609.

Ploessl, Donna M., Marcia L. Rock, Naomi Schoenfeld, and Brooke Blanks. 2010. "On the Same Page: Practical Techniques to Enhance Co-Teaching Interactions." ***Intervention in School and Clinic***. doi:10.1177/1053451209349529.

Pratt, Sharon. 2014. "Achieving Symbiosis: Working through Challenges Found in Co-Teaching to Achieve Effective Co-Teaching Relationships." ***Teaching and Teacher Education*** 41: 1–12. doi:10.1016/j.tate.2014.02.006.

Pratt, Sharon M., Sarah M. Imbody, Lindsay D. Wolf, and Amanda L. Patterson. 2017. "Co-Planning in Co-Teaching : A Practical Solution." ***Intervention in School and Clinic*** 52 (2): 243–49. doi:10.1177/1053451216659474.

Rampey, B. D., G. S. Dion, and P. L. Donahue. 2009. "NAEP 2008: Trends in Academic Progress." ***National Center for Education Statistics***.

Raskinski, Timothy V. 1990. "Effects of Repeated Reading of High-Frequency Words and Phrases." ***Journal of Educational Research*** 83: 147–50.

Richmond-Cullen, Catherine, Dona Bauman, Vanessa Ferrance, and Sonya Kunkel. 2017. "The Sustainability of Inclusionary Practices : A Case Study" 16 (5): 1–13.

Rivera, Echo A., Susan D. McMahon, and Christopher B. Keys. 2014. "Collaborative Teaching: School Implementation and Connections with Outcomes among Students with Disabilities." ***Journal of Prevention and Intervention in the Community*** 42 (1): 72–85. doi:10.1080/10852352.2014.855067.

Roden, Lea Susann, Arthur J. Borgemenke, and William Holt. 2013. "Improving the Academic Achievement of Students with Disabilities." ***NATIONAL FORUM OF SPECIAL EDUCATION JOURNAL*** 24 (1): 1–7.

Rubin, Beth C. 2006. "Tracking and Detracking: Debates, Evidence, and Best Practices for a Heterogeneous World." ***Theory into Practice***. doi:10.1207/s15430421tip4501_2.

Scruggs, Thomas E., Margo A. Mastropieri, and Kimberly A. McDuffie. 2007. "Co-Teaching in Inclusive Classrooms: A Metasynthesis of Qualitative Research." ***Exceptional Children*** 73 (4). Council for Exceptional Children. 1110 North Glebe Road Suite 300, Arlington, VA 22201. Tel: 888-232-7733; Fax: 703-264-9494; e-mail: cecpubs@ cec. sped. org; Web site: http://www. cec. sped. org/AM/Template. cfm? Section= Publications1: 392–416.

Sweigart, Chris A., and Timothy J. Landrum. 2015. "The Impact of Number of Adults on Instruction: Implications for Co-Teaching." ***Preventing School Failure*** 59 (1): 22–29. doi:10.1080/1045988X.2014.919139.

Toledo, Cheri, and Sharon Peters. 2010. "Educators' Perceptions of Uses, Constraints, and Successful Practices of Backchanneling." ***In Education*** 16 (1): 1–15.

U.S. Department of Education. 2018. "College- and Career-Ready Standards | U.S. Department of Education." Accessed January 30. https://www.ed.gov/k-12reforms/standards.

Walsh, James M. 2012. "Co-Teaching as a School System Strategy for Continuous Improvement." ***Preventing School Failure: Alternative Education for Children and Youth***. doi:10.1080/1045988X.2011.555792.

Walsh, James M. and Barbara Jones. 1995. "New Models of Cooperative Teaching." ***Teaching Exceptional Children*** 36 (5): 14–20.

Whatley, Janice. 2009. "Ground Rules in Team Projects: Findings from a Prototype System to Support Students." ***Journal of Information Technology Education*** 8: 161–76.

Wilson, Gloria Lodato, and Craig A. Michaels. 2006. "General and Special Education Students' Perceptions of Co-Teaching: Implications for Secondary-Level Literacy Instruction." ***Reading & Writing Quarterly***. doi:10.1080/10573560500455695.

Wood, Claire A. and Daniel Perlman. 2017. "A Multifaceted Partner Presentation Assignment for Improving Educational Outcomes Among College Students." ***International Journal of Teaching & Learning in Higher Education*** 29 (2): 201–15.

Zimmer, Ron. 2003. "A New Twist in the Educational Tracking Debate." ***Economics of Education Review***. doi:10.1016/S0272-7757(02)00055-9.

At the time of this book's publication, the information cited is the most current available and/or the original source material. All information has been verified as of March 2018. The author and publisher do not provide any guarantee or warranty regarding the information provided by any sources cited here, nor do we take responsibility for any changes to information or websites that may occur after verification. If you find an error or would like to alert us to a change to any resource cited herein, please contact us online: http://susanfitzell.com/contact-susan-fitzell/

APPENDIX

How to Facilitate a Successful Book Study

Individual Book Study

This book is designed to serve as both a functional reference as well as a textbook that can be used as part of a formal course, individual book study, or guided group study.

Completing the book study as an individual is a simple process.

Read each chapter.

Consider the Chapter Review/Discussion Questions and jot down or record your reflections.

Note: If you intend to obtain a Verification of Completion for this course, you may need to provide copies of your responses to these questions.

Group-Oriented Book Study

We encourage you to complete this book study as part of a community of learners, where possible:

- Department or grade level teams.
- Core academic teams.
- Vertical teams (across grade level), by subject area.
- Any other reasonable grouping technique that works for your campus or activity.

Steps:

1. Each group will need a group facilitator or team leader.
2. Determine your groups or teams.
3. Clearly outline a timeline of reading goals.
4. Set dates and times to meet for group discussion of Review/Discussion Questions and application of strategy ideas.
5. Establish ground rules. Use the section in the book on setting ground rules for students as an action-learning activity for the group. Simply adjust the activity for adult learners.

Tips for Being a Good Facilitator

- Create a relaxed atmosphere for the group.
- Treat everyone with respect.
- Consider having a co-facilitator, especially for larger groups.

Remember that the term "facilitator" means "to make easy." Your job is to make it easy for everyone to participate. This will help participants feel comfortable and foster an atmosphere of helpful cooperation for everyone, including you.

Be prepared: Understand the Chapter Review/Discussion questions. The facilitator is responsible for keeping the discussion on target and allowing everyone to have a voice in discussion.

First Meeting

- Be sure all group members have a book.
- Have all group members introduce themselves, if necessary.
- Be sure everyone understands the study's purpose and goals.
- Review the course requirements, proposed timeline, and meeting schedule.

All Meetings

- Ask group members to bring their books and notes to every meeting.
- A good way to start is to review the Review/Discussion questions and go over the pages of the book that may apply to the questions.
- The goal of group meetings is to be sure all members have completed the chapter exercises, promote discussion, and foster an environment of mutual motivation and cooperation.

Review/Discussion Questions and This Guide

- This guide and the questions offered in each chapter are meant to promote reflection. Let discussion flow and progress naturally.
- If conversation wanders from the topic, return to the discussion questions, but remember that good discussion is sometimes more important than covering all the questions.
- Try to involve everyone.

Leading Discussions

- Pose one question, or scenario, at a time to the group.
- Pre-select the questions or scenarios to discuss, based on group and school needs. Write each on an index card and pass them out to the group members. Each participant (or team of two or three) takes a card and addresses the question or scenario on his or her card.
- Have participants model strategies discussed in the reading to address questions or scenarios (mind maps, mnemonics, snapshot devices, etc.).

Group Discussions Without a Facilitator

If the group facilitator is unable to attend and no alternate has been designated, continue with the meeting and discussion without him or her.

- Take turns going around the room, allowing each group member to talk about his or her experience or reflections on the reading. Set a time limit for discussion of each participant's comments.
- Hand out index cards. Ask everyone to write a question or observation; then select one or more to discuss. Set time limits for discussion of each card.

Book Study Activities

Fishbowl Activity

The fishbowl exercise allows the facilitator to demonstrate how a book study works, and what good facilitation looks like.

Ask for a few volunteers (six to eight max) and seat them in a circle with an experienced facilitator inside the "fishbowl." (You can facilitate this group or have another skilled facilitator do it.) The other participants can sit or stand around the small group to observe. The facilitator begins by welcoming everyone, initiating introductions, and explaining the facilitator's impartial role.

The facilitator will help the group set its ground rules. Then the discussion begins and continues for several minutes. During the discussion, the facilitator should introduce some typical opening session questions such as personal concerns about the issue, and some questions that help people consider different viewpoints on the issue (typical of later study circle sessions). During the fishbowl, the facilitator should demonstrate some paraphrasing, clarifying, summarizing, or other common facilitation techniques. Involve the entire group in debriefing the exercise, using the questions below.

Post these questions where everyone can see them in the debriefing demonstration after the fishbowl activity.

What did the facilitator do to:

- Set a positive tone?
- Explain and help the group set the ground rules?
- Help people connect their concerns and values to the issue?
- Manage the discussion process? For example, what interventions did he or she use? Were those techniques effective? Would another approach have been better?
- Help advance the group's understanding of the content?
- Make sure several different views were considered?
- Bring out some of the complexities of the issue?

- Try to involve everyone in the discussion?
- Help participants identify areas of general agreement?

Time	Facilitator Activities	Participant Activities	Techniques & Equipment
30 min	Provide information on *<insert topic>* for research	Identify reference material for *<insert topic>*	Pairs, text, flip chart paper, markers.
10 min	Collect and comment on sources and debrief activity	List sources Discuss aids to process	Whole group

Search-Pair-Share

Purpose: To increase the amount of information sharing from a search.

Activity Explanation and Instructions

Facilitator: When an activity to address a specific standard is needed that also meets the needs of all learners, it may be difficult to locate one. It is easier when material has been previewed, and references are organized in advance.

Objective: Identify the topic to be addressed: ***<insert topic>*** and create a list of suggestions from the text to address that issue or topic while meeting the needs of different participants.

Techniques/Equipment: Written text materials, flipcharts, and markers, etc. Monitor and encourage participation.

Process: In pairs:

- Find as many activities, ideas, etc. to address ***<insert topic>*** in the text within the next [ten] minutes.
- Summarize the activity/idea and main points.

Group Success: All participants can explain the main points.

Accountability: Pairs share their references and information with the whole group. A combined list of references is created.

Debrief: What were the differences you saw in how your pair and other pairs searched for references? How did this affect the length of the compiled list?

Time	Facilitator Activities	Participant Activities	Techniques & Equipment
25 min	Provide section/chapter information on reading & guide activity	Describe information on *<insert topic>*	Pairs, written information
10 min	Ensure comprehension Debrief activity	Answer content questions Discuss group process	Whole group

Pair, Read, Respond

Purpose: To increase comprehension by using shared readings.

Activity Explanation and Instructions

Objective: Describe ***<insert content>***

Time: Thirty-five minutes (5 min. set up, 2x10 for pair reading, 10 min. debrief)

Techniques/Equipment: One copy of ***<insert content>*** information to each person. Monitor and encourage participation.

Process: Individually, silently read each paragraph or section and then, in pairs:

- Take turns describing the content of the reading to the partner. Discrepancies in understanding are discussed as needed.
- When each pair finishes, they might discuss the entire passage.

Group Success: Both people in the group can describe the passage content.

Accountability: Randomly answer questions on content.

Debrief: Was this an effective means of covering this material for you? Why or why not?

What Worries You?

Purpose: To bring out fears so they can be addressed and handled. Change is difficult. So much is at stake for teachers in today's classrooms that, sometimes, putting those fears out on the table for discussion is the best way to address them.

Time	Facilitator Activities	Learner Activities	Techniques & Equipment
10 min	Pose *<insert topic area>* and ask for "nightmares" Guide activity	Identify the worst-case scenarios that you can imagine for *<insert topic>*	Pairs, 5x7 cards, markers or felt pens
10 min	Collect cards for reference Debrief activity	Discuss scenarios and perceptions	Whole group

Activity Explanation and Instructions.

Facilitator: What we do not know how to deal with may make us quite nervous.

Objective: Identify imaginary but realistic worst-case scenarios for ***<insert topic>*** situations.

Time: Twenty minutes

Techniques/Equipment: Large sticky notes or 5x7 cards, colored markers or felt pens.

Process:

- Individually: Each participant writes out a <insert topic> scenario that he or she dreads (real or imagined).
- In pairs: Discuss the worst case for each scenario.

Group Success: Both participants can identify with the feelings of the other.

Accountability: Scenarios are described to the whole group. Group posts scenarios for review.

Debrief: How does discussing "worst-case scenarios" change your perception of what might happen and what you might do about it?

Is Homogenous Tracking Better Than Heterogeneous Grouping?

I created this report a few years ago discussing educational tracking. It defines types of tracking in detail and includes data regarding the process of tracking and its effect on students.

Introduction

Educational tracking remains a controversial issue in American schools. The term itself has fallen out of favor over the years to be replaced with more descriptive terms that appear to disguise the reality—yet it is still tracking. Labels such as "streaming," "homogeneous grouping," "curriculum differentiation," and "leveling" avoid the baggage that the term "tracking" evokes. In its most general form, tracking is a practice applied in many countries whereby students from kindergarten to the college level may be grouped according to one or more of the following: past achievement, academic ability, intelligence, and teacher recommendation (S. Kelly & Price, 2011). Heterogeneous grouping is reflected in classrooms with mixed achievement and ability levels. Homogeneous grouping is reflected in classrooms sorted according to achievement and ability levels.

While they are often used synonymously, it is important to differentiate "tracking" from "ability grouping" in some of the literature (T. Loveless, Farkas, & Duffett, 2008). Tracking is considered a school-based system that streams students into classes of different levels of the same curriculum, or different curricula altogether, based on a combination of factors. Ability grouping has a dual reference:

1. It is one of the factors considered in tracking, and it is mostly used to reflect academic ability.
2. It is also considered a more classroom-based and initiated practice at the discretion of a teacher who applies it for a short period of time, often less than a year, for instruction purposes.

Ability grouping has shown to increase the reading and early literacy growth in kindergartners, for instance (McCoach, O'Connell, & Levitt, 2006).

In this report, we will focus on tracking as a wide practice of placing students in classrooms based on past achievement and academic ability. The evidence examined here will explore current views, incidence in studied schools and school districts, and the impact of tracking on student achievement.

Current Limitations in Evidence

It is difficult to quantify how many schools, school districts, or school systems across the country incorporate tracking or curricular differentiation. This is one of the weaknesses of this area of study. Some of the challenges faced in data collection are:

1. The lack of a unified definition of tracking within school districts and across cities or states.

2. Varying policies and applications of tracking from school system to school system, and even from school to school within the same system.

3. Even within the same school, formal policy may differ, depending on the subject.

4. Differing policies as to whether students are bound to a track for a limited period or throughout their studies.

Consequently, with this variance, in practice and definition, it is difficult to draw conclusions on how tracking affects public school students across the nation.

Tracking students is even more difficult to define when it occurs at pre-registration, whereby students who test at set levels are not allowed into certain schools. Charter schools have been accused of incorporating admission policies that "skim" strong students and deny admission to low-ability ones. Some charter schools have also introduced "multi-class" curricula whereby a class is offered at different levels (e.g., basic, intermediate, advanced) (Booker, Gill, Zimmer, & Sass, 2009). Tracking is now often embedded in multi-level course design and offerings, especially at the higher grades. Tracking policies and applications also vary by schools, grades, and subjects (e.g., math or English).

In addition, tracking is started in some schools as early as fifth grade with honors and gifted courses. These are not enrichment courses for gifted students. Rather, they are courses that segregate students based on test scores. Sometimes, this practice separates students by removing them from their local school and assigning them to a separate school.

A significant limitation in earlier tracking studies is the lack of comparative analyses of the same curriculum and teaching approach in homogeneous and heterogeneous classrooms. Instructional quality is accepted as seminal to student achievement and advancement. Despite this, many studies that support tracking do not factor into their conclusions how instructional quality and approaches are important in this achievement beyond the structural differences between the two types of classrooms.

Challenges in Tracking

In the United States, tracking has faced and continues to face two challenging, and often competing, tasks. First, public school districts must strive to provide all students with an equal learning opportunity despite their ability.

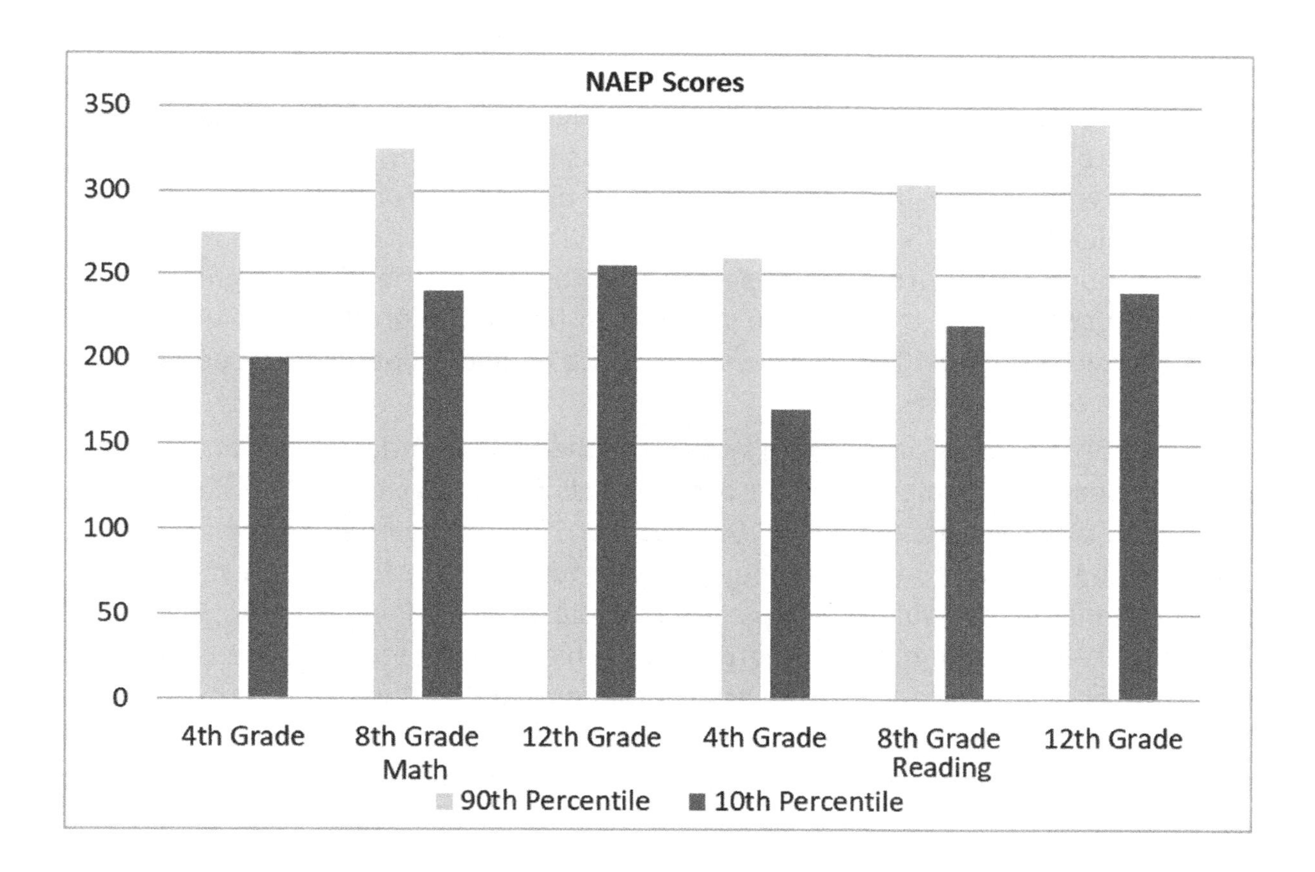

Second, teachers and schools are urged to recognize the need for different pedagogic approaches to address students' differing learning styles, motivation, cognitive abilities, and even English language competency. American schools offer tracking to deal with these two tasks, since there are wide achievement gaps among students. According to the National Assessment of Educational Progress (NAEP), by the time public school children enter the fourth grade, those who are reading at the 10 percent level are testing six grade levels or more than children in the bottom 10 percent. In mixed level classes, the teacher and curriculum must teach both levels of students and provide challenging enough material for skills' development. Figure 1 also illustrates the wide differences found across math and reading scores in grades four, eight, and twelve (Rampey, Dion, & Donahue, 2009). The top achieving students, 90th percentile, and the bottom achieving ones, 10th percentile, maintain a gap in their scores from elementary school through the final year of school.

In addition to existing gaps in achievement, tracking is often self-imposed. According to the Fordham Institute (T. Loveless et al., 2008), high-achieving students are more likely to seek and attend schools that group students based on academic ability. In his study on high-achieving students across the nation, Fordham found that more than 78 percent of students at the 90th percentile attended a school that tracks math students in the eighth grade. This figure is lower for average and 10 percentile students at 71 and 66 percent, respectively.

Many research studies on tracking have described the practice as necessary in fostering academic achievement across all levels (Tom Loveless, 1999; Lucas, 1999). Yet, other results from the 1970s to the 1990s have been critical, claiming that tracking seemed to benefit high-ability groups while offering only mediocre, if any, benefits in low-ability groups (Tom Loveless, 1999; Peng & Fuchs, 2015) (Loveless, 1999). Some have even argued that high-ability students are likely to perform worse in heterogeneous classes than in homogeneous ones (Lucas, 1999). This has been especially the case as the issue of tracking is one that is mired in socioeconomic complexities of race, poverty, poor school funding, and class marginalization.

What is critical to note, however, is that, overall, research has been inconclusive on the practice of tracking and its ability to influence achievement and reduce educational consequences of socioeconomic inequities in providing quality education to all.

Recent Policies and Practices in Tracking

Middle Schools

Tracking often begins in middle school (although some school districts start in elementary school) on a limited basis and serves as a bridge between the largely heterogeneous classrooms of elementary school to the tracked ones of high school. The percentage of tracked students in middle schools has changed over a fifteen-year period from 1992 to 2007 as shown in the NAEP figures below in Table 1:

Table 1

NAEP National Tracking Data (Percentage tracked, 8th grade)			
Mathematics	**1992**	**1996**	**2007**
Schools	73	71	75
Black students	66	64	66
White students	75	73	78
Hispanic students	63	61	70
English Language Arts	**1992**	**1996**	**2003**
Schools	48	31	43
Black students	54	39	51
White students	46	33	39
Hispanic students	49	38	59

Table 1 illustrates that tracking eighth grade students has only slightly changed in schools for mathematics over a fifteen-year period. The same is true for ELA, although the trend has seen a decrease in the number of tracked schools in 1996 below 1992, only to see it rise again in 2003. Within racial groups, math tracking in eighth grade reflects greater tracking for White students and slightly less so for Black and Hispanic students. With ELA, Hispanic students have the greatest rate of tracking (59 percent) while White students have the lowest (39 percent).

Loveless (2009) studied recent evidence from middle school tracking in Massachusetts. The state has led the nation in the twenty-year period from 1990 to 2010 in changing tracking policies and practices in classrooms. In his study, Loveless examined results from the 2009 state middle school survey. The goal was to analyze within-subject and within-grade tracking at middle schools as well as the position of high achievers in these schools. Loveless also compared tracked schools and detracked ones (defined as no tracking in math classes) to discover any differences in student achievement. He concluded that tracked schools did better than detracked ones, and that the practice has been largely dismantled in Massachusetts middle schools. This is especially the case with English, science, and history classes. However, the practice remains, in a limited form, in math classes. The Massachusetts middle school survey had the following characteristics:

Of the 295 schools surveyed, 128 responded (a 43.4 percent response).

Achievement data was collected and compared for 1995, 2005, and 2008.

It posed three (3) essential questions to guide the analysis:

How has tracking changed in middle schools since the 1990s?

Why did some schools "detrack" while others did not?

Do tracked and detracked schools differ in the number of high-achieving students they produce?

From the sample of schools that responded, a variation existed in tracking and detracking by location as seen in Table 2.

Table 2

Massachusetts Tracking Data: Community of School		
School community	Tracked	Detracked
Urban	35.7%	64.3%
Suburban	63.6%	28.6%
Rural	28.6%	71.4%

As illustrated in Table 3, Massachusetts had higher math tracking and lower English tracking than the national averages.

Table 3

NAEP Massachusetts Tracking Data (Percentage tracked, 8th grade)			
Mathematics	**1992**	**1996**	**2007**
Schools	88	85	83
Black students	62	72	71
White students	90	88	86
Hispanic students	80	63	72
English Language Arts	**1992**	**1996**	**2003**
Schools	60	41	38
Black students	41	27	31
White students	61	44	40
Hispanic students	58	35	34

Table 4 shows the change in average number of tracked levels per subject from 1991 to 2009. The figures show that English, history, and science were detracked at a higher rate than math in that period.

Table 4

Average Number of Track Levels (Subjects, 8th grade)				
Subject	1991	1995	2005	2009
Math	2.99	2.59	2.36	2.30
English	2.38	1.86	1.39	1.33
History	2.11	1.66	1.20	1.14
Science	2.16	1.72	1.23	1.18

Table 5 further shows the percentage of middle schools with tracking in the four academic subjects, and how those figures changed from 1995 to 2009. The data reflects the detracking of English, history, and science at faster rates than math. In 2009, history and science classes are taught at only one level in most schools (89.8 percent and 86.7 percent, respectively) while math is taught at one level at 15.6 percent of middle schools. English has seen the most detracking effort with a change from 30 percent of schools in 1995 to 4.7 percent in 2009 offering at least three levels of instruction in the eighth grade.

Table 5

Percentage of Middle Schools with Tracking in Academic Subjects						
	1995			2009		
	1 Level	2 Levels	3+ Levels	1 Level	2 Levels	3+ Levels
Math	15.2	30.3	54.5	15.6	49.2	35.2
English	55.1	14.9	30.0	72.7	22.7	4.7
History	67.7	9.4	22.9	89.8	7.0	3.1
Science	62.2	14.2	23.6	86.7	9.4	3.9

According to Loveless (2009), principals of the 128 middle schools surveyed said that when it came to influential actors in tracking policy in Massachusetts, district policy makers, school administration, and teachers (35.2, 43.8, and 29.7 percent, respectively), were considered "great actors." Following closely and considered "great actors" were research literature and No Child Left Behind (23.4 and 15.6 percent, respectively).

The influence of tracking on student achievement has fueled much of the controversy surrounding the practice (followed by its socioeconomic implications). According to Loveless (2009), middle schoolers in tracked and detracked schools have shown different levels of achievement in math as illustrated in Table 6. These differences are the largest in those on opposite ends of the achievement scale. For instance, among the seventeen schools that are detracked (with only one level of math instruction in eighth grade), 15.8 percent of students scored as "Advanced." Comparatively, among the forty-three schools with three or more levels of math instruction, 26.6 percent of students scored as Advanced. Tracked and detracked schools also differed significantly in students who scored as "Failing" in math (14.8 vs. 26.2 percent, respectively). The figures show that tracked schools produced more high-achieving students in math than detracked schools and reported fewer failing students.

Table 6

Distribution in Achievement, 8th Grade Math (Year 2007-08)				
Number of math Tracks	Advanced	Proficient	Needs Improvement	Failing
1 (n=17)	15.8%	29.3%	28.8%	26.2%
2 (n=66)	18.6%	31.9%	28.7%	20.7%
3+ (n=43)	26.6%	34.5%	24.1%	14.8%

High Schools

Sean Kelly (2007) sampled 92 of 351 North Carolina high schools to gain information on tracking. The study examined curriculum guides to learn more about tracking policy and practice differences among the schools. Particularly, Kelly documented consistencies and variability in the use of tracking in these schools and found common tracking practices, as well as wide variability. For instance, almost all the schools tracked English because the course is mandatory across the four years in the state. In forty-one of the ninety-two schools, English was differentiated into two track levels based on academic ability while twenty-nine schools differentiated the course into three levels. Finally, twenty schools differentiated English into four levels. An example of three tracking levels in a school is one that offered honors, college prep, and tech prep English classes.

In mathematics, tracking was even more complex because it was not based on differential ability alone but on course offerings. Most schools in the sample had similar math curricula. Some schools streamed students into tracks based on their test scores in algebra upon high school entrance. For some students, this track marked the remainder of their high school careers. For example, students who had low scores in algebra in ninth grade were placed into less rigorous course offerings than calculus in the senior grades. Even with low-ability students, several levels in algebra were offered, with some students given the option to complete the mandatory ninth grade course over two years.

Out of the ninety-two schools, thirteen had policies that eliminated mobility from lower to higher tracks for courses beginning in ninth grade. For instance, students who entered a technical preparation course in English in the ninth grade were not allowed to take Honors English classes the remainder of their high school careers. Within low-ability classes, students were allowed to move between courses. Another nine schools eliminated mobility beyond the tenth grade while eighteen schools eliminated mobility beyond the junior year of high school.

Tracking in the sampled schools was based on both prior achievement (minimum grade policy) and academic ability (standardized test score policy). Nearly 30 percent of the schools had a required minimum grade policy in English, math, and science (twenty-seven out of ninety-two schools). For standardized test score policies, nearly 23 percent of schools had one for English (twenty-one out of ninety-two schools) while 21 percent had them for math and 9 percent had them for science. Prior achievement and academic ability were not the only criteria for tracking students into high-ability and low-ability streams. Schools also had more subjective measures such as teacher recommendations. For instance, 43 percent of schools in the sample required teacher recommendation for placement into higher level English classes while 50 percent did so for science classes.

Recent Evidence of Tracking Impact on Achievement

The controversy surrounding tracking is often based on two factors: student achievement and instructional quality. The decision whether to conduct homogeneous groupings whereby students are tracked by academic ability and past achievement relies on a number of factors as illustrated by the Massachusetts and North Carolina examples.

However, emerging evidence shows the impact of homogeneous versus heterogeneous groupings on achievement. Burris, Heubert, and Levin (2006) studied the impact of an accelerated mathematics curriculum in heterogeneously grouped middle school classes in a suburban school district in Long Island, New York. The study also wished to examine students' likelihood to complete advanced high school math courses and do well in them. The study showed that heterogeneous groupings of mixed-ability and achievement students did not hamper the effect of the accelerated curriculum. All student groups, including those at low achievement levels, as well as minority and low socioeconomic status students, were more likely to complete advanced math courses.

Furthermore, the performance of the high-achieving students within heterogeneous classes was similar to their previous performance in homogeneous ones. Thus, unlike earlier research (Lucas, 1999) that showed a negative effect on high-achieving students when mixed with initially low-achieving ones, this study showed that these high achievers can thrive in a heterogeneous environment.

The evidence is also interesting in comparison to the Massachusetts data (Loveless, 2009), which shows tracked math classes producing greater percentages of high-achieving students. The question is whether those same high-achieving students will continue to thrive in a heterogeneous environment as the Long Island students have.

Zimmer (2003) found that homogeneous classrooms in math and English provided advantageous atmospheres in high schools across all ability groups. His results also showed that low-ability students in tracked classes performed better than those who were placed in heterogeneous classes. When these results are viewed in light of the Loveless (2009) and Burris et al. (2006) studies, it becomes clearer why there are challenges in reaching a consensus on whether tracking endures as a good policy to improve student achievement and instructional quality.

Despite the Zimmer (2003) results, it is unclear why performance in math and English classes was favorable in homogeneous classrooms. While Zimmer reports that some positive gains are made from tracking for low-achieving students, the author holds that these gains are mostly from tailored instruction (which he terms "achievement targeted instruction"). Furthermore, the author claims that although negative peer effect exists (from being isolated from high-achieving students), this effect is outweighed by the tailored instruction. This analysis by Zimmer is common to many studies that support tracking benefits for low-achieving students whereby the benefits are not directly attributable to the tracking mechanism or structure; rather, they are attributed to instruction differences (Rubin, 2006). Thus, comparative analyses of curriculum rigor and teacher training and performance are often not done in both homogeneous and heterogeneous classrooms to isolate these instruction elements and evaluate tracking independently. In other words, the Zimmer study does not indicate why achievement-targeted instruction would not be equally effective in a heterogeneous environment while allowing low-achieving students also to gain from positive peer effects.

Boaler (2006) has addressed this very issue of instruction quality in a strong support of detracked environments. According to Boaler, an urban high school (Railside School) of ethnically diverse students with varying abilities was able to bring about high mathematics achievement in a heterogeneous environment through complex instruction and a reform-oriented approach employed by teachers. In this study, the mathematics department was matched and compared to two other schools' (both less urban) mathematics departments that continued with tracking and traditional teaching methods. Over a four-year period, the author collected information, including 600 hours of classroom observations and student assessments in addition to questionnaires and interviews.

Boaler (2006) found that instruction in the detracked mathematics classroom had a central quality of complex instruction: ***multiple ability treatment***. In most traditional mathematics classrooms, the author argued, students are assessed on a unidimensional scale that emphasizes the execution of procedures correctly and quickly. According to Boaler, this narrow assessment means that some students immediately grasp the execution of these mathematics procedures and become high achievers while others do not, creating a hierarchy in the mathematics classroom. At Railside, mathematics classrooms avoided this singular assessment of success by expanding task requirements that recognize and reward different abilities. These requirements included open-ended problems that expanded upon important mathematical concepts and offered multiple solution paths. The unique aspect of this department's approach to the detracked mathematics classrooms was the autonomy given to teachers to create the algebra curriculum themselves, which allowed them to adapt problems from different curricula. Students responded to this unique instructional approach by recognizing different problem-solving techniques and practices.

The four-year study by Boaler (2006) also illustrated other instructional practices that contributed to the success of low-achieving students. These practices, considered "equitable," included techniques such as assigning roles in group work and assigning competence on intellectual tasks to low-achieving students. The goal of assigning competence is to provide feedback to the student that is "public, intellectual, specific, and relevant to the group task" (p. 43). Other instructional techniques emphasized student responsibility for learning, high expectations of achievement, and the importance of effort over ability. The study revealed that all the instructional elements outlined (complex instruction + equitable practices) were instrumental in the high achievement of low-ability students in a heterogeneous mathematics classroom. According to the author, "mixed-ability teaching and providing high level learning opportunities" (p. 46) were key to high student achievement at Railside School.

Similar to Boaler, Horn (2006) also studied the specific practices and structures shared by two detracked mathematics departments to gain a greater understanding of their success factors. Hoar followed a British (Phoenix Park) and an American school (East High School), both urban and diverse, as they became successful in improving the achievement of students designated as low-ability. The two schools were also successful in having more of these students enroll in and succeed in advanced mathematics classes than their counterparts in tracked classrooms. Horn found that teachers in both schools moved away from mathematics curricula that emphasized basic terms and procedures' practice.

Instead, the schools focused on important mathematical ideas in an effort to counteract previous low achievement. Similar to Railside School in the Boaler study, instruction included a significant component of group-worthy problems. These problems had a number of qualities, including important mathematical concepts, multiple tasks, allowing for multiple student-led representations, and several possible solution paths.

Conclusion

These two studies illustrate that instructional qualities and teaching approaches are central to the success of low-ability students in heterogeneous classrooms. Supporters of tracking have long held that these students fail in mixed-ability classrooms for a number of reasons, including their inability to cope with the complexity of the regular curriculum (Loveless, 1999; Lucas, 1999). Supporters also hold that tracked classrooms for low-ability students allow for instruction tailored to their achievement levels.

However, the above studies show that mixed-ability teaching and high quality learning environments are the key to success for low-achieving students. In a heterogeneous classroom, these environments lead to the high achievement of students while allowing them to gain from equitable practices and positive peer effects of learning alongside high-achieving students. Although the overall debate on tracking benefits is claimed to have inconclusive results, recent evidence shows that instructional quality and approaches may be the deciding factors in the achievement of all students, especially low-ability ones, and not structural differences of separating by ability in homogeneous classrooms.

Enrichment Activities: SDI & Challenge Activities in the Mixed-Ability Classroom

One of the biggest challenges teachers face when teaching a multi-ability class, where some students are working at the honors level and other students are struggling, is to teach all of those students at an appropriate level and still maintain classroom control, engagement, and interest.

When Chunking Lesson Plans®, a strategy whereby you divide your lesson plan into chunks of approximately ten minutes or less, you can have a ten-minute chunk of time with three ability-based groups, each doing work at its level of instruction. In this scenario, one group could be your SDI, or re-teach group, another group might be working on practice items, while the third group would be working on enrichment activities that challenge and accelerate learning.

While teachers typically focus on the group of students who are receiving SDI, or being re-taught the material, other students need activities that keep them engaged and behaving appropriately. It is typical for students to work on practice activities after instruction in the classroom without much need for teacher attention. This group is not much different from the group that might be doing the odd numbers on page 35 after a lesson on how to work an algebraic equation. Teachers are used to this scenario and may lightly supervise students in this group. In reality, this does not change the chunking strategy. The difference is that teachers are teaching one group of students while their other students are engaged in the practice activity.

The real challenge is what to do with the students who are ready to move beyond the current level of instruction. How do you give those students something more challenging that enriches their learning, but doesn't cause them to feel resentful that they are doing harder work, more work, or boring work?

It seems logical that we might give these higher-achieving students more difficult problems to solve, more challenging work to accomplish, and longer and more demanding essays to write. They are capable, so the temptation is to challenge them with these types of assignments. However, what often happens is that students become resentful, start to misbehave, and then go home and complain to their parents that they are being discriminated against because they have to do more work than other students in the classroom. The key is to give students challenging activities that are fun, engaging, and take learning up a level in a way they find stimulating and motivating.

These activities can be used to challenge students for a ten- to twelve-minute chunk of time while you are re-teaching another group of students.

Ten-Minute Acceleration Center Activities Across the Content Area

- **A WebQuest Challenge:** Send students on a WebQuest to answer an open-ended question about the topic you just taught. WebQuests move students beyond just the facts. They require students to use prior knowledge and stimulate curiosity that promotes an investigation of the topic at a deeper level. An excellent resource for Web Quests can be found at Tommarch.com. Also, check out webquest.org.
- **Be a Character Detective:** Research a key person (scientist, author, historical figure, mathematician, etc.) to come up with a theory as to why he or she is notable. What prompted the person to do what he did? What events or people in her life influenced her? Where would the world be if his or her life had been different? Students can present their findings and conclusions in a quick presentation (via screencasting, a skit, a song, an iMovie or Animoto trailer, or a mind map).
- **What Is the Source of That Theory?** Use Wolfram Alpha to research background information on a theory in geometry, algebra, or science, and present that information to the class in a creative manner.
- **Visual Research and Analysis (math):** Use Google images to find structures that include a specific shape, such as a parabola, and determine the formula for that particular shape. Consider how a shape might contribute to the structural integrity of objects such as chairs or tables.
- **Video Curation and Analysis:** Find videos on the topic of instruction that present the knowledge in a unique or entertaining way. For example, find music videos that explain the difference between metaphor and simile. Or find videos, for example, that present the prologue to a Shakespearean play in three different styles (a skit created by students, professional production, a dramatization uploaded by a teacher). Analyze how the different presentations provide the viewer with differences in perspective on the piece of literature.
- **Analyze that App:** Provide students with a rubric to analyze a device app, or a video, or an instructional website. Have them use the rubric to create a "top three" list of resources for the other students in the class on any given topic.

- **Create a Whiteboard Movie (Screencasting):** Instruct students to create a whiteboard movie using an app such as Explain Everything, and show two sides of an issue, both sides of an argument in a debate, or two different characterizations of a social situation.
- **Karaoke Mnemonics:** Students choose a karaoke version of a popular song so they have the music without words. Create new lyrics to sing the concept just taught so they will remember the lesson.
- **Dramatize Dry Text in Person or with Video:** Show students an episode of Real Actors Read Yelp and have them use the movie app on their device to dramatize content area reading that would typically be very dry, similar to what the actors have done with the Yelp reviews.

Some of the great teachers in my network also had excellent enrichment ideas:

- **Reading Comprehension Acceleration Activity for Language Arts, English, and Reading in the Content Area:** Choose books slightly above students' reading level that will challenge their thinking on point of view or a historical issue. Instruct students to meet "book club style" to discuss the text. Encourage students to make connections to past instruction and suggest points to discuss in the upcoming lesson(s). For example, choose several books from a specific time period such as ***Sadako and the Thousand Paper Cranes***, ***I Survived Pearl Harbor***, ***How Baseball Saved Us***, ***I Survived the Nazi Invasion of 1944***, and ***Number the Stars***. These all give a different child's point of view about World War II. Students get a 360-degree view of events during that time and draw their own conclusions based on their reading and discussion. ***Contributed by Chrystal Williams, Clara Love Elementary, Justin, Texas***.
- **Vocabulary and Content Specific Terminology:** Choose a key term discussed in your lesson and have students research the term to gain more detail. For example, when Felicia Thomas was teaching pre-Civil War events through to the Civil War there was minimal time in the lesson to discuss thoroughly the role of an abolitionist. The acceleration group researched the term to identify and respond to the who, what, when, where, why. ***Contributed by Felicia Thomas, Joseph Martin Elementary, Hinesville, Georgia. Twitter: @fthomas_jme***
- **Background Knowledge for Current Topic:** Have students read informational articles and create questions for a classmate or parent based on their reading. ***Also contributed by Felicia Thomas, Joseph Martin Elementary, Hinesville, Georgia. Twitter: @fthomas_jme***
- **Computer Classes—Application, Problem Solving, Analysis, and Synthesis:** After providing an overview of the key components of high-end computer systems via teacher presentations and video tutorials, Lawani uses a "Who Wants to be a Millionaire" style quiz to reinforce learning for about five minutes. Then he splits the class into groups of three or so and gives each

group a different kind of computer system, for which they must research and identify the key components they would use, depending on the purpose for which their computer will be used. He allows five minutes for the research and then facilitates a question and answer period to monitor and evaluate their understanding. ***Contributed by Lawani, Lewisham Southwark College***.

- **Create Game Questions to Reinforce Learning and Peer Review with the Class:** Instruct students to create questions (about five) to be used for a study guide, quiz, or test, or to play (my favorite) Kahoot (Kahoot.it). Students create questions relevant to what has been taught and must include an answer key. This can be done individually or as a group. ***Contributed by Janna Ramirez, Lyman Hall Elementary, Hinesville, Georgia. Twitter: @ JhalesRamirez***
- **Go Deeper Through Creating Models That Teach:** Have students use apps like Wixie, ExplainEverything, or Educreations to go deeper into a standard and/or learning target. Challenge them to create video learning models for students who need extra practice. ***Contributed by Janice Brennan, Taylors Creek Elementary School, Hinesville, Georgia. Twitter: @jbrennan_tce***
- **Offer Students Choices for Enrichment:** Janice Brennan offers her students choices that accelerate learning. Examples of Acceleration Centers she provides include Boggle Your Mind, a figurative language matching game, a vocabulary-independent word study for a novel the class is reading. Ten minutes is the ideal time limit and Janice's students love the timed aspect. ***Also contributed by Janice Brennan, Taylors Creek Elementary School, Hinesville, Georgia. Twitter: @jbrennan_tce***

Enrichment Using Technology in the Classroom—Nine Ways to Use Google Images to Teach Vocabulary

Contributed by Amanda McNinch, Struthers City Schools

Susan's note: Some teachers struggle to use technology effectively in the classroom. During a program I did in Columbus, Ohio, I met a wonderful teacher, Amanda McNinch, who shared how she uses Google images to support vocabulary. Amanda was kind enough to outline her strategies so I could share them here.

Technology in the Classroom Using Google Images

Every one of these ideas could be used in any subject area, and there are a number of ways you might apply these strategies in your classroom. Please comment below and add your ideas to this list!

1. Continuum of meaning—Have students search a word with degrees of meaning, such as "anger." Then have them pick five images and order them (from least to most angry); then compare their images with their peers.
2. Continuum of meaning, antonyms—Just like #1, but use antonyms like "hot" and "cold."
3. Continuum of personal application, close to their lives/far from their lives—For example, use the word "regal." Students might find an image to represent their cat and an image of Princess Diana to illustrate both ends of the spectrum.
4. Have students make a personal image "glossary" of content vocabulary using Google images instead of verbal-linguistic definitions.
5. Play "Memory" of words for visual representation. Keep words, definitions, and visual representations of words visible so ***no one*** guesses!
6. Play a match game of words and definitions to visual pictures that the teacher finds. This can be used as formative assessment.
7. Post a current events type Google Image. Challenge students to make a link from a vocabulary word to the image, and defend it. Class votes on funniest, best, most meaningful, etc. for prizes or points.
8. Post a word and its meaning. Students find example and non-example images, and explain why each image fits, or not.
9. Post an image and ask students to find and explain the "most interesting" (or any other qualifier) word to describe that image.
10. Students love to use technology, and they have fun with these activities!

About the Author

Susan Gingras Fitzell, M.Ed., CSP, has been consulting, writing and presenting since 1993 and has spent over fifteen years onsite in organizations throughout the United States working hand-in-hand with teachers, management, and employees helping them to increase productivity, learning, and problem solving to reach their goals.

She has authored over a dozen books and is one of only 650 Certified Speaking Professionals in the world today. Susan is a dynamic, nationally recognized speaker as well as an innovative change agent, compassionate coach, and effective productivity and learning expert. After working with Susan, clients are more efficient, productive, and effective.

She is a black belt in kickboxing and a student of kung fu. Her family members pride themselves on being geeks and her two adult children have both earned degrees in mechanical engineering using the strategies Susan shares with her clients.

Other selected titles by Susan Gingras Fitzell, M.Ed.:

- 100+ Tech Ideas for Teaching English and Language Arts
- Special Needs in the General Classroom: 500+ Teaching Strategies for Differentiating Instruction, Third Edition
- Paraprofessionals and Teachers Working Together: Highly Effective Strategies for Inclusive Classrooms, Third Edition
- Free the Children: Conflict Education for Strong & Peaceful Minds
- Memorization and Test-Taking Strategies
- Motivating Students to Choose Success
- Please Help Me with My Homework! Strategies for Parents and Caregivers (English and Spanish)
- RTI Strategies for Secondary Teachers
- Transforming Anger to Personal Power: An Anger Management Curriculum for Grades 6 through 12
- Umm Studying? What Is That? Learning Strategies for the Overwhelmed and Confused College and High School Student
- Use iPads and Other Cutting-Edge Technology to Strengthen Your Instruction

Bring Susan to Your School for Consultation or In-Service

Susan Fitzell, M.Ed., CSP, has nearly twenty-five years of expertise as a teacher, educational consultant, and leadership coach. She is a sought-after speaker, educating and inspiring thousands each year, and she is the author of over a dozen books on collaborative teaching, ed-tech, learning strategies, and inclusion.

Susan's keynotes and workshops are interactive, content rich, dynamic presentations. She customizes to meet her clients' needs to ensure relevance to the client organizations' dynamics.

Choose from four customizable topics:

Motivating Students to Choose Success

Learn practical strategies to motivate your students to make positive choices, put forth their best effort, & realize they are in control of their own destiny.

Co-Teaching & Collaboration for All

Maximize the skills of co-teachers and specialists in your inclusive classrooms with ***new***, concrete implementation approaches that take the guesswork out of collaboration.

Differentiation Strategy Blast

Discover a variety of brain-based, research supported, "implement tomorrow" strategies that maintain rigor, maximize time, and increase success for all learners.

Paraprofessionals and Teachers Working Together

Four mini-workshops in one day to strengthen critical skills needed for success in the classroom: 1. Build a Strong Foundation for Success, 2. How to Collaborate Successfully, 3. Positive Behavior Management, and 4. Academic Support

Launch your conference or benefit with Susan's Keynote:

Differentiated Instruction: Why Bother? Aka: Inclusion: Why Bother?

Shift mindsets that challenge successful differentiated instruction and inclusive practices. The motto of this powerful keynote is "Good for all, critical for the students with special needs."

Send an inquiry to sfitzell@susanfitzell.com

Or via her website www.SusanFitzell.com

School Professional Development License Agreement

IF YOU DID NOT DO IT YET, DO NOT FORGET

GET YOUR BONUS RESOURCES HERE:

http://Bonus398.susanfitzell.com

DID YOU FIND A TYPO?

Although this document has been thoroughly reviewed and edited, there is always a chance that we missed something. If you find a typo or other issue in this book, send it to me in email at sfitzell@susanfitzell.com and you will be entered into our monthly prize drawing.

Made in the USA
Columbia, SC
19 June 2020

11476308R00176